PENGUIN

In Wr

Adam Phillips, formerly Principal Child Psychotherapist at Charing Cross Hospital, London, is a practising psychoanalyst and a visiting professor in the English department at the University of York. He is the author of numerous works of psychoanalysis and literary criticism, including most recently *Unforbidden Pleasures* and *Missing Out*. He is General Editor of the Penguin Modern Classics Freud translations, and a Fellow of The Royal Society of Literature.

IN WRITING

Adam Phillips

PENGUIN BOOKS

PENGUIN BOOKS

UK | USA | Canada | Ireland | Australia
India | New Zealand | South Africa

Penguin Books is part of the Penguin Random House group of companies
whose addresses can be found at global.penguinrandomhouse.com.

First published by Hamish Hamilton 2016
Published in Penguin Books 2019
001

Printed and bound in Great Britain by Clays Ltd, Elcograf S.p.A.

A CIP catalogue record for this book is available from the British Library

ISBN: 978–0–241–97923–5

www.greenpenguin.co.uk

MIX
Paper from
responsible sources
FSC® C018179

Penguin Random House is committed to a
sustainable future for our business, our readers
and our planet. This book is made from Forest
Stewardship Council® certified paper.

In memory of Richard Poirier and J-B Pontalis,
who encouraged me

Not every human being has the luxury of not being a fanatic.

Nancy Bauer, *How to Do Things with Pornography*

Sometimes it seems that a line or so was simply added by the actor into his part even if it did not always make sense in the fuller context of the play.

Tiffany Stern, *Making Shakespeare*

Only works of propaganda are addressed to a wider audience.

Pierre Hadot, *Philosophy as a Way of Life*

. . . 'culture' as balm, 'identity' as pacifier.

Maureen N. McLane, *Critical Mass*

CONTENTS

CONTENTS

PREFACE

It is often amazing to people who like writing that most people are not at all interested in it. A lot of people, of course, find it useful, but it doesn't give them the pleasure people who 'love reading' can feel; nor the sense that people who study or teach literature can have that reading and writing are somehow essential to the lives they want to live. Whatever the appeal of writing is – and it must be considerable given its staying power – it is not clear how it is best served; other, that is, than by writing itself. Nor indeed what is being served in the valuing of it.

Like any minority interest that, because it is a minority interest, is felt to be perpetually under threat, this can prompt defences (and idealizations) of the so-called humanities that often betray, in their vehemence and the nature of their claims, a lack of confidence in writing; as though without considerable justification it might disappear; as though it can't hold its own against its competitors; as though we might be in danger of losing interest in language, or in the right sort of language. So when people defend 'literature' now it is difficult for them not to sound like people defending a religion, or a political ideology, or a local hospital. Instead of believing that literature, rather like psychoanalysis, is just for the people who like it – that it makes them feel alive in ways they prefer; that it sustains what they care about; that it creates interest and engagement and curiosity; and creates jobs they want to do, and institutions, like universities, and libraries, and publishing houses, which they value – it can be made to sound like a life-support system, or preparation for a moral beauty contest. Exaggerated claims prompt the suspicions they are intended to dispel. The best defence of literature is writing that appeals to people, but in ways they find difficult to articulate. It's worth wondering what we fear might happen to literature if we no longer defended it.

Because writing can only ever be as good as its readers make it, it is always tempting to blame the audience (people don't read enough, or properly; they don't read the right things, and so on). But it is misleading to be only cross with the people who don't share your pleasures (or your values). People read and write to find out if there is a group of like-minded people; and, if there isn't, to try to make one. Writing needn't be a world-domination project – successful writers aren't like rock stars or celebrities – but just the attempt to find enough people who are interested in what matters most to you. So the whole notion of the successful writer is always contentious, and reading can be one of the things we do in which we don't have to worry about success. That a writer engages our attention, and how or why he or she does, are the only things that matter. And these things matter because of the thoughts and feelings and conversations and lives to which they can lead.

Both literature and psychoanalysis can help us work out what are the conversations we crave that may get us the lives we want. It is only worth having relationships that bring out the best in us, and both literature and psychoanalysis can give us a clue about what these relationships might be, and about what the best in us is. But commitment to psychoanalysis narrows the mind – over-organizes our attention – in ways that an interest in literature can avoid. The extraordinary range of tones and rhythms and voices and sentences that is literature exposes the limits, and the limitations, of psychoanalysis, and its descriptions of what a person is, and can be. So I have always admired writers – like, say, W. H. Auden, or Randall Jarrell, or William Empson, or Louise Glück, or Richard Rorty, or Marion Milner, or Stanley Cavell, or Wendy Brown– who could be interested in psychoanalysis without having to be committed to it. Writers who could, however inexplicitly, use psychoanalysis, among many other things, to make something of their own. Psychoanalysis is at its best when it is unpredictably useful; when it inspires something other than total devotion, and so stops just repeating itself. The problem with (and for) psychoanalysts has always been that they have to believe in psychoanalysis.

Like all essentialist theories – all theories that, because they know where they start from, set strict limits to where they can go – psychoanalysis makes a cult out of what could be just good company. It is very difficult to go on being interesting and interested – to go on seeing and listening differently – if you are trapped in a vocabulary. It is very difficult to avoid the seductions and grandiosities of generalization if you always already know what you are looking (or reading) for. This is why psychoanalysis applied to literature can be so stupefying. It all too easily assumes, as the critic Mikko Tuhkanen writes, that 'works of art are like queer adults, who, according to psychoanalysis, haven't quite got their stories straight'. Psychoanalysis is just one way of wondering what we are doing when we are trying to get our stories straight.

The essays in this book are written in the belief that psychoanalysis has something to offer our reading and writing (and the living of our lives), without being quite sure what that is; while being quite sure that literature has far more to offer, which is not more of the same. Psychoanalysis, of course, has its own so-called literature, just as literature could be described as having an interest in psychology (though reading literature, in all its diversity, can make you wonder what psychology could possibly be). But neither need be a commentary on the other; we can just allow for the fact that they have overlapping preoccupations. That they both contribute, as much else does, to our repertoire of descriptions.

Through psychoanalysis we can learn how to speak more freely without needing people to agree with us; indeed, we can speak freely only when we don't need people to agree with us (it was left to Freud's inspired colleague Ferenczi to wonder why it is that we can't say whatever we want to anyone, and not just to a psychoanalyst). And in reading literature, as opposed to propaganda, something other than agreement is being sought. If people don't have to either agree or disagree with each other, what else could they be doing together? In both psychoanalysis and what we have been taught to call literature we can experiment with the need to believe and be believed. And, if we want freer speech, to experiment with what we want it for.

Psychoanalysis for Poets

> . . . the physical is important as well as the spiritual and I don't doubt
> that a thousand derangements are the result of our misunderstanding
> of the physical. Freud says his object is to substitute a conscious for
> an unconscious – a normal for a pathogenic conflict and we must
> do this if we can. A knowledge of abnormal conditions is a help in
> understanding normal conditions . . .

> Marianne Moore to Bryher, 18 April 1921

> Ezra has written me and speaks most disrespectfully of America.
> Defiance being a form of dependence according to Freud, we
> perhaps should be honoured.

> Marianne Moore to Bryher, 9 May 1921

Writing on Jean Cocteau in *The New English Weekly* in 1935, Ezra
Pound reports that Pirandello was '*concerned*' while Cocteau was
writing *Oedipe*, for Cocteau's danger of tackling that subject without
a plop into Freud, or it may have been only a passing thought
that floated up over the luncheon table, in brief conversation, but it
ended with the Italian's shrug: "No, on the whole no, he won't fall
into the Freudian mess. Il est trop bon poete." ' Which, Pound adds,
'is emphatically true'. Cocteau was too good a poet to fall into the
Freudian mess; the danger of tackling Oedipus without a plop into

Freud may have been a passing thought over lunch, a mess being a meal, a muddle and a soiling and a 'company of persons eating together'. To be in Freud's company when writing about Oedipus threatens to spoil something; as though Freud has turned the Oedipus myth into something one could fall into. Whatever Freud had done to it, in Pound's view he had spoiled it for poets. What do you have to do to do that? 'In an age beset with cranks we have I suppose heard of Freud,' Pound wrote in 1937, reviewing the Jefferson–Adams letters; a bit rich perhaps coming from him. But Pound was more than convinced that Freud was unconvincing, a crank, someone no one should be taken in by: 'yr / Freud all bunk,' he wrote to H. D. in 1954, after her *Tribute to Freud*, '. . . instead of sticking to reading list left by Dante / . . . You got into the wrong pig stye ma chere. But not too late to climb out.'

It may be useful to think of reading lists as being the right or wrong pigsty; but Freud in Pound's view – and he is characteristically drastic though not unrepresentative of the first generation of Anglo-American modernist poets – needed to be discredited as a pernicious influence. Freud was a crank who narrowed the mind and distracted attention from what really mattered: 'for every man with an anxiety state due to sex', Pound writes, 'there are nine and ninety with an anxiety state due to lack of purchasing power, or anticipation of same': we should not use sexuality as a distraction or a refuge from the real anxiety, which is economic. 'It is typical of a bewildered society,' Pound goes on, 'that it should erect a pathology into a system.' With this erection, as with the plops, Pound wittingly or unwittingly writes in a suggestively Freudian way in casting aspersions on Freud; as though Freud was contagious, in Auden's words, 'a whole climate of opinion / under whom we conduct our different lives' whether we want to or not. So psychoanalysis, which is about how things get in under our radar, itself gets in under our radar; it comes to represent, among other things, language we may not be able to protect ourselves from, a language unduly contagious. But Freud was not, in the generations eager to make it new, part of the right version of the new; his work, and those who were impressed by it, were symptoms of the bewildered society, not a way of addressing this bewilderment. Psychoanalysis pre-empted the realer engagements, was actually, itself, a form of repression. In a London Letter for the *Dial* in August 1922 Eliot had written that the conclusion of May Sinclair's novel *The Life and Death of Harriett Frean*:

> extracts as much pity and terror as can be extracted from the materials; but because the material is so clearly defined (the soul of man under psychoanalysis) there is no possibility of tapping the atmosphere of unknown terror and mystery in which our life is passed and which psychoanalysis has not yet analysed.

That 'not yet' makes the point. For Pound, Freud makes people write about sex when they should be writing about economics; for Eliot, Freud makes us write too definitively about unknown terrors and mysteries ('the material is so clearly defined'). Psychoanalysis is the wrong language in the wrong place; too prescriptive, too knowing. For Pound and Eliot, Freud's work exemplified the very things it was attempting to cure. Fears about language, we might say, were being mapped out. Fears about language as distracting and distracted.

If, as Lyndsey Stonebridge has written, 'The relation between modernism and psychoanalysis in France has . . . its own history which, from Breton through to the Tel Quel group . . . is characterised by a continual affirmation of the radical potential of both the avante-garde and psychoanalysis,' the same is not true of the relation between Anglo-American modernist poets and psychoanalysis, which is characterized at worst by outright dismissal, and at best by a wary disregard. Cocteau, who was French and interested in psychoanalysis, was, in the view of Pirandello and Pound, who were not, too much of a poet to fall into the Freudian mess. He was too good a poet to plop into Freud when tackling the subject of Oedipus. H. D.,

3

an American modernist poet who valued Freud greatly – and who we will come back to – had, in Pound's view, virtually fallen into the wrong pig stye ('not too late to climb out') instead of sticking to the right reading list left by Dante. What is the Freudian mess, and what kind of wrong reading list was psychoanalysis for these modernist poets? Why Dante rather than, instead of, Freud? What is it about Freud's work that is supposed to be insidiously undermining or misleadingly seductive for the poet? These plops and falls and erections and pig styes have obvious associations. Clearly, psychoanalysis is not being treated as harmless.

While the psychoanalysts, beginning most notably with Freud, were for the poets and poetry, the poets have never, in quite the same way, been for psychoanalysis – other, that is, than the surrealists. 'The poets and the philosophers before me discovered the unconscious,' Freud famously wrote on the occasion of his seventieth birthday. 'What I discovered was the scientific method by which the unconscious can be studied.' 'At the beginning I was utterly at a loss,' Freud wrote in *Civilization and Its Discontents*, 'and the first clue that I had came from the philosopher-poet Schiller who observed that the mechanism of the world was held together by hunger and love.' There are many such moments in Freud – and in his followers – when poetry and poets are cited as both precursors and unofficial collaborators in the psychoanalytic project; as though what Freud calls generically 'the poets' are taken to be allies, fellow-travellers in the same timely cultural conversation as the psychoanalysts. As though there is something they are doing together even though this something is rarely spelled out (or spelled out as anachronistic banality, exploring the depths of the modern psyche, and so on). It is, though, also worth taking seriously Freud's preference for what he calls, more in the tradition of German Romanticism, the philosopher-poets, Goethe being pre-eminent for Freud; philosophy adding something to poetry that Freud needed, or Freud thought that poetry needed to be akin to psychoanalysis; or poetry making the philosophy that Freud tended to be wary of more palatable. But my point is the simple one: poets, right from the beginning, are invoked by psychoanalysts, whether pathologized or idealized or both, as exemplary and inspiring figures in the way that Freud and his followers were not and are not by poets. And this would probably not be worth mentioning were it not for two things: firstly, and most obviously, that Freud's work is contemporaneous – and in a certain sense, of a piece with – modernism in the arts. And secondly – most succinctly formulated if not inaugurated by Lionel Trilling's great essay 'Freud and Literature' – because of the rediscovery of Freud by the poets for the poets by the poet-critics Empson, Auden and Jarrell, and by the American critics Burke, Bloom and Hartman. There is a Freud, that is to say, that is rediscovered and used by a later generation of the literary. 'Of all mental systems,' Trilling wrote – in an essay first published in 1940 and revised and republished in 1947, and so neatly spanning the war – 'the Freudian psychology is the one that makes poetry indigenous to the very constitution of the mind. Indeed the mind, as Freud sees it, is in the greater part of its tendency exactly a poetry-making organ.' This, of course, cuts both ways – if Freud has discovered that we are all poets, we just have to work out now what makes some people better poets than others; or we have to work out why we still call some people poets and not others. It is not exactly that people are suffering from inhibited sexuality, it is implied, but from the inhibitions, symptoms and anxiety around their poetry-making organs. The poet, we might think – at least according to Trilling, the critic; poets are not cited to support this view – finds in psychoanalysis the science most germane to her practice; not only is the psychoanalyst self-evidently in favour of the poet, the poet can now welcome psychoanalysis as having recognized her exemplary significance and status. Habit, Pater wrote, is a form of failure; in Trilling's view of Freud, insufficient verbal inventiveness is a form of failure. Psychoanalytic patients were people who didn't realize how tellingly they spoke, or who couldn't speak tellingly enough. Though there was, despite Trilling's point, and as

5

he well knew, more to poetry than expressive power; it is, for example, as Eliot remarked, a form of punctuation. It is not entirely clear what it means to say that the mind is a poetry-making organ and not to add that the mind does not always or often think or speak in poetic forms. We know what Trilling means, and we don't know. A later formulation from his essay 'Art and Neurosis' — 'Freud, by the whole tendency of his psychology, establishes the naturalness of artistic thought' — seems more compelling because it is vaguer.

Psychoanalysis, we can now see, found its way into literary criticism but not in a comparable way into poetry. And perhaps we have not been sufficiently struck, or perplexed, by the fact that critics could apply psychoanalysis to poetry in a way that poets, on the whole, did not. Certainly poets then, as now — with notable exceptions — have not been explicit or forthcoming about psychoanalysis as a significant inspiration for, or presence in, or influence on, their writing. Just as, at its inception, it was not as inspiring as it might have been to what Freud called 'the poets' with the notable and telling exception of the surrealists in France. It is no longer sufficient to say — even if it is sometimes part of some truth — that psychoanalysis was merely resisted by the poets; though it is worth wondering what about Freud's work, what about psychoanalysis, might feel threatening rather than inspiring to the poet without the assumption that the poet is wrong to be threatened. What kind of perceived danger could psychoanalysis be to what Trilling called, in his strange phrase, the poetry-making organ? The question being perhaps a version of Karl Kraus's aphorism that psychoanalysis is the symptom of what it purports to be the cure. What is it that a particular vocabulary, certain words in a certain context, certain kinds of conversation, certain kinds of writing, can do that might spoil — rather than foster or prompt or provoke — someone's poetry-making? As though a certain kind of language — call it psychoanalytic language — could be bad for poetic language? These could be, say, justifiable fears of being dominated by someone's vocabulary, which would mean being dominated by their jargon, by their morality and their life-aims; or it could be fear of expression foreclosed by pathologizing; fear of attention being narrowed; fear of a world consisting only of know-alls and know-nothings. And clearly, when one thinks of even its most impressive adepts and acolytes, psycho-analysis has in various ways colonized their writing, and indeed their characters; and this despite the fact that psychoanalysis cultivates an acute awareness of the singularity of individual histories; that psychoanalysis is the science of the individual voice, despite the fact that there are so few individual voices within it. Indeed one thing psychoanalysis might be showing us, or warning us, is how languages can take over. Or, to put it the other way round – developmentally – shows or warns how language begins by taking over, and shows what we can and can't do with or about that fact.

Psychoanalysis never lets go, but in a quite different way from the poems and the poets that haunt us and that we return to. What is the difference – which is not entirely a difference, or entirely to do with the fact that poetic voices are both older and more various than psychoanalytic voices? Languages that stick can call up our most ambivalent feelings even though we never quite know what they stick to. And these questions, sufficiently historicized, may be as pertinent now as they were in the early twentieth century when Freud's work was first being translated into English; the *Three Essays on the Theory of Sexuality* was first translated in 1910, *The Interpretation of Dreams* in 1913, *The Psychopathology of Everyday Life* in 1914. It is a question of both the dangers of psychoanalysis, and what, to put it psychoana-lytically, is a facilitating environment for poetry. What is bad for poets about psychoanalysis, and what is good for poetry? Are certain kinds of language, certain kinds of exchange, harmful to poets and poetry? After all, it's not as though poets in general, if such a group exists, claim philosophers, or anthropologists, or historians as their own. And yet what is distinctive – and this is not of course unique to poets – is the hostility Freud's work occasioned. Psychoanalysis may be something many people don't want, but why, it may still be worth wondering, would these modernist and later poets not want it? Or why wouldn't they just ignore it? After all, Freud doesn't need to be mentioned, so in referring to him what do they imagine they are doing? What exactly is the conversation they are joining in to, and why are they bothering? If we can work out what is bad for poets about Freud, we may have more of a clue about what we imagine is good for them, whether or not it is, as Pound thought, the reading list that Dante left.

This traditionally has been the moment when people, often 'artists', start talking about their fear that if they are cured they will be cured of their art, if they lose their devils they will lose their angels, and so on. In actuality there is no risk of cure – 'we're on earth and there's no cure for that' – and I take it that this fear has always been another way of locating whatever it is about ourselves that can sabotage our inspiration; another way of saying that we can never know beforehand whether a relationship, an exchange, will be good for us in the way we want it to be good. Or another way of saying what Keats said, that we 'hate poetry that has a palpable design upon us', while psychoanalysis, which may or may not sometimes be poetry, certainly has a palpable design upon us. Whether, or in what sense, psychoanalysis is for poets – is good for them, is on the side of their poetry; whether and why psychoanalysis has been an object of suspicion for poets more than an object of desire – is something to do with the nature of psychoanalysis and the fears it evokes, and something to do with how certain traditions of poetry, and not only poetry, predisposed poets to think in a certain way of the once new science of psychoanalysis, and of poetry. Why, in short, should psychoanalysis and poetry be linked at all? What have they got to do with each other? Other, that is, than the fact that Freud and his followers have had a mostly unreciprocated love and admiration for what are still called, in psychoanalysis, the poets? Why, to put it pragmatically, have poets after Freud been unable to make more use of psychoanalysis, when psychoanalysts have been able to make so much use of them? Why do psychoanalysts idealize poets when poets do not tend to idealize psychoanalysts? Or, what is it about poets and poetry that can make analysts so servile? There is, one could say, in psychoanalytic language, a sado-masochistic relationship – if one can speak so generally – between psychoanalysts and poets; the analysts admire, desire and idealize the poets, while the poets, often enough, are not that interested in psychoanalysis, or actively disavow it. Love, Lacan remarked, is only real if it is mutual.

Psychoanalysis, we could say, as a newer thing than poetry, likes the way poetry can legitimate it; but poets, of course, do not need psychoanalysis to legitimate what they do. And yet once, at the very beginnings of psychoanalysis, Freud's work seemed so promising for the arts, and possibly even for poetry. 'Freud's promise,' Michael Levenson writes in his book *Modernism*,

> was that even obscure and atypical neuroses would eventually be revealed as intelligible and that the most eccentric conduct would fall within the laws of the psyche. Although he held to the vocation of science, and resisted 'wild analysis,' his work was an invitation to other uses, with the case studies encouraging a view of selfhood as deep, extravagant, and desirous. Furthermore, the celebrated, central technique of therapy – the free associations of the patient – was a spur to narrative experiment. Freud rigorously demanded the application of law-like principles, but for many artists, writers, and musicians, the great example of his work was the image of life beyond the law. In the 1920s, the surrealists took Freud as an inspiration for their use of dreams and automatic writing as essential sources of artistic creation. But well before Surrealism emerged, psychoanalytic ideas (and images), especially where they converged with the anti-rationalism of Nietzsche, suggested the power of singularity rather than the force of law.

Levenson's suggestion that Freud's work 'was an invitation to other uses', that 'the great example of his work was the image of life beyond the law', a 'view of selfhood as deep, extravagant, and desirous', seems applicable to the arts in general as a kind of liberation from older forms,

9

a new-found commitment to what Levenson calls 'anti-rationalism' and the 'power of singularity'. And it is instructive to be reminded now that Freud's work was once thought of as liberating, revisionary, genuinely transgressive. Certainly, when we think of the so-called great Anglo-American modernist poets, we think of the power of singularity, of the distinctiveness of individual voices, but not always of a celebration or welcoming of the anti-rational, deeply desirous and extravagant self in its psychoanalytic incarnation (we may think of the self of right-wing sympathies, or the Lawrentian self, say, but this is not the psychoanalytic version). We can read the effect of Freud's work on so-called traditional narrative – or just see the simultaneity of Freud's work with modern narrative experiment – but no comparable effect on the form and content of poetry. The confessional poets in America, clearly affected by what Philip Rieff called 'the triumph of the therapeutic', were still called confessional, something patently theological and not psychoanalytic. A post-Freudian poetry might have said something more or something else about sexuality, or about the putative death-instinct; it might have had a new post-Romantic sense of the tendentiousness of childhood memories; it might have found in psychoanalysis different forms of self-justification, new ethical ideals, a new repertoire of ways of describing how the past informs and deforms the present; new imaginings of the allure of transgression, or of the kinds of relationships people might be able to have. But this has been truer, as I say, of the criticism of poetry than of the poetry itself. And the surrealist experiment, in which Freud was distinctly uninterested, was always a paradoxical, though sometimes witty, misreading of his work in its attempt to recruit the unrecruitable unconscious, to do by day what the dream-work does by night. Freud at least created a context in which dreams could be rather more interesting than they usually are, or in which more interesting things could be said about them. What Levenson writes of Freud's work as an 'invitation to other uses' rings truer for narrative, for drama, for literary criticism, but not in the same way for Anglo-American poetry.

The poets may have read Freud, but they have not been, on the whole, his champions; H. D. and Auden, who I will come to – along with Empson and Jarrell – being the notable exceptions.

It is possible, though I am not knowledgeable enough to know this, that the poetry in this tradition, or rather, in these traditions, was peculiarly resistant, rightly or wrongly, to psychoanalysis. I don't really know why this is, or quite how true it is; it is clear that Freud was read or read about, and that he became, however indiscernible in their poetry, a part, however minimal, of their dream-work, of their cultural equipment, if only agonistically. Certainly none of the great modernist poets, other than H. D., wrote essays on Freud or on psychoanalysis, any more than poets tend to do now (though D. H. Lawrence of course wrote great, elaborate critiques of Freud's work). But rather than coming to larger historical or literary or sociological conclusions, I want to look briefly at three specific instances in which we can ask, and speculate about, what the poet might want from the psychoanalyst; what psychoanalysis or a psychoanalyst might have that a poet might want; what psychoanalysis might be able to do for the poet and his or her poetry. What psychoanalysis could be for poets. The psychoanalyst in each instance being Freud, the poets being respectively: Bruno Goetz, whom Freud saw briefly in 1904–5; the poet H. D. who saw Freud in the 1930s and wrote her remarkable account *Tribute to Freud*; and W. H. Auden, whose great elegy to Freud is essentially perplexed by what Freud and psychoanalysis might be for poets, among other people. These cannot, of course, be taken to be exemplary instances, or historically representative, but they do show Freud and a poet before the Great War, between the wars, and after the wars. For Freud we are always in the wars.

The German poet Bruno Goetz begins his 'reminiscences of Sigmund Freud' on the defensive, as though he had to start his account of his brief treatment with Freud in 1904–5 by addressing the criticisms of people like Pound; as though there was some kind of consensus about Freud and his work, and that all these suspicious misgivings needed to be dispelled. 'Whenever I hear people talk about Freud's alleged intellectualism, his biased methods and his reductive thinking,' Goetz writes,

> my reaction is to say, But what you are trying to say isn't right, or rather, it's only half the truth, since it leaves out the most important element: Freud the man as I knew him during my years as a student in Vienna, when I had a few conversations with him which made a profound impression on me. As a man Freud had greater breadth, richness, complexity, and – I'm glad to say – more inherent contradictions than his teaching.

A poet himself – he went to see Freud to treat his 'attacks of acute facial neuralgia' when he was a student at the University of Vienna and, as he says, 'writing his first important poems' – Goetz is saying that Freud is not accurately represented by his writing, or his reputation. The issue of writing, that is to say, is immediately in play. Having been referred to Freud, Goetz quickly reads *The Interpretation of Dreams* and is appropriately appalled. 'At first I was deeply shocked by it,' he writes:

> I found his manner of interpreting dreams scandalous since it destroyed the dream vision as such (which ran counter to the whole of my artistic sensitivity, especially when I thought of this procedure being applied to poetry) and conjured up from the shattered wreckage a new interrelationship of meaning which both disturbed and secretly attracted me.

When Goetz meets Freud – his symptoms, of course, are soon cured – he confronts him in some trepidation about this supposedly reductive type of psychoanalytic interpretation:

> I took a moment to compose myself and then I asked:
>   'What happens when you analyse a poem? Do you not then resolve its component parts until there is strictly speaking nothing

left of it and in this way take us to the brink of nothingness? I am sorry if this question sounds impertinent, but this does bother me.'

'Why do you think it is impertinent?' Freud replies:

'I have constantly asked myself the same thing. You put the question to me as a poet who feels that his existence is threatened . . . I, however, am a psychologist not a poet. When I enjoy a poem as poetry I certainly do not analyse it, I let it make its effect on me which is purely that of edifying me. The function of art in society is to edify, to build us up when we are in danger of collapsing. When, however, I approach a poem as a psychologist, as far as I am concerned, it is from that moment no longer a poem but rather a hieroglyphic and problematic psychological text which I have to decipher, and which in doing so I am bound to dismember. The psychological manner in which with luck I apprehend it has nothing to do with the work of art before me. I merely use it as an invaluable means of gaining scientific knowledge. It is natural that you as an artist should thereby feel injured and misunderstood. Well, I quite understand how you feel. But you must forgive me since I am also a man of science . . .'

Much, of course, can be made of this, as of the whole brief but fascinating account of how Freud actually worked. It is a paper that should be better known. But there are two things I want to stress that are, I think, pertinent to the matter in hand. First, and most obviously and endearingly, Freud's explicit sense of and sympathy with Goetz's fears and doubts about psychoanalytic interpretation. But then there is Freud's distinction between the poem and the scientist's use of it: 'The psychological manner in which with luck I apprehend it has nothing to do with the work of art before me.' Presumably he means that it has nothing to do with the work of art as a work of art. It is almost as though Freud is preaching a kind of pragmatic pluralism, though he wouldn't have called it that; a poem, like any work of art, can be used, can be redescribed from different points of view. Freud as psychoanalytic scientist wants to use the poem for 'gaining scientific knowledge'; but in a different context, as a non-psychoanalytic reader – what we might call a common reader – Freud lets the poem have its effect on him, which he describes as edifying. Meaning is a function of use. A poem, like any other cultural artefact, has many aspects, can be redescribed with differing intentions in mind. What Goetz the poet wants from Freud the psychoanalyst is cure of his symptoms, reassurance that Freud doesn't mind impertinent questions, that he is keen to see things from Goetz's point of view, and that he won't by psychoanalytic interpretation be taken, as he puts it, 'to the brink of nothingness'; even though that might be an interesting place to be taken (and is indeed a place favoured by many Lacanian analysts).

'The function of art in society,' Freud says to Goetz – easily shedding his analytic neutrality and reticence – 'is to edify, to build us up when we are in danger of collapsing.' Like psychoanalysis, one might think, an affinity is being intimated. And indeed it might be better to think of psychoanalysis as one of the arts, and so as edifying; edifying in Richard Rorty's distinction in *Philosophy and the Mirror of Nature* between philosophers like Dewey and Wittgenstein whose 'aim is to edify – to help their readers or society as a whole, break free from outworn vocabularies and attitudes, rather than to provide "grounding" for the intuitions and customs of the present'. Pound and Eliot and H. D., Yeats and Lawrence, one could say, wanted to provide a 'grounding' in the way that Moore and Stevens and Ashbery do not. And psychoanalysis is similarly divided between essentialists and revisionaries. Freud, at least in his encounter with Goetz, is on the side of breaking free from outworn vocabularies and attitudes. 'I don't want to impose my ideas on you,' Freud says to Goetz in Goetz's account:

> you are very young and the devil knows where you will end up. That is another reason I am not going to analyse you; you must make your

own way. For my part I remain what is known as an old-fashioned honourable atheist, trying to help people by helping them gain insight into themselves. That is *my* good conscience. *You* must try your own way.

'You are very young and the devil knows where you will end up': perhaps Freud believed that the young, or that young poets, make Faustian pacts. But, at least from Goetz's meeting with Freud, we can say that there are two things the psychoanalyst can do for the poet, two things the poet might want from the psychoanalyst. First, the psychoanalyst can help dispel the poet's paranoid fantasies about what psychoanalysis will do to him, and through this what other things (and people) might do to him. And secondly, the analyst can refuse to psychoanalyse him. But it has to be an analyst – in this case *the* analyst – who doesn't do the analysing. In this brief encounter Freud says one thing about Goetz's poems: 'they are very fine but shut in on themselves. You hide behind your words instead of letting them carry you along.' He asks Goetz briefly about his father and his love affairs, and makes a few observations about Goetz's character. 'It was,' Goetz writes, 'as though someone had opened a floodgate within me.' In Freud's presence – what Goetz calls Freud's 'wonderfully kind and warm gaze' – Goetz discovers in himself an appetite to talk. 'The main thing,' Freud finally says to Goetz, 'is never lose heart. And *never* have yourself analysed. Write good poetry, if it is in your power to do so, but don't become shut in on yourself or hide yourself away. One always stands naked before God; that is the only prayer we can still offer.' Freud was too much of a poet to analyse Goetz. The poet must come to the psychoanalyst with all his suspicious expectations and assumptions intact, and the analyst must show the poet that it is otherwise than he imagined. And he does this through engaged conversation informed by a few psychoanalytic preconceptions. The success of a psychoanalysis is as much to do with what the analyst has the wit not to analyse, as with what he analyses. And this depends, of course, partly on the analyst's sense of what psychoanalysis is good for. Freud clearly positions himself on the side of Goetz's poetry and on the side of Goetz's sense of himself as a poet.

In the modern 1974 edition of H. D.'s *Tribute to Freud*, published by Godine and then New Directions, we are confronted, once again, right at the beginning – this time in Norman Holmes Pearson's interesting Foreword – with the hostility of her modernist contemporaries to Freud. H. D. is quoted as saying that her close friend D. H. Lawrence 'was instinctively against Sigmund Freud', and Freud remarks to her that Lawrence impressed him as being 'unsatisfied but a man of real power'. We are told by Pearson that 'Pound's belligerent disapproval of Freud' had 'cooled their friendship' (Pearson and H. D. had been lovers as well as friends). And once again, as with Goetz, the Freud we meet in H. D.'s *Tribute* – possibly unlike the Freud met by Lawrence and Pound in his writing – is not someone one would necessarily avoid or need to disparage. What H. D. calls Freud's 'charming way to fall in with an idea, to do it justice, but not to overstress unimportant details' seems unimpeachable both in its charm and in its attentiveness: 'I had expected to meet,' she writes, 'the rather remote, detached, and much abused scientist, [but] I found the artist. Sigmund Freud said, "Ah, you tell this all so beautifully." ' H. D.'s Freud is not dogmatic – 'Freud says there are always a number of explanations for every finding' – and she experiences him more like a fellow-writer: 'I must find new words,' she writes, 'as the Professor found or coined new words to explain certain as yet unrecorded states of mind or being.' Indeed Freud is presented by H. D., albeit in quasi-religious terms, as the analyst of dogmatism and its pernicious effects: 'He did not wish to prove people wrong,' she writes, 'he wanted only to . . . show them that others had imposed ideas on them that might eventually prove destructive.'

As with Goetz, Freud is keen to acknowledge her as a poet, and all that that might entail for her. Before their meeting in 1932 he writes to her:

> Dear Mrs. Aldington [as she then was], I am not sure of your knowing German so I beg to accept my bad English. It may be especially trying to a poet. You will understand that I did not ask for your books in order to criticize or to appreciate your work, which I have been informed is highly praised by your readers. I am a bad judge on poetry especially in a foreign language. I wanted to get a glimpse of your personality as an introduction to making your personal acquaintance.

The following year he would conclude a letter to her, 'I confidently expected to hear from you that you are writing, but such matter should never be forced.' Freud as a writer, and an aspiring writer himself, understands something about how writing works.

It is, as many people have noted, what psychoanalysts call an idealized portrait; but the risk in saying this is that it is complicit with the psychoanalytic suspicion of idealization that tends to underrate just how productive some idealizations can also be (think, for example, of parenting, of being in love, of religious transfiguration). The analysis worked for H. D.; that is, she valued it in her own terms and felt it to have been important in her life, and in her life as a writer. Like Goetz she had partly expected, or been encouraged to expect, that Freud would be dogmatic, reductive in the scientific way, and unable to take her on her own terms. Instead of speaking on her behalf, he encouraged her to speak and write for herself. The sign that her analysis worked was that H. D. didn't become a Freudian, she just appreciated what he had done for her. Freudians are people who have been unable to recover from Freud's effect on them.

What is striking in both Goetz's and H. D.'s accounts is not that Freud turns out to be a wonderful, warm, inspiring and sympathetic man rather than a scientific crank full of fanatical bunkum, but rather how symmetrical or complementary these accounts are. It may be that Goetz's and H. D.'s accounts were reactive to, or compensatory for, the dismissal and disparagement of Freud that were current. But it is also an abiding and by now familiar element of the psychoanalytic effect that psychoanalysis, and Freud himself, are either exorbitantly prized or unduly vilified. After reading Goetz and H. D. you could be forgiven for thinking that a meeting with Freud was an experience worth having, and perhaps especially useful for a troubled writer, or for those troubled writers. But then with psychoanalysis there is the clinical experience of psychoanalytic treatment, and the reading experience of psychoanalytic texts. And it was, of course, mostly the psychoanalytic texts – what were loosely called the ideas – that were turned against; what Eliot called contemptuously, 'the soul of man under psychoanalysis' was not a soul worth saving. The soul of man under psychoanalysis is a soul oppressed – the allusion to Wilde's title links psychoanalysis with socialism – but what exactly is it oppressed by? And what is it oppressed by that is of particular danger to the poetry-making organs of modernist poets?

Clearly the question of why poets might, in the best and the worst senses, resist psychoanalysis is part of the larger question of why anyone, of why a whole culture, might have misgivings about it. And so it might tell us something useful about what poetry, or modern post-Freudian poetry, is assumed to be if psychoanalysis is deemed to be something that poets should steer clear of (just as it is telling us something about our picture of what human nature is or should be if psychoanalysis is taken to be something that can pervert or mislead it). Psychoanalysis as the saboteur of the poetic is one of its more intriguing and disturbing incarnations. Possibly more revealing, in its way, than psychoanalysis – as it was for Goetz and H. D. among the very few – as the facilitator or even the inspirer of the poetic. Psychoanalysis may have, for a time – let's say, at least in Britain and America between the 1950s and the early 1980s – been embraced, albeit ambivalently, by the wider culture informing its language and many of its social practices. In literary criticism and what became cultural studies – in the work of Wittgenstein, in the work of Cavell, in the work of Rorty, just to take philosophy alone – Freud is a significant presence. Psychoanalysis, I think it is true to say, has never had a comparable status or influence among the poets. And we should perhaps wonder in what sense, if at all, this is of any interest. And this is where Auden comes in. Auden as the only modern British or American poet – other, that is, than Empson and Randall Jarrell, who were both significantly influenced by Auden – who keenly and consistently, at least for a time, takes Freud up as a necessary adjunct and inspiration for his poetry. For Auden, Freud was as essential as the landscape and the climate. What, we can briefly consider by way of conclusion, was he essential for?

Auden's relationship with Freud is a subject for another essay. But when he writes in an essay of 1935, 'Psychology and Art Today' – which includes a section entitled 'What would be a Freudian literature' – that 'the importance of Freud to art is greater than his language, technique or the truth of theoretical details' we are left in no doubt about just how impressed the young, radical poet was by Freud. He begins his essay by implicitly comparing 'the influence of Freud upon modern art' with the influence of 'Plutarch upon Shakespeare'. But nothing Auden says in this telling essay is specifically about poetry; it is about the arts in general. He has wanted, as he puts it, 'to show what light Freud has thrown on the genesis of the artist and his place and function in society, and what demands he would make upon the serious writer'. But he does mention in his conclusion, as among Freud's 'obvious technical influences on literature', 'the use of words in associational rather than logical sequence'. And we can read this influence in Auden's early poetry; Freud allows for and encourages the truth-tellings of association in preference to the more supposedly defensive logical sequences of coherent narrative and phrasing. But by the time Auden comes to write his great elegy to Freud he has become a no less inventive but more discursive poet. And it is in this poem, perhaps unsurprisingly, that Auden, unlike the first generation of modernist poets, is thinking about, among many other things, what psychoanalysis is for poets. And there will be no comparable meditation on this until Robert Pinsky's wonderful 'Essay on Psychiatrists' in his appropriately entitled first book, *Sadness and Happiness*, of 1975.

For Auden, Freud's death had inspired an elegy, but what had poets as poets lost, if anything, from Freud's death, while gaining such a great elegy? It is worth noting, as John Fuller does in his wonderful Commentary on Auden's poetry, that, as he puts it, 'This poem appears, incidentally, to be the first that Auden wrote in syllabic metre, under the influence of Marianne Moore.' Auden, that is to say, wrote a different kind of poem for the death of Freud. 'Syllabics', James Fenton writes, refers 'to a kind of poetry in which the principle of organisation of the line is by number of syllables *and nothing else . . .* For the most part, though, counting the syllables seems to be something that works, if it works, for the poet. It is a private method of organization.' In telling us of the public shared loss and legacy of Freud, Auden is also, inevitably, saying something about a more private loss; after all, Freud has left us his writing, and it isn't a personal relationship exactly that is being mourned. Indeed the poem opens by asking a question about the privacy of grief:

> When there are so many we shall have to mourn,
> when grief has been made so public, and exposed
> to the critique of a whole epoch
> the frailty of our conscience and anguish,
>
> of whom shall we speak?

Freud made it clear in his writing – much of which, unsurprisingly, as he got older, was about mourning and loss – that one of the people of whom we speak when we mourn is inevitably ourselves. It is as if Auden is wondering here just how self-revealing his elegy might be;

just as it might be one of the oppressions of psychoanalysis to make us feel that whatever else we are talking or writing about we are always also talking and writing about ourselves; or even worse, that we are really only talking about ourselves. The question – even in an elegy, and perhaps particularly in an elegy for Freud – is: of whom shall we speak? If Freud is, in Auden's words, 'a whole climate of opinion' who, 'like weather . . . can only hinder or help' and 'quietly surrounds all our habits of growth', he becomes, as a writer, somehow inescapable, something any writer might both fear and desire; someone who invades our privacy by redescribing it. This being surrounded, this medium, this language in which one must live, could leave one feeling, like Blake – though wrongly – that one must 'create' one's own system or be 'enslaved' by another man's. Paradoxically, for his fellow-writers, Freud's language might be too captivating, or captivating in the wrong way; Freud might have done something with language that could feel enviable, or intimidating, or distracting, or radically misleading. Freud's writing, whatever else it had done, had certainly exposed just how contagious a language can be. And Auden's elegy is celebrating this contagion in terms of the benefits it has brought. Unlike the younger Auden, it should be remembered, who had written in his journal in 1929, 'The trouble with Freud is that he accepts conventional morality as if it were the only one.'

Auden, who managed as a poet to give knowingness a good name, refers to 'wit' and 'conceit', and indeed to Dante in the poem – as for Pound, Freud and Dante once again juxtaposed – but there is only one moment in 'In Memory of Sigmund Freud' that poetry is referred to explicitly, as it were: one moment when poetry and psychoanalysis are linked, in the name of Freud.

> He wasn't clever at all: he merely told
> the unhappy Present to recite the Past
> like a poetry lesson till sooner
> or later it faltered at the line where

      long ago the accusations had begun,
      and suddenly knew by whom it had been judged,
      how rich life had been and how silly,
      and was life-forgiven and more humble,

      able to approach the Future as a friend
      without a wardrobe of excuses, without
      a set mask of rectitude or an
      embarrassing over-familiar gesture.

A scene is being described – a poetry lesson deemed to be 'like' a psychoanalytic session – in which something is revealed through a faltering that opens up the future. After this sudden knowledge the future can be approached without alibi or pretence, 'without a wardrobe of excuses, without / a set mask of rectitude or an / embarrassing over-familiar gesture'. But if this poetry lesson is akin to a psycho-analytic session in which Freud 'told / the unhappy Present to recite the Past', what is this 'poetry lesson'? Auden clearly wants us to attend to it because the line-endings make us stop and start, noticing what has happened and what is happening in this lesson; and, of course, because a poetry lesson is being referred to in a poem which we are in the process of reciting to ourselves as we read it. A number of questions are soon raised without being resolved: is this poetry lesson one in which someone is learning about poetry, or learning to write a poem, or to recite an already existing one? And which poem is it? In what sense is learning to recite a poem a poetry lesson, any more than learning to recite psychoanalytic theory is a lesson in psycho-analysis? When the unhappy Present is told to recite the Past, the implication is that the past is already known – is available to be recited – so the past must be like a poem we already know but can't quite recite; we falter at a certain line – the line 'where / long ago the accusations had begun' – and at our faltering, at our pause or hesita-tion or slip something is revealed. It is a strange situation because the so-called patient is learning to recite a poem that she has already written (or at least that no one else has), and already knows; the past, Auden intimates, is a poem we have written but never got quite right; or, the past is a poem we tend to forget, one we learn to recite but where we falter, where we can't remember or get it wrong, or disclose our history to ourselves; or at least the bit of our history that has made the future so difficult. The point of this poetry lesson is that where the recitation fails, where we falter, the important thing is revealed; the sudden knowledge occurs not where the poem fails, but where our memory of the poem fails. Freud reveals, in Auden's view, that the past is a poem that we keep failing to remember; and that we need those poetry lessons called psychoanalysis to learn to recite the poem, and to see where we falter. It is an extraordinary and wonderful idea that our personal pasts are a poem that we have to learn to recite. The poem has already happened – or rather, we must assume, has already been written; the question is whether we can recite it; and whether we can let ourselves falter. It is an interesting idea that we have our histories off by heart, and that if psychoanalysis is like a poetry lesson then our histories are in some way like a poem.

As in Trilling's account of Freud, we are all already poets; what is not explained is why or how some people actually then become poets, while most people do not. Auden, in this poem, wants us to think of psychoanalysis as like a poetry lesson in which we learn to recite something like a poem that we keep forgetting. We all have a past which is like a poem which we can more or less recite; though we were not aware of writing it and not aware that it was a poem. Poets are people like us, but also people who actually write poems. They show us how it is done, and indeed what a poem is, and in this sense they can help us with our psychoanalysis, and so with our sense of the past.

But what, at least in this version, is Auden suggesting psychoanalysis can do for poets? Well, one thing it can do is give them an analogy for – another way of picturing or describing – what they might be doing in writing or reading a poem; or at least, what they might be doing in a poetry lesson. Poetry is attentive, in a way psychoanalysis cannot be, to the difference between articulating something as well as one can – against resistances – and getting better. Between the voicing of something and the curing of something. Poetry wants to do something to us but unlike propaganda and psychoanalysis it needn't have, and often doesn't have, stated aims. Psychoanalysis, by definition, has stated aims; and this is the best and the worst thing about it, the bunkum and the boon. If psychoanalysis is like a poetry lesson, a poetry lesson – in the fullest sense of that phrase – might be, as Auden suggests, like a psychoanalysis. But a lesson in getting something right in words, as right as one can make it; and a lesson in the importance of faltering; and a lesson in the value of unstatable, unknowable aims. This is what I think, or I hope, that Auden meant when he wrote in his great elegy that Freud 'would have us remember most of all / to be enthusiastic over the night'. But this, of course, once again, is just another reminder of what poetry can do for psychoanalysis.

Tribute to H. D.

This is no rune nor riddle,
it is happening everywhere;

H. D., *Tribute to the Angels*

One of H. D.'s last entries in 'Advent' – the notebook that she kept during her analysis with Freud – is about fairy tales. She has been remembering the Greek myths that were read to her when she was seven by a Miss Helen. Those stories, she writes, 'are my foundation or background, Pandora, Midas, the Gorgon-head – that particular story of Perseus and the guardian, Athene'. H. D.'s parents were pious Protestants, but like many of her modernist contemporaries she was turning cultures of myth into what Freud had called, in a famous and timely essay, 'a family romance'. Disillusioned with the real parents, the child chooses parents she would prefer to have had – typically grander, more impressive ones – and believes they are in fact her parents. The family history is complemented as it were by other histories; genealogies are chosen, inheritances are found and fashioned. Not satisfied imaginatively by the religion of her parents, H. D. found other myths (and indeed wonders several times during her analysis with Freud whether she will be the founder of a new religion). H. D., it seems, from a very young age, was seeking alternative foundations and backgrounds. She was using what she could find to tell her own stories.

H. D. became a writer with an extraordinary gift for finding and forming the connections and affinities she needed to articulate her vision. There was Christianity, Greek and Egyptian mythology – she would write a book-length poem entitled *Helen in Egypt*: she was always a born Freudian in her ability to so freely associate – and then there was her encounter, as a middle-aged woman, with Freud, and his Jewish history. For Freud, as for H. D., there was something belated and diminishing about Judeo-Christian culture ('The Professor said that we two met in our love of antiquity') but there was something about all religions, all mythologies, all compelling fictions that needed, in Freud's view, to be interpreted, to be redescribed. New links needed to made between apparently disparate phenomena; between, say, spellbinding parents and entrancing gods, between symptoms and inspiration, between sexuality and hope. As H. D. herself realized, they were both, as modernist writers, wanting a revitalization of culture, a renewal through language. For Freud, and for H. D. in the troubled period of her life, psychoanalysis was a means to this, but not an end. It was not a new religion, but a method; a method summed up in H. D.'s brief reference to fairy tales in her notebook:

The miracle of the fairy tale is incontrovertible; Sigmund Freud would apply, rationalize it.

It is an apparently simple remark, but like many of the sentences in her *Tribute to Freud*, which is an unusual mixture of poetry and prose, it needs noticing. If something is incontrovertible it can't be opposed, or argued against, or disputed, or denied (and the controversy that was psychoanalysis is somewhere in the background here); Sigmund Freud – his whole name authorizing the point – would 'apply, rationalize it', acknowledge the miracle by transforming it, by seeing it as a metaphor for something that matters (the wish to change, and to change the world); a mere comma separating the two words suggests that to apply might also be to rationalize, which may not necessarily be a bad thing. 'Rationalization' has received bad press largely because of psychoanalysis, but it is worth remembering, as H. D. does here, that in Freud's minting of the word we only rationalize things that are disturbing and important. Our rationalizations are our personal mythologies.

So what would it be to apply, to rationalize, a miracle? That is H. D.'s question, in a book riddled with questions and answers (she calls Freud her 'answerer', but is also clear that the aim of psychoanalysis is to enable the patient to find and formulate her own questions, and not be fobbed off with answers that can't work because they don't). Freud, in H. D.'s view, is not exactly disputing the miracle of the fairy tale, he is using it differently; as a poet might use, or apply, a myth. This is what H. D. went to see Freud for: to find new applications, new rationalizations – bearable redescriptions of unbearable things – for the material that mattered most to her. This material was her recent traumatic history, and the mythologies and symbols which she had made and used to keep herself going. What H. D. wanted to talk about with Freud was her life during one world war and before another, interwoven with childhood memories and dreams; a life in which both her parents and a brother had died, in which she had miscarried, been seriously ill and borne a child; a life in which her marriage and various love affairs had fallen apart, as she herself had, and in which she had made herself a remarkable avant-garde writer (Barbara Guest's wonderful biography of H. D. tells the story with extraordinary vividness and tact). In *Tribute to Freud* H. D. tells the story of someone trying to make a new kind of sense of living in the aftermath of a catastrophe, with the (accurate) foreboding of there being another catastrophe in the offing. And one of the many touching things about H. D.'s relationship with Freud in this book is her wish to protect Freud, the great realist, from knowing too much about the Nazi threat. In delegating both her fear of the future and her wish not to know about this fear to Freud she could sustain him in her mind as the powerful figure she needed. The strange title of her remarkable novel about the First World War, *Bid Me to Live* – written in 1927 – was the demand she brought to Freud.

It is of interest, given her predilection for something like a collective unconscious – what she refers to in her *Notes on Thought and Vision* of 1919 as the 'universal mind' or the 'over-mind'– that it was Freud and not Jung or a Jungian that H. D. had wanted to see (you could always tell a Freudian from a Jungian by their attitude to fairy tales). And it is not incidental that Ezra Pound and D. H. Lawrence, who had both been immensely influential in H. D.'s earlier life, were in different ways fiercely and determinedly anti-Freudian. Knowing what was good for her, which meant knowing what was good about herself, H. D. could also be undistracted by men. She saw meeting with Freud as an opportunity so she could make it one. Indeed it is one of the many boons and benefits of *Tribute to Freud* that it makes us wonder why so few of the great modernist writers found Freud's work useful, or only useful agonistically (H. D. found it both). *Tribute to Freud* should be read, that is to say, not merely for what it tells us about Freud – though it tells us much that is of great interest – but for what it shows us and tells us about what H. D. made of Freud, and was making of herself; and making of herself through what she could make of Freud.

Freud, as he says to H. D. – and the Freud in his late seventies that H. D. saw was remarkably candid about his work – had 'struck oil'; but he had, in H. D.'s view, opened up his discovery rather than confining, or foreclosing, or over-owning it. 'He himself – at least to me personally,' she writes '– deplored the tendency to fix ideas too firmly, to set symbols, or to weld them inexorably . . . it was he who "struck oil" but the application of the "oil", what could or should be made of it, could not be regulated or supervised by its original "promoter".' The unconscious, which H. D. calls 'the hieroglyph of the unconscious . . . this vast unexplored region', is an extraordinary resource (at once like oil, and something that oils things); it needs to be deciphered and thus requires trained reading, but not the Jungian fixing of symbols; and it can only be 'promoted', in its several senses, but not strictly defined, or proven. And it is also worth noting how she applies the word 'application'; because it is part of her poetic method in this book, as in her poetry – and psychoanalysis is a method only in the sense that poetry is – to reiterate words and phrases and sentences throughout the text, as indeed happens during psychoanalysis. Without repetition there is no improvisation, and no history. And there is no poetry and no psychoanalysis without following the wording, and its patterns of sound and sense. In *Tribute to Freud* H. D. has the vagrant incisiveness of someone – a writer, in fact, whose writing is an account of a speaking – who can make her associations tell because of her belief in her listener. Freud having, as Foucault remarked, the most famous ears in history.

It is easy now for a psychoanalyst or a so-called patient to be struck in H. D.'s account by just how unorthodox a Freudian Freud was: he lends H. D. books, introduces her to his family, shows her his art-objects, talks about another patient, and generally gossips with her. There is an ease and a friendliness and a sense of real enjoyment in the way Freud works with H. D., that is not at all incompatible with the seriousness of the project, and that is the real lesson of the master (it reveals how strangely professionalized and hemmed in the psychoanalysts quickly became, caricatured and discredited rather than engaged with). And it is equally easy for the contemporary reader to distrust H. D.'s patent, almost awestruck, admiration of Freud: 'with the Professor,' she writes,

I did feel that I had reached the high water-mark of achievement; I mean, I felt that to meet him at forty-seven, and to be accepted by him as analysand and or student, seemed to crown all my other personal contacts and relationships, justify all the spiral-like meanderings of my mind and body. I had come home, in fact.

You don't need to be Sigmund Freud, as it were, to read this as the child's idealization of her parents ('I had come home, in fact': or rather in fantasy, because no home is quite like that). There is a glancing acknowledgement when the first sentence is qualified by 'I mean', that she might have reached a 'high water-mark of achievement' with Freud and not merely by just meeting him. H. D.'s admiration for Freud gave her an appetite to speak, not to submit; an appetite to write, but not in Freud's language. H. D. never became a Freudian, or even a follower; she simply went on being the writer she was becoming.

Read closely it is clear that despite, or because of, her being so impressed by Freud – and Freud explicitly encourages this – H. D. goes her own way and gets what she seems to want from the analysis (when she refers to Freud's 'infallibility' she knows what she is doing, and she knows the irony of what she is saying). One of the things she gets, of course, from the analysis is her *Tribute to Freud*, a piece of writing so artfully akin to a person speaking on the couch that it can and should be read, at least in the first instance, with no scholarly annotation or commentary, the reader, like the analyst, picking things up as she goes along. Indeed, H. D.'s tribute, whatever else it is, is that rare thing, an account of a genuine collaboration, a testimony to the pleasure H. D. and Freud took in each other's company.

What analysts call 'idealization' – often misleadingly, and often misleadingly equating it with a kind of masochism – may be one of the preconditions for collaboration (as it is for parenting, and for falling in love, and indeed for reading and writing). Psychoanalysis could be an 'after-education', to use one of Freud's words, in collaboration; it could be the aim of a psychoanalysis to enable the patient and the analyst, like Freud and H. D. in this unique account of an analysis, to take such pleasure in each other, to be free to be so interested and interesting to each other. H. D., like Freud, but in a quite different way, was able to use psychoanalysis as a means to her own ends, but without needing to know beforehand what they were. 'My discoveries are not primarily a heal-all,' H. D. reports Freud saying to her. 'My discoveries are a basis for a very grave philosophy. There are very few who understand this, there are very few who are capable of understanding this.' H. D., it seems, was one of the very few.

Barthes by Himself

One, really, doesn't have the right to assume anything about anyone.

Joe Brainard, *Diary 1969*

'No need of a story,' Beckett wrote in 'Texts for Nothing', 'a story is not compulsory, just a life.' But in an autobiography you can't have one without the other. It is not compulsory, though it goes without saying now, that everyone has a story and will probably want to tell it (and should be free to); that there is every need for a story; that the one thing everyone does have inside them is an autobiography, and that they might even suffer from not telling it. And yet once you start even telling the story of your day, Barthes writes in *Roland Barthes by Roland Barthes*, 'you constitute yourself, in fantasy, as a "writer", or worse still: you constitute yourself.' You get stuck with the self you have made up; the story becomes compulsory. In an age of autobiography in which life stories – lives recovered in words – have become our inspirational literature, there is always the risk of fixing ourselves. The quest for singularity, the therapy of becoming oneself, might be a form of arrested development; or as Barthes might say, arrested language. There is always the allure of what he called, in *Camera Lucida*, 'the impossible science of the unique being'.

'A certain pleasure is derived,' Barthes wrote in *The Pleasure of the*

Text, 'from a way of imaging oneself as individual, of inventing a final, rarest fiction: the fictive identity.' The idea of an identity of course assumes that there is something, or someone, that one is identical to, as though one's identity is always one's elusive double. For Barthes the only identity is a fictive identity, and we always have various doubles; this fictive identity, Barthes adds ominously, is the way we 'stage our plural'. Autobiography, then, as an invention, a staging, a fiction. And it has to be rare and final because no one writes more than one. You can't be a professional autobiographer. All writing may in some sense be autobiographical, but only an autobiography tells the conventional story of a life. *Barthes by Barthes* shows us, and sometimes tells us, just how compulsory the conventions can be in the conventional stories of a life.

These stories must, for example, give an account of the parents (in *Barthes by Barthes* the parents are rarely evoked, either as characters or as absences); they must contain childhood memories, the person's likes and dislikes (as *Barthes by Barthes* does, but also, like many things in this book, as a list); there must be something, however understated, about a person's so-called sexuality (in *Barthes by Barthes* there is a quietism, an abstraction in Barthes's allusions to his life as a gay man); and the story must make some sense of a life, find a meaning or a pattern in its inevitable repetitions (in *Barthes by Barthes* repetition is repeatedly discussed, but only as an idea, as an issue). An autobiography must, in other words, be what Barthes called a readerly text, one that doesn't make it too difficult for us, one we know how to read. An autobiography has to tell us a story in which we know where we are.

And yet, as Barthes's narrator writes in this extraordinary book – a book that begins, he tells us at the very beginning, after he has finished it, and in which so many of our expectations about autobiography are undone – 'anyone who speaks about himself gets lost'. Psychoanalysis has always been divided about whether we should be better at losing ourselves, or better at not doing so, but autobiography has traditionally been about the finding and describing of selves. Barthes wants us to bear in mind that the words we have for ourselves leave us at a loss. In other words, *Barthes by Barthes* – at least nominally an autobiography – is written by someone who wrote in a famous essay of 1967, 'The Death of the Author', that a text 'has no other origin than language itself, language which ceaselessly calls into question all origins'; and indeed that the text 'is henceforth made and read in such a way that at all its levels the author is absent'. Barthes by Barthes by no one, or nothing, but language. An autobiography without an author that is the autobiography of an author, of a life lived in writing, in which language, more often than not, is the subject.

But everyone, as we know, has a life story – it is seemingly the most democratic of genres – and everyone's life story is different (though every autobiography, and biography, is similar in that it is a revelation of uniqueness). It is a convention of these genres that their subjects should be unconventional in some way; autobiography signifies a heroism however ordinary ('my body is not a hero', the author remarks in *Barthes by Barthes*, just to make sure the reader doesn't jump to the wrong conclusions). The genre makes its own claims on us; it speaks on our behalf. Indeed, nothing persuades us more of the life of the author than his autobiography. A world without life stories is unimaginable now; taking and making a history is where most of the so-called disciplines and professions start from, though without always being overly aware of what they are doing by doing this ('What right,' Barthes asks appropriately in this book about his past, 'does my present have to speak of my past?'). The story is compulsory but the meaning of it is not; the subject is not always clear, and clarity has its own conventions (*Barthes by Barthes* is a book about what it is to make something clear). The story can always and only be interpreted, can always be read differently, and evidence never speaks for itself – or rather, as Barthes writes, 'the true violence is that of the self-evident'. An autobiography is a life made only of words; Barthes wants us to wonder why it goes without saying that there must be something (or someone) in it. And, indeed, why we want to recognize ourselves at all.

The obvious, for Barthes, was a fetish, a way of warding something off; a sign of how apathetic we can be about our pleasure. 'That which goes without saying,' Barthes the semiologist wrote in *Criticism and Truth* in 1966, '. . . never raises questions of method, since a method is, in a quite contrary way, the act of doubt by which one asks oneself about chance or nature.' As a critic Barthes always read for whatever supposedly was beyond question in a text. That which goes without saying, the obvious, the self-evident, the taken for granted – what Barthes calls *doxa* in *Barthes by Barthes*, 'Public Opinion, the mind of the majority, petit bourgeois Consensus, the Voice of Nature, the Violence of Prejudice' – is beyond question, which means, for Barthes, beyond interpretation. But what goes without saying is always said in a language. Semiology, the science of signs that Barthes championed in his own idiosyncratic way, was a reading of culture as a set of languages, and of meaning as something made by a system of signs ('the object of all his work', he writes in *Barthes by Barthes*, 'is a morality of the sign'). A sign system is a consensus in which there has never been an initial agreement; a language is a contract that no one has ever signed. So methods of interpretation are required to make sense of the methods, the assumptions, of language and its effects. It is not a matter of finding what things mean – or, as we say, really mean – but of showing how meaning is made (in contemporary autobiography, for example, the singled-out childhood memories are taken to be the essentially formative experiences, the set pieces that signify The Significant). 'It is necessary to posit a paradigm,' Barthes writes in *Barthes by Barthes*, 'in order to produce a meaning and then to be able to divert, to alter it.' Language as a system, and language as loophole. When Barthes came to write an autobiography – *Barthes by Barthes* was published in 1975, the year he was elected a member of the Collège de France, the year he established himself, so to speak – it was always going to be an improvisation.

Reading Barthes's early writing could make you feel that languages were like cults, and that semiology was the only way out; and, indeed, that semiology could be a pleasure to read, that there was a pathos, an eroticism about signs, that semiology was for the sophisticated, not merely for the technically minded. 'It seemed to me,' Barthes wrote in his *Leçon*, 'that a science of signs could stimulate social criticism,' and it was in *Mythologies*, the book that made him famous – and the book most reprised and referred to in *Barthes by Barthes* – that Barthes performed his eccentric scepticism, his acts of doubt about the *doxa* that he referred to, slightly confusingly, as the myths of contemporary French culture. The Eiffel Tower, Steak and Chips, Striptease, Toys, the World of Wrestling, the Brain of Einstein, French Wine, among many others, were read as coded messages that needed to be unscrambled to expose the often absurd and exploitative ideologies that informed them.

Interpretation, in Barthes's earlier writing, was a form of disillusionment, the unmasking of a cultural fantasy life that masqueraded as the reality principle; language was something that needed to be exposed. 'It is true that wine is a good and fine substance,' Barthes writes in *Mythologies*, and a version of this particular truth is returned to in *Barthes by Barthes*, 'but it is no less true that its production is deeply involved in French capitalism whether it is that of the private distillers or that of the big settlers in Algeria who impose on the Muslims, on the very land of which they have been dispossessed, a crop of which they have no need, while they lack even bread.' Stylishly – without jargon and apparently without method – Barthes used the methods of psychoanalysis, Marxism and semiology to unmask the props of bourgeois life. Myths were the forms of reassurance the culture used to entrap people in forgetful consumption and political naïveté. 'The very principle of myth,' Barthes writes in *Mythologies*, is that 'it transforms history into nature', a process into a fact; 'it abolishes the complexity of human acts, it gives them the simplicity of essences'; once something becomes a myth, in Barthes's terms, 'it is natural and goes without saying'. Myth promotes 'nothing but the popular and age-old image of the perfect intelligibility of reality'. The Barthes of *Mythologies* was an angrier, more politically outraged writer than the Barthes of the later work (in *Barthes by Barthes* politics is often an irritant, something that is so real to him that he wants to find a way around it). But *Mythologies* is the best introduction to *Roland Barthes by Roland Barthes* because autobiography as a genre, as Barthes knew, is our modern myth *par excellence*. Nothing reassures us more about who we are – even when they disturb us, or particularly when they disturb us – than our life stories. Nothing makes us more intelligible to ourselves. But a life story may be a myth we hide our lives in, or hide something about our lives in; not a cover-up, which would suggest there was something essential to be revealed, but a fixation; a fantasy of describing an essential self where there is neither a self nor an essence ('You are a patch-work of reactions,' Barthes describes himself while describing the reader; 'is there anything primary in you?' he asks, perhaps wistfully). There is no avant-garde of autobiography (even though psychoanalysis once promised to be this, the psychoanalytic life story quickly became part of the *doxa*). It is not news now to say that there is no such thing as the self; it is news, however, to show how this works in the practice of writing. In this book Barthes wants to show us how the self forms and performs itself in language, as what he calls an effect of language; how it, as a plural, is literally made up; how, as Barthes writes, it can 'grasp [itself] only by means of an image-repertoire', as a drama of signs.

Barthes's favourite motto, he tells us on several occasions, was *Larvatus prodeo* (I advance pointing to my mask). There is in Barthes's writing an ironic self-consciousness that knows it can't always see what it is showing other people, but is always acutely aware of the audience, and of the reader as part of an audience, as sociable rather than solitary. It is important to remember, when reading *Barthes by Barthes*, his early interest in the theatre – at university in Paris he helped found a theatre group to perform classical plays – and his lifelong interest in Brecht. Because *Barthes by Barthes* is a staged and stagey autobiography of a Brechtian kind ('While writing *Roland Barthes*,' Barthes said in an interview, 'I wasn't sure at one point that I'd have enough to say, and I considered – if only as a fantasy – inserting passages from Brecht'). It is informed, that is to say, by that wariness of extended, continuous narrative that is essential to the episodic nature of Brecht's epic theatre.

Barthes by Barthes is fragmentary for strategic reasons, which are reasons of pleasure. 'Discontinuity of discourse,' Barthes wrote in *Brecht and Discourse* (published the same year as *Barthes by Barthes*), 'keeps the final meaning from "taking",' which is then reiterated in *Barthes by Barthes*: 'a superior rule: that of the breach (heterology): to keep a meaning from "taking"'. If a meaning 'takes' – if a particular image of ourselves, or anything else, begins to stick – if it becomes settled, definitive, essential, it becomes part of the *doxa* (in *The Pleasure of the Text* Barthes contrasts '*doxa*, opinion' with '*paradoxa*, dispute', what is current with what is contentious). And for Barthes there is a terror of getting stuck, of being immobilized, that is everywhere in his writing and which may or may not have been compounded by his two long hospitalizations as a young man for tuberculosis between 1934 and 1935, and, intermittently, between 1941 and 1947. So *Barthes by Barthes* is an autobiography that can be dipped into and skimmed – cruised, to use Barthes's word. The reader is invited, indeed tempted, to move around in the text, without ever losing the place or the plot.

In *Barthes by Barthes* no meaning, no event, significant or otherwise, is dwelt on – there are no privileged moments that are without question – as though the story of a life would be distorted by the assumption of there being themes, or continuities, or self-evidently important memories, or virtually anything else of which a life is supposed to consist (there is, for example, no mention in the book of Barthes's half-brother; no love affairs are described; and lovers and friends are given initials like so-called patients in psychoanalytic case histories, one of the many languages of autobiography alluded to, and parodied, in the book). In his epic theatre, Brecht writes, he 'regards nothing as existing except in so far as it changes, in other words, is in disharmony with itself'. The fragments in alphabetical order of *Barthes by Barthes* – in which an arbitrary system, by replacing the usual developmental story, exposes its arbitrariness – keeps the disharmony going; we can't easily get a picture of the author (or his book), or jump to conclusions, or even come to them. In this auto-biography, in which no one is doing anything as conventional as growing up, we keep jumping to new beginnings (the only heir of *Barthes by Barthes* is J-B Pontalis's remarkable autobiography, *Love of Beginnings*, in which the writing of many autobiographies is proposed). Barthes has no truck with autobiography as the successful or failed progress myth called development. He has to, as he says in this book, '*rewrite* myself', as one might rewrite successive drafts of a book, not with a view to getting it right but to take up positions in relation to himself. So he writes for and against his pleasures while always insisting on them: perversion, for example, is celebrated in this book – 'perversion, quite simply, makes happy; or to be more specific, it produces a *more*' – but Barthes is never an improper writer, there is nothing that sounds like perversion in his book; in a work so much about the body, bodies are rarely described. *Barthes by Barthes* is full of definitions written by someone who goes in fear of definition, and defines the fear: 'to name is to pacify'. Positions are taken up but mustn't be allowed to take, as though he also fears fascination, and is wary of how charmed one can be by oneself (he describes *Barthes by Barthes* as 'the book of my resistance to my own ideas'). So the reader, to whom the writer is unusually attentive in this book, is never allowed to settle into a conventional autobiographical narra-tive, into 'the perfect intelligibility' of a remembered life, into the myth of honesty.

And by the same token, neither is the writer, who is more like a

Brechtian actor than a conventional autobiographer. 'The actor,' Brecht writes in 'A Short Organum for the Theatre', a text much admired by Barthes, 'has to discard whatever means he has learnt of getting the audience to identify itself with the characters which he plays. Aiming not to put his audience into a trance, he must not go into a trance himself.' The writer as so-called autobiographer must not identify with the character in his book – must not assume they are the same or even similar – and the audience must not be allowed to identify with him either, or be lulled into a state of inattention; they must be helped, by the writer, to keep their wits about them, to go on having their own thoughts, to go on interpreting – which means to go on being surprised ('The dramatic theatre's spectator,' Brecht writes, 'says: Yes, I've felt like that too . . . The Epic theatre's spectator says: I'd never have thought it'). The muddles and mystiques of empathy are to be avoided, and the writer must be as conscious as he can be of the kind of appeal he makes to the reader. 'This work [*Barthes by Barthes*] would be defined,' he writes, 'as: *a tactics without strategy*,' intimating that conventional autobiography is a strategy supposedly without tactics, 'innocently' selling us something essential about a self.

So the reader in *Barthes by Barthes* is continually being reminded that that is what he is. Barthes, who is always (as unobtrusively as possible) pedagogic – and who loves the unobtrusive, and so can only hate violence – is all too often telling the reader, in the nicest possible way, how he should be reading his book; or rather, how the writer depends upon him for his effects. 'The ideal would be,' he writes, in *Barthes by Barthes*, 'neither a text of vanity, nor a text of lucidity, but a text with uncertain quotation marks . . . This also depends on the reader, who produces the spacing of the readings.' In a text of uncertain quotation marks no one would be quite sure whose words were whose. The reader would have to be alert, not spellbound but bound by something else to keep reading. Barthes was always interested in new kinds of attention, in new forms of attentiveness. His hedonism was a curiosity, not a nostalgia. He wants us to revise our pleasures. And reading and writing are emblems, for Barthes, of these pleasures.

But of course enthusiasm for the new can never be new now. *Barthes by Barthes*, among many other things – and the text is, in one of Barthes's favourite images, kaleidoscopic – is a new kind of book about novelty; novelty as myth, and novelty as an object of desire. About how we might sustain our pleasure without losing our interest, and about how we might sustain our interest without losing our pleasure. Brecht, Barthes said in an interview, 'was the first to provide me with a theoretical right to pleasure . . . I discovered in him that ethic of both pleasure and intellectual vigilance.' In this book that 'consists of what I do not know' – a book of endless disclaimers in which the author is always disidentifying himself – it is this ethic of pleasure and intellectual vigilance that is the sustaining thread. Every fragment in this book is alert to something, and takes pleasure in the attention it gives and takes and takes away.

But the book also takes pleasure in telling the reader what to do (a writer, after all, cannot be unassuming, he has to make his voice felt; on virtually every page of *Barthes by Barthes* there are italics). Even before it really begins – at the beginning before the beginning – there is an instruction that sounds like a stage direction: 'It must all be considered as if spoken by a character in a novel.' And just in case we forget, the instruction is repeated, with a difference, towards the end of the book, in a section entitled 'The Book of the Self': 'All this must be considered as if spoken by a character in a novel – or rather by several characters.' 'As if' because it isn't a novel, and it isn't spoken; and, of course, for Barthes, it is no longer self-evident what a character is anyway, other than something made with words, and something plural. Language was always Barthes's obscured object of desire (in an uncharacteristically grandiloquent moment in this book, Barthes refers to himself, so to speak, as 'the visionary and voyeur of language'). *Barthes by Barthes* is his celebration of language as possibility. In a society ridden, he once wrote, by two moralities, platitude and rigour, what kind of life stories can be told? 'What he writes,' Barthes writes in this book, in his third person, 'proceeds from a corrected banality.' Perhaps our life stories are a banality that needs correcting. The death of the author means the death of the autobiographer. But it also means, at least in *Barthes by Barthes*, with all its fragmented authority, the quicker life of language.

Against Biography

For Hermione Lee

Necessity does everything well.

Ralph Waldo Emerson, 'Gifts'

I

Emerson began his first published book, *Nature*, in 1836 with what became a famous declaration of independence, a declaration far more grandiose and ambitious than its original, originality being at once the point and the problem. 'Our age is retrospective', he writes,

> It builds the sepulchres of the fathers. It writes biographies, histories, and criticism. The foregoing generations beheld God and nature face to face; we, through their eyes. Why should not we also enjoy an original relation to the universe? Why should we not have a poetry and philosophy of insight and not of tradition, and a religion by revelation to us, and not the history of theirs? . . . why should we grope among the dry bones of the past, or put the living generation into masquerade out of its faded wardrobe? The sun shines today also . . . There are new lands, new men, new thoughts. Let us demand our own works and laws and worship.

43

Emerson, who famously believed that all history was biography, also believed that there was something radically wrong with the contemporary forms of history and biography. We don't know how Emerson knows that the foregoing generations 'beheld God and nature face to face', but we do know that a certain kind of immediacy is being called for; and that, in his view, biography, history and criticism give us nothing first-hand. They bar us from what matters most, God and Nature, and we are enervated. Emerson is describing a radical estrangement from the sources of our being; as criticisms of biography go this seems drastic. If you no longer like biography – or history, or criticism – what is it that you then like? Emerson likes originality and that means being able to experience oneself as new to the world; unprecedented by the life stories of other people, and not using the past as a refuge.

If his age is retrospective, and is merely building the sepulchres of the fathers, then the age is effectively entombed, and retrospect is entombing. They are sepulchres of the fathers, not for them, so we have imposed this task on ourselves. We worship the dead so we can turn a blind eye to the living; our devotion to the past is an evasion of the future. And it is biography, history and criticism – biography first on the list – that prevent us having and enjoying an original relation to the universe; in Emerson's view we already have this original relation to the universe but can't allow ourselves to acknowledge it. And he proposes this, we should note, as a question about pleasure 'Why should not we also enjoy an original relation to the universe?', as though this original relation is an enjoyment too far. As though the enjoyment is as much of a problem as the original relation. What kind of pleasure, then, is an original relation to the universe, and that biography sabotages?

Why, Emerson asks, do we bother with the past at all – 'grope among the dry bones of the past' as he puts it – associating the biographers and historians and critics with necrophiliacs; as though we have eroticized the past to make it desirable; as though we want to make the present – new lands, new men, new thoughts – a nostalgic period piece, a costume drama, putting the 'living generation into masquerade out of its faded wardrobe'. If a masquerade is, in the definitions of the usefully entombing *OED*, 'a masked ball . . . acting or living under false pretences, a travesty . . . to pass oneself off under a false character', then there is an active and knowing deception going on, however entertaining, in our biographies, histories and criticism; and even the clothes used are already faded. What is it about living in new lands, about being new people or having new thoughts that would drive people to these lengths (to write all these biographies and histories)? What would make people so phobic of the present and the future that they would write and read these biographies and histories, that they would have to make the past – and the dead, as Emerson stresses – such a paramount and exclusive object of desire? And why would they want conservation always to trump innovation, or prefer restoration to improvisation? Emerson wants us to be on the road, not too much in the library. 'Our age is retrospective. It builds the sepulchres of the fathers. It writes biographies, histories, and criticism.' What is wrong with biographies, histories and criticism – a virtual description of a liberal arts education – and what should we be writing? Could there be biographies, histories and criticism that would facilitate this original relation, or are these genres, at least as traditionally conceived, inherently pernicious and distracting? It would, of course, be the parasitism of the past that Freud would formalize. If you put the living generations into a masquerade by dressing them in old, second-hand clothes, they are all dressed up with nowhere to go. Life stories, Emerson suggests, are all too easily death-in-life stories. 'Before the immense possibilities of man, all mere experience, all past biography, however spotless and sainted, shrinks away,' Emerson writes in 'The Over-Soul'; '. . . we have no history, no record of any character or mode of living, that entirely contents us'. Our accounts of our lives, our own and other people's, cannot encompass our possibilities, and therefore they cannot really encompass our lives. When Emerson writes, 'we have no history,

45

no record . . . that entirely contents us', he means we have no such stories that either satisfy us, or do justice to the content of our lives. Because for Emerson our lives are our possibilities, our biographies diminish the lives they describe; even our so-called experience is not sufficiently telling. What do biographies have to say about people's possibilities, however immense they are taken to be?

It is clear that a man who would write a book called *Representative Men*, who greatly admired Carlyle, and who wrote in his journal for 1847, 'All biography auto-biography. I notice the biography of each noted individual is really at last communicated by himself', was not so much against biography – or indeed retrospection – but preoccupied by them. And preoccupied above all by what would eventually be formulated by the American Pragmatists who were among Emerson's successors (and that would become a question for the related arts of biography and psychoanalysis): if it was not the past, in and of itself that was, as it were, the problem, was it the uses of the past? How, then, is the past to be used? Both how are we using it, and how would we like to use it? The past was not merely an inheritance, a legacy, a burden or a boon but it was rather something – in its forms of transmission, as cultural tradition and as trauma – that could be used in different ways. It need not be the enemy of our freedom, but its source; the past – the personal and the cultural past – could be described more as an artefact than a fate; more as a tool than a necessity; the various available determinisms need not be the be-all and end-all. Or these determinisms – God, for Emerson; instincts, or genes, or transgenerational histories for many of us – could be described in ways that opened rather than foreclosed the future. For Emerson biography was a way of talking about the fundamental thing – our sense of possibility. Emerson is wondering here whether biography, say, can or does change our sense of the shape, and the shaping of, a life; and why it might want to do this rather than merely obeying the conventions of the past.

The past could, for example, be used – in biography, history and criticism – to pre-empt the future, to estrange us from the present, as

Emerson believed was happening in what he called his new but un-approachable America. Unapproachable because in his view no one dared approach it without the preconceptions of the European past, the very preconceptions that had made the founding and the finding of America so imperative. For Emerson we use the past to prevent ourselves from having an original relation to the universe, and to prevent ourselves from enjoying that original relation. A relation being someone to whom we are related, and so reminding us, intriguingly, of family members, and making us wonder what kind of original relations we have, and have with them. Biographies, which are all about families, are, Emerson wants to persuade us, something we should be against if it is an original relation to the universe that we want. Biographies are for conformists, for people who want to compare themselves with other people in order to be the same as them or different. We read them for self-measurement, to identify and disidentify with their subjects. And there is certainly nothing original in doing that. Or perhaps there could be but it hasn't yet been done in a way that allows us to be the new people that we have it in ourselves to be.

'What is it that interests us in biography?' Emerson asks in his journal on 19 January 1834:

> Is there not always a silent comparison between the intellectual & moral endowments portrayed & those of which we are conscious? The reason why the Luther, the Newton, the Bonaparte concerning whom we read, was made the subject of panegyric, is, that in the writer's opinion, in some one respect this particular man represented the idea of Man. And as far as we accord with his judgment, we take the picture for a standard Man, and so let every line approve or accuse our own ways of thinking & living by comparison.

What else might we be doing with each other if we weren't comparing ourselves with each other? And what of the silent comparison between the intellectual and moral endowments portrayed in biographies and those of which we are unconscious, rather than conscious, as Emerson says? There is certainly a suggestion here that the effects of biography are incalculable, whatever else they are. But Emerson implies, in writing about the biography as the exemplary life, that biographers are Platonic propagandists, finding subjects who represent the idea of man (not woman), so we can have a picture of what Emerson can only abhor, Standard Man. And Standard Man is there to approve of us or to accuse us. The biographer and her subject are essentially judging us; and that is why we like biography, because we want to be judged. And the criteria for judgement – just like the criteria for internal self-criticism – can come from nowhere but the past. All judgement is sepulchral. It is a worshipping of the past through the enactment of its value-judgements. In reading biographies we are being examined. And we are being examined with standards from the past. Emerson, that is to say, wants us to wonder how we use biography as a way into wondering how we might better assess ourselves, use the past to open the future, rather than to conceal it, or to travesty it. What are biographies telling us about, other than about the past, or the past as it was supposed to be? Biographies trade in outmoded evaluations of character. Except, of course, when they do something else.

Biography, Emerson also believes in his determinedly self-contradictory way, can work by affinity. Because we can sometimes see ourselves in a biography, we can be consoled and consolidated in ways that inspire our going on being. 'The great value of Biography,' he writes in 1835,

> consists in the perfect sympathy that exists between like minds. Space & Time are an absolute nullity to this principle. An action of Luther's that I heartily approve I do adopt also . . . Socrates, St Paul, Antoninus, Luther, Milton have lived for us as much as for their contemporaries if by books or by tradition their life & words come to my ear. We recognize with delight a strict likeness between their noblest impulses & our own. We are tried in their trial. By our cordial

approval we conquer in their victory. We participate in their act by
our thorough understanding of it.

The phrase 'thorough understanding' may give us pause here; about,
perhaps, the wishfulness or wilfulness of the affinities Emerson is
promoting. They do, after all, even ablate Kant's fundamental categories of space and time. And, indeed, the idea of these great men having
lived 'for us', and their biographies revealing this, has an ambiguity
that undoes Emerson's intention; it would be sepulchral to say merely
that they have lived instead of us, or instead of our needing to have
our lives. But where there is perfect sympathy, when there is the
meeting of like minds, space and time are supposedly an absolute
nullity. We may regret that Emerson, as a man of his time, couldn't
see himself in any women; but this Emerson is so certain of his own
mind that he knows it when he sees it in others. The great thing about
identification is that it reassures us about who we think we are; the
all-too-limiting thing about identification is that it reassures us about
who we think we are. Emerson wants to have it both ways, but partly
by saying, paradoxically, that we need to find other people who
have our own original relation to the universe, or something akin to
it; that originality requires a degree of solidarity (intimating that
if you were too original you might feel stranded). This Emerson wants
heroes, because they are like him, and wants their trials because
they are his. So in a sense, in this nullity of time and space, there is no
tyranny of the past, no redundant old models to baffle the future,
because the like-minded are in a perpetual present that leads to an
open future. And their biographies – stories of their lived lives –
reveal this to us. Emerson is inspired by these men, who are alive
only in their writings and in their biographies, to be more originally
himself. He will, as it were, repeat their originality by not repeating
their work. Biography can inspire when it is the biography of those
with whom we feel an affinity. And we recognize an affinity, Emerson
intimates, by the desired but unpredictable future to which it leads.

Emerson's question is: what is the best use we can make of other people's lives in our own lives? Biography and history address this question directly – but they can also, of course, tempt us to forget the future. And this is Emerson's dilemma about biography – what it can tell us, if anything, about the future, about our possibilities: what kinds of futures can it help us to make? 'What is it that interests us in biography?' Emerson asks, and it is a striking and peculiarly difficult question to answer; partly because what we might want from biography, biography may not be able to give us. And partly because, as Emerson intimates, what we want from biography tells us something about what we want from our relations with other people, with our contemporaries. Biography, that is to say, is a remarkably evocative and provocative issue. As we know now, as the inheritors of more biographies than anybody else in history, biography is an obscure object of desire; a bit like pornography in that people are either very enthusiastic about it, but sometimes with real misgivings, or they really dislike it. Indeed one of the most interesting things about biography as a genre is the kind of argument it provokes; the kind of contradiction it exposes in ourselves, as it did in Emerson. About our interest in the lives of others, and our wondering about this interest; our wondering what stories about the lives of others have to tell us about the lives of others and ourselves. And with biography – unlike history or criticism, but like pornography and psychoanalysis – there is always the intrigue of curiosity and the hesitations about voyeurism, about privacy, about intrusiveness; and so about the use of other lives as an exploitation of other lives. Emerson, as we have briefly seen – as a way of working out what you might be against if you are against biography – was both for and against. For, because biography might let us know about something we can use, for the future, that will enable our original relation to the universe, even if it only shows us what is no longer of any use in the description of character; and against, in so far as biography, by providing compelling and plausible accounts of a life, merely reinforces our compelling and plausible accounts of a life, giving us tradition but not insight, routine formulations without what Emerson calls 'revelations to us'. By providing an elaborate account of a unique life history and the person who lived it biographies tell us nothing new about life histories or about what a person is, and could be (for Emerson there is a real sense in which a person is who they could be). 'Why should not we have,' Emerson wrote, 'a poetry and philosophy of insight and not of tradition?' What, then, would a biography of insight and not of tradition be like? What is insight if it is counterpoised against tradition?

Emerson wasn't sure whether he was calling for an end to biography, or for a new kind of biography, or even for new ways of using biography. But it was the so-called insights of biography, and the traditions they came out of, that Freud was to be famously excercised by. Indeed Freud believed, I think – like Emerson, but for similar and different reasons – that biography was the enemy of the future. But by the future Freud meant psychoanalysis. Another way of saying this is that only biographers and the Catholic Church made him quite so rancorous, quite so intemperate and extreme in his criticism. Like Emerson, Freud believed that biography was dangerous – dangerous in its restrictiveness, in its truth claims, in its effects. But Freud, unlike Emerson, had a (secular) theory about the hidden allure of whatever we need to discredit, of whatever we feel endangered by. And it is this that makes Freud's writing against and about biography so revealing both about biography and about himself; and, indeed, so revealing of his understanding of psychoanalysis, of which there could never be, by his own definition, in Emerson's words, 'a thorough understanding'. Without biography and biographers Freud would not have been able to clarify something of his sense of what psychoanalysis and psychoanalysts were. And perhaps then, by the same token, psychoanalysis may be able to clarify something about biography, and what it is not. Freud's misgivings about biography were, as we shall see, Emersonian, in that Freud believed that the biographer misleads through the deceptions of prejudice; and that the deceptions of prejudice are where we can locate the tyranny of the past.

II

Obviously, we are all inclined to believe that we are ourselves.

Jacques Lacan, *The Seminar of Jacques Lacan Book II*

As a young man Proust was an avid reader of Emerson. 'Since his youth,' his biographer William C. Carter writes, 'Proust had felt a profound affinity with writers in English'; and Emerson was, he writes, one of Proust's 'favourite Anglophone authors'. (Proust, at twenty-two, describes himself in a letter to Reynaldo Hahn as 'still in bed, drunk with reading Emerson'.) I mention this because Proust seems to take up some of Emerson's doubts and dealings with biography, and because, of course, one of the many effects of Proust's great novel is to raise questions about the uses of biography. All the biographies of Proust, as is well known, are plagued by the biographers' attempts to work out whom, among the many people he knew, his fictional characters are based on. Indeed Proust biographies are written as if, despite frequent disclaimers to the contrary, Proust's novel is a fictionalized autobiography – as if there were any other kind – and that Proust's extraordinary and eccentric life was the key to understanding the novel. In the reading and the readings of Proust the so-called biographical fallacy – the belief, to quote the University of Houston website, that 'one can explicate a work of literature by asserting that it is really about events in its author's life' – is clearly alive and well.

So it is not entirely surprising that Proust's narrator in the novel has many things to say, both obliquely and more explicitly, about writing about lives, one's own and other people's. Indeed his novel could be read as one long suspicion about the uses and abuses of biographical truth; or, as the critic Ingrid Wassenaar puts it rather more ironically in her book *Proustian Passions*, the novel is 'a linguistic experiment . . . set up to monitor self-justification'. So I want to look briefly at Proust's novel as a way of linking Emerson's misgivings about biography to Freud's contempt for biography via some of the reflections in *In Search of Lost Time* about sexual jealousy. Biographical research is what we do, biography is what we become intensely interested in, Proust's narrator insists, when we are sexually jealous; our lust for biography is initiated by sexual jealousy. People read and write biographies because when they are really interested in someone they can't bear feeling left out. We are interested in other people only because they can betray us; and they betray us by excluding us. This, put rather crudely, is what Proust's narrator seems to be proposing (and, of course, it is something a Freudian might say).

Proust, as is well known, writes at elaborate and often fascinating length about sexual jealousy as the instigator and the inspiration for our desire for knowledge about other people. Once we sense that someone we desire could betray us – and that is what someone we desire is, in Proust: someone who can betray us – we need to know them, and know about them; with a view to possessing them. And once, of course, we possess them, Proust tells us, we no longer want them. Possession, one of Proust's favourite words, is the cure for desire. So the person we love, in Proust's account, is playing hide and seek with us; and we, supposedly, are trying to rid ourselves of our desire for them. 'What an extraordinary value the most insignificant things take on,' the narrator in *The Prisoner* says, 'as soon as the person we love hides them from us!' And yet even if Albertine, the person the narrator loves, 'had told me the truth every time I asked, for example, what she thought of a person, the answer would have been different each time.' And these ineluctable facts turn him into something akin to a biographer:

Her confessions were so few and stopped so short that they left between them, in so far as they concerned the past, great blanks which it was my duty to fill in with the story of her life, which I therefore had to learn.

Why does he have to learn it? To make a bearable, liveable future for himself. There is the need to know Albertine, and the impossibility of knowing Albertine (and knowing here means knowing in a way that would make it impossible for Albertine to betray him). As for Emerson, the past is of any significance only in terms of the future it makes possible. It is to free himself from his obsession with Albertine – which, by totally organizing his life, is foreclosing it – that the narrator has a duty, to himself, to fill in with the story of her life what Proust calls 'the great blanks' in her own story. In this predicament there is a kind of biographical imperative, to find out about 'that unknown life we hope to possess in the act of possessing' the beloved.

The biographer may or may not be akin to a haunted lover, may or may not be wanting to cure himself of his preoccupation with his subject. Writing a biography, or any kind of historical reconstruction, may be prompted by an abiding sense of being left out of something one wants to be included in. And none of this may be true for any given biographer. Each case must be different, whatever the overlaps. But what Emerson and Proust and Freud want us to wonder about is what the biographer wants, what the biographer feels deprived of, what kind of account the biographer might give of her curiosity; and then, what the reader of biography might want or, in Proust's terms, even crave. The Proustian narrator hates his need for Albertine, and his self-cure is to fill in the gaps in the story of her life; to know her as thoroughly as possible in order to possess her. (Biographical knowledge, knowledge about someone's life, as the answer to dependence: why do we want to know people? So we can create the illusion that they are within our control, like our other belongings.) He doesn't, of course, literally, write her biography; he, as it were, does the research for it. And famously, at the end of *In Search of Lost Time* the narrator is about to embark on writing the story of his life, which we have just, at least in part, read. If not quite redemptive, Proust intimates that biographical research, biographical writing, might save us from something. And what it might save us from is entrapment; it might release us from the futile stuckness of passion, from an alluring inertia, a riveting paranoia that paralyses us with eternal vigilance.

And yet – and this is where Proust also concurs with Emerson and, as we shall see, with Freud – biography can itself be entrapment. There can be no foreseeable end to the biographical researches of the jealous lover; he can become possessed by the need for possession. And a biography, of course, can entrap its subject – and its readers – in a story of a life; and can be, in that sense, to use Emerson's word, 'sepulchral'. A biography can entomb its subject through its fixity, through the finish of its account. So Emerson's question would be: what kind of biography could give us an original relation to its subject, and so an original relation to ourselves and our futures? To put it as simply and as melodramatically as possible – Emerson, Proust and Freud raise the alarm about biography. Each of them is alarmed by the kinds of biography they have, and about the desire to write and read biography; and each of them has an abiding belief in the value of life stories. They are so in love with life stories, one could say, that they want only the best; they don't want to be fobbed off. Wherever there is idealization there is a romance under threat. Such is their wish to believe in life stories they are continually suspicious. And in Freud's case, rather more than suspicious.

III

Slipshod methods do not inevitably produce misleading results.

Tim Lewens, *The Meaning of Science*

For Freud the best life stories are the ones told in psychoanalysis, in the psychoanalytic way. All other life stories are rationalized self-deceptions. And if we want to understand why this is so we just need to read biographies. What is wrong with biography shows us what is so right about psychoanalysis. Indeed, without biography – without biography as what psychoanalysis is not – psychoanalysis would be difficult to explain. And yet, of course, it would be Freud who would show us that we repudiate, that we disown and discredit, only where we feel a dangerous affinity. The biographer, we might say, is what the psychoanalyst is trying not to be. When and if he is akin to a biographer he is failing as a psychoanalyst.

The psychoanalytic method is, fortunately, easily explained, as we shall see. But we should note, though, that there is no comparable biographical method. Nor is the biographer trying to cure anybody of anything; nor indeed is biography a form of medical treatment. Freud, in other words, is threatened and rather obsessed by something that, to all intents and purposes, seems to be no rival. No one who might seek out an analysis would, in all likelihood, read or write a biography instead. Nor is it likely that someone would choose to write a biography rather than have an analysis. The analyst wants to cure; the biographer wants to write a good biography. Psychoanalysis and biography are competing, if they are competing at all, for very different things. But it is the biographer Freud selects initially for a rival. What are biographers doing then that Freud wants to invalidate? And what is Freud recruiting biography and biographers to say?

Unsurprisingly perhaps, given the nature of the discipline he invented, Freud himself wrote both biographical studies and bio-graphical speculation about the great dead; most often, it should be noted, about people he greatly admired. As though psychoanalysis might in some way bring him closer to them, by way of biographical conjecture. He was notoriously interested in what biographical evidence there was that Shakespeare was the author of his own plays; Michelangelo, Moses, Dostoyevsky, among others, were subjected by Freud to what was being called by its critics, 'pathography': the use of biography to pathologize its subjects, to explain their works through the problems, or even the illnesses, in their lives. And Freud was concerned, rightly as it turned out, that psychoanalysis might be unduly reductive when applied not to patients but to so-called great men (Freud wrote of women mostly as patients, but not as subjects of biography). And he also feared that the resistance to pathography could turn people against psychoanalysis. As though pathography exposed the worst excesses – or even the basic presuppositions – of psychoanalysis.

'It would be futile to blind ourselves to the fact,' he wrote in his most notorious biographical study – the appropriately entitled 'Leonardo da Vinci and a Memory of His Childhood' (1910) – 'that readers today find all pathography unpalatable':

> They clothe their aversion in the complaint that a pathographical review of a great man never results in an understanding of his importance and his achievements, and it is therefore a piece of useless impertinence to make a study of things in him that could just as easily be found in the first person one came across.

The real problem with pathography is that it makes everybody sound the same; the distinctiveness of the individual dissolves into his symptomatology. Clearly what Freud is worrying about here is that psychoanalysis merely tells us that we have different solutions to the same problems; and even the solutions aren't that different, but merely the array of familiar and recognizable symptoms that psychoanalysis can diagnose and describe because they are general. Leonardo da Vinci was just like us, he just found more culturally prestigious solutions to his problems. How do you stop the individual getting lost? And getting lost above all in generalizing descriptions?

And yet, Freud believes that the problem is not in the pathologizing of the pathographers and the inner superiority of their diagnoses, the problem is actually the opposite; the problem is biographers. It is not that pathographers implicitly disparage their subjects, it is that biographers explicitly idealize them. Biographers, that is to say, have the kind of problem that psychoanalysis was invented to address. With no apparent irony, at this moment in the text, Freud becomes the pathographer of biographers in general. And what is unleashed in Freud is an unusual rancour and contempt; indeed, what is unleashed is the kind of scapegoating, the kind of demonization, that psychoanalysis was also invented to address. 'Biographers,' Freud writes, more than willing to use the language of the pathographers,

> are fixated on their heroes in a quite special way. In many cases they have chosen their hero as the subject of their studies because – for reasons of their personal emotional life – they have felt a special affection for him from the very first. They then devote their energies to a task of idealization, aimed at enrolling the great man among the class of their infantile models – at reviving in him, perhaps, the child's idea of his father. To gratify this wish they obliterate the individual features of their subject's physiognomy; they smooth over the traces of his life's struggles with external and internal resistances, and they tolerate in him no vestige of human weakness or imperfection. They thus present us with what is in fact a cold, strange, ideal figure, instead of a human being to whom we might feel ourselves distantly related. That they should do this is regrettable, for they thereby sacrifice truth to an illusion, and for the sake of their infantile fantasies abandon the opportunity of penetrating the most fascinating secrets of human nature.

What are we to make of this, which is a patently absurd generalization about biography and biographers, and seems to be describing, if anything, many people's misgivings about anything akin to hagiography? Perhaps one way of reading this is as part of Freud's growing critique of religious belief and the wildly unrealistic idealizations it entails. But two things are clear: firstly, that Freud believes that biographers, all biographers seemingly, are 'enrolling' their subjects into 'the class of their infantile models', and 'for the sake of their infantile fantasies' sacrificing truth and 'the opportunity of penetrating the most fascinating secrets of human nature'. And secondly, though this is implicit for Freud, psychoanalysts are not – unlike virtually everyone else – marooned in their radically distorting infantile fantasies, and they are therefore the ones that have been able to take up the opportunity of penetrating the most fascinating secrets of human nature. Life stories do contain the most fascinating secrets of human nature; but not the life stories biographers tell.

The problem that the biographer fatally suffers from, and from which the psychoanalyst is significantly exempt, is infantile fantasy. And this is a problem, in Freud's view, because our earliest fantasies colonize and convert reality into versions of our desired and undesired past. That is, they lead us to radically and wishfully over-simplify. We read and experience reality as though it was a version of our preferred past. This produces what Freud calls cold, strange, ideal figures with 'no vestige of human weakness or imperfection'. Biographers, then, are like children: their perception is distorted by wish. People who read and write biographies are people who have never grown up and can't face the reality of other people, or acknowledge how complicated people are. Freud is against biography and biographers because, wittingly or unwittingly, they mislead us; they give us the wrong picture of what people are really like. They are, as Emerson said in a different way, addicted to the past at the cost of the future. Biography is the news that never stays news; biographers want to stop time. And we should note also that both Emerson and Freud write about fathers and not mothers; the age, Emerson wrote, 'builds sepulchres of the fathers'. Contemporary biographers, Freud suggests, build sepulchres to the wished-for fathers of childhood. For both of them the past is being used in perniciously distracting ways. People are being described in biographies that no longer exist or may never have existed. By presenting us with false pictures of a life, biography is the saboteur of people's development.

There is, apparently, a crisis of biography for these men that bespeaks a larger crisis. As though writing about biography was writing about things of ultimate and urgent importance; as though biography wasn't simply one among many genres of writing, but the genre where writers locate their fears about writing, and about the influence of writing (and indeed their hopes, by implication, for their own writing. To be against biography for them is to be for the kind of writing they do; they assume theirs is a productive antagonism). They take biography, we might say, with exemplary seriousness; or rather, they take biography with alarming seriousness. When they write about biography nothing less than the future is at stake, the future development of the human race. They are determined that the readers of biography should not be fooled; we are all too vulnerable to biography and its seductions, and vigilance is required. What then for Freud is the worst that biography can do?

In 1936 Arnold Zweig wrote to Freud asking if he could write Freud's biography; and Freud replied, in what became a famous letter, that he had found the time to reply only because he had been 'aroused by the threat that you wish to become my biographer'. Zweig was a writer Freud admired, and he knew that Zweig had better things to do than write a biography, even his biography. Indeed Freud claims in his letter that by refusing Zweig he is protecting him from a fatal temptation; protecting him from doing something actually self-destructive. Freud encourages Zweig not, I think, with false modesty, that Zweig has 'so many more attractive and important things to do', including 'survey the brutal folly of mankind from the height of a watch tower'. Freud, in other words, is warning Zweig off from the kind of involvement biography entails, but also alerting him to the sense in which his writing of Freud's biography would be both a self-betrayal and betrayal of Freud. One of the worst things biography can do, in Freud's view, is bring out the worst in both the biographer and his subject. 'No, I am far too fond of you to allow such a thing to happen,' Freud writes,

> Anyone turning biographer commits himself to lies, to concealment,
> to hypocrisy, to flattery, and even to hiding his own lack of under-

standing, for biographical truth is not to be had, and even if it were it couldn't be used. Truth is unobtainable; humanity does not deserve it, and incidentally, wasn't our Prince Hamlet right when he asked whether anyone would escape a whipping if he got what he deserved?

It is clear, as from the quote from Freud's essay on Leonardo, that writing about biography undoes Freud, makes him uncharacteristically irrational and over-insistent, in a way that Freud himself has taught us how to read. To turn biographer is to expose oneself as thoroughly disreputable – a liar, a cheat, a hypocrite and a flatterer – trading in something that doesn't actually exist ('biographical truth'), and if it did exist would be no use. Indeed there is such a thing as truth, but we can't have it ('truth is unobtainable'); which prompts the obvious question, how does Freud know, if it is unobtainable? Freud then adds that humanity doesn't deserve this unobtainable truth anyway; and anyway, how could he know, and why don't they – humanity, everyone on earth – deserve it? Because they couldn't bear it, because they are better off as liars? And, if everyone got what they deserved – presumably the account of themselves that they deserved – they would be punished. To put it as simply as possible, no one comes out of this well. And then Freud adds, as the next paragraph to his letter, an illuminating association:

> Thomas Mann's visit, the address he presented to me, and the public lecture he delivered for the celebration, were gratifying and impressive events. Even the Viennese colleagues celebrated me and betrayed by all manner of signs how difficult they found it.

What being celebrated reveals is the envy of your colleagues. It seems as though over thirty years of practising psychoanalysis had not restored Freud's faith in human nature. Biography is the problem because it exposes what we are really like; it exposes biographers as ignorant and duplicitous and their subjects as requiring good cover stories. Biography – its writers, its subjects and its readers – reveals us at our worst. It is what might be called a symptomatic genre, exposing everything that is most disreputable about us. We have biography that we may not perish of the truth. Which is, of course, unobtainable, so we wouldn't recognize it if we saw it. Biography, in other words, over-exposes Freud, and not merely psychoanalysis. The worst thing about biography is that it over-exposes its critics.

We know that Freud, even as a younger man, didn't want a biography written about him; and that he is rather terrified (i.e. mocking) of his, perhaps presumptuously assumed, future biographers; and, of course, we can speculate about why this might be. And it is equally evident that in writing about biographers and biographies he is writing about what he doesn't want psychoanalysts and psychoanalysis to be (on the well-worn psychoanalytic principle that you are what you say you are not). And yet, in some way, the most interesting thing about Freud's writing on biography is that something about biography so disturbs him. Just as Freud said that we never know what it is about a joke that amuses us, we never quite know, I think, what it is about biography that upsets Freud. It just makes him say absurd things such as that biographers are committed liars but truth is unobtainable, or that biography presents us with cold, strange, ideal figures, when he knows we know this to be not always, or even often, true. We just know that biography is something Freud determinedly needs to discredit. The biographer is his negative ideal; biography is what psychoanalysis must not be.

When we speak of biography we speak about what we want lives, and life stories, and truth-telling to be. For Freud, truth-telling about lives, such as it was, could be done only by the person himself, through the method of free association, responded to by a psychoanalyst. In his 'Two Encyclopaedia Articles' Freud writes of the patient being encouraged to

> make a duty of the most complete honesty, while on the other hand
> not to hold back any idea from communication even if 1) he feels that

it is too disagreeable, or if 2) he judges that it is nonsensical or 3) too
unimportant or 4) irrelevant to what is being looked for.

This, in a nutshell, is the psychoanalytic method, a method of
free association that facilitates a quite different way of telling a life
story: telling a life story by not telling a life story, but by saying
whatever comes into your head. And yet, in some ways like the biographer, the analyst is giving the fragmentary discontinuous speech
of the analysand a new narrative coherence. A new story is told out
of an old story differently told. The biographer's material is not often
the direct speech of her subject, is not only spoken, and is not only
spoken by the subject. Freud puts his money on the couple, so to
speak; the biographer puts her money sometimes on the couple, but
also on whatever else.

Clearly, someone who believes in psychoanalysis – or even in
free association – need not be so virulently against biography. They
could, for example, in a more liberal pluralistic way, think of themselves as having interestingly overlapping preoccupations: both about
the ways of telling life stories and the purposes of telling life stories;
about what people might be wanting in the telling of a life story – both
one's own and other people's – and what they take a life story to be
(what would make us think that a story was not a life story, say, and
if it wasn't a life story what might it be about? What makes us think
that a life story isn't much good, or has been badly told? And so on).
But Emerson, Proust and Freud – among many others – want us,
above all, to be suspicious about biography; and by being suspicious
about biography they tell us a great deal about what they fear. Indeed,
their suspicion about biography is one of the best ways they have of
telling us what they want.

Johnson's Freud

METHODIST. *n. s.* [from *method*]

1. A physician who practises by theory.

2. One of a new kind of puritans lately arisen, so called from their profession to live by rules and in constant method.

Samuel Johnson, *A Dictionary of the English Language* (1755)

In Chapter VI of *Rasselas* (1759), 'A dissertation on the art of flying', the prince talks to the man referred to as 'the artist' about the 'sailing chariot' the latter is building. '[R]esolved to inquire further before he suffered hope to afflict him by disappointment', Rasselas pursues his sceptical enquiry in his search for realistic hope, the implication being that disappointment is created by false expectation, and that, while life isn't inherently disappointing, we can still be disappointed. ' "I am afraid," said he to the artist, "that your imagination prevails over your skill, and that you now tell me rather what you wish than what you know." ' In an anticipation of William Empson, the artist, defending his belief, replies: 'He that can swim needs not despair to fly,' and that 'We are only to proportion our power of resistance to the different density of the matter through which we are to pass.' For sense 1 of 'resistance' Johnson has, in his *Dictionary*, 'The act of resisting; opposition' and, in sense 2, 'The quality of not yielding to force or external impression'. He cites the Bible, Bacon, Waller and Locke; the affinity

64

with *Rasselas* is evident in his illustrative quotation from Newton's *Opticks* (1704): 'But that part of the *resistance* . . . is proportional to the density of the matter, and cannot be diminished by dividing the matter into smaller parts, nor by any other means, than by decreasing the density of the medium.' Resistance depends upon, is proportional to, the density of the matter that has to be resisted. It would be unrealistic to be disappointed by the density of the matter.

Clearly it was not part of Sigmund Freud's originality to show us that perception is distorted by wish or, as Rasselas puts it, to the artist, 'you now tell me rather what you wish than what you know'. And resistance was the heart of the matter for Freud, the ways in which the patient, and not only the patient, resists what he knows with what he wishes. Freud, like Johnson, has to be mindful of the density of the matter, of what the analyst and the patient are up against. 'The unconscious – that is to say "the repressed",' he writes in *Beyond the Pleasure Principle* (1920), 'offers no resistance whatever to the efforts of the treatment. Indeed, it itself has no other endeavour than to break through the pressure weighing down on it and force its way either to consciousness or to a discharge through some real action. Resistance during treatment arises from the same higher strata and systems of the mind which originally carried out the repression.'

The ego – Freud's figure for a part-function of consciousness – has to have what Johnson called, in defining sense 2 of 'resistance' in his *Dictionary*, 'The quality of not yielding to force', from the repressed instincts, or to 'external impression', from the interpreting analyst. Resistance is the name of the game, and such is the density of the matter – the determined and horrified repudiation of forbidden or unacceptable desire, and of forbidden or unacceptable external reality by the individual, his life organized to refuse its acknowledgement – that a great deal of work has to be done understanding the density of the resisting medium, the person's defensive system. (Johnson writes in *Rambler* 4 of youth needing to be 'initiate[d]' into what he calls 'the art of necessary defence'. Indeed, it is the analyst's job to nudge the patient, to give him a good description of how he goes about not seeing things. 'There is no doubt,' Freud writes, 'that it is easier for the patient's intelligence to recognize the resistance and to find the translation corresponding to what is repressed if we have previously given him the appropriate anticipatory ideas. If I say to you: "Look up at the sky, there's a balloon there" you will discover it much more easily than if I simply tell you to look up and see if you can see anything.' When Johnson and Freud write about resistance they write about flying, about the strange matter of air. It was, we should remember, the artist who claimed to understand 'resistance' in *Rasselas*; the man who, eventually, 'waved his pinions awhile to gather air, then leaped from his stand, and in an instant dropped into the lake'.

I have made this detour into Freud's writing just to make an obvious and simple point; it is worth wondering what is gained – and perhaps more importantly what is lost – in the making of such links. We might wonder, for example, what is being resisted in the courting and claiming of echoes and shared preoccupations. Especially when Johnson is, or was, or can be so easily, cast as a secret sharer of Freud's, despite the obvious disparities of time and place, of genealogy and profession. So, for example, in Donald Davie's Introduction to *The Late Augustans: Longer Poems of the Later Eighteenth Century* (1958), he has this to say about Johnson that easily finds favour with Freud's picture of the (modern) human predicament. 'This man,' Davie writes,

> who, as critic, insisted on the necessity for common sense to control the flights of the imagination, was the same whose imagination so peopled his solitude that he implored his friend's company in the middle of the night. The man whose vivid emotional life is recorded in his private prayers, whose tender sensibilities led him to maintain for years a household of waifs and strays and unfortunate eccentrics, is the same whose verses observe disciplines equalled in strictness only by Pope's. And this is not paradoxical. For it is the mind which

knows the power of its own potentially disruptive propensities that needs and demands to be disciplined.

It is a touching portrait in the service of a poetics; and it could be said that, after Freud, psychoanalysts – and not only psychoanalysts – also divided into those who were on the side of the potentially disruptive propensities of the mind, and those who were rather more interested in the discipline side of things; and what it might mean to be on those sides, so twinned and interanimating as they are. Both Freud and Johnson, it should be said, were among those so struck by the potentially disruptive propensities of the mind that their money was, fairly and squarely, on the disciplines required. 'For it is the mind which knows the power of its own potentially disruptive propensities,' as Davie says, 'that needs and demands to be disciplined.' Clearly, how Johnson and Freud described the mind and those disruptive propensities, and indeed what constituted realistic (or truthful) discipline is, as we say, culturally and historically specific. It is intriguing to read Johnson's 'Prayers' and Freud's *Future of an Illusion* (1927), or his *Civilization and Its Discontents* (1930), together, but it reveals almost a different cosmology – a different description of where the stress is, and where the stress should fall. Where, for example, Freud makes the most sweeping generalizations about religion, in his insistent attempt to demystify it, Johnson is most particular about its necessary truths and essential consolations. Freud generalizes to discredit, Johnson generalizes to credit. Johnson warns himself away from 'loose thoughts'; Freud encourages them.

Johnson advises us famously in his 'Life of Cowley' that 'Great thoughts are always general, and consist in positions not limited by exceptions, and in descriptions not descending to minuteness.' (Freud, it should be noted, thought biography impossible, whereas for Johnson it was both instructive and exemplary.) 'The business of a poet,' Imlac argues in *Rasselas*, 'is to examine, not the individual, but the species; to remark general properties and large appearances: he does not number the streaks of the tulip, or describe the different shades in the verdure of the forest.' If we can avoid, in our descriptions, descending to minuteness, and look for the species not the individual, then, in Johnson's eighteenth-century aesthetic, we can make our links and connections wherever they are truthfully pertinent; pertinent, that is, to a putatively universal human nature, bearing in mind Philip Davis's description of Johnson as 'so particular a generalizer'.

Johnson's aesthetic frees us, in a way that Freud's does not. For the psychoanalyst it is not great thoughts that are general but defensive ones. Great thoughts may or may not be general for Freud – Freud was interested, as a scientist, in particulars in the service of generalities – but they are, clinically, the least revealing; it is the exceptions, the descending to minuteness, the examining of the individual, that Freud is after. Johnson, that is to say, encourages us to read Freud in a way that Freud cannot encourage us to read Johnson. Johnson might recommend that we read Freud for abiding truths about human nature, or at least to find out whether Freud has such truths to tell. Freud believes that the patient is at his least truthful in the speaking of general truths. Freud, one might say, is interested in what generalization is about, what psychic needs it might serve. He gives us a language in which we can redescribe what people might be up to when they generalize. Freud, indeed, has a method for finding out how people use general truths to hide themselves in. He was not of William Blake's party – 'To Generalize is to be an Idiot' – but a distinctive difference is discernible in these shifting criteria.

So when T. S. Eliot in his well-known lecture 'Johnson as Critic and Poet' tries to give an account of how we are to read Johnson, it is the historical question that vexes him; he is insistent that we reduce Johnson if we try to make him modern, and render Johnson our contemporary. 'If we censure an eighteenth-century critic,' Eliot writes,

for not having a modern, historical and comprehensive appreciation, we must ourselves adopt towards him, the attitude the lack of which we reprehend; we must not be narrow in accusing him of narrowness, or prejudiced in accusing him of prejudice. Johnson had a positive point of view which is not ours; a point of view which needs a vigorous effort of imagination to understand.

Part of this vigorous effort of imagination, Eliot believes, requires that we not be bewitched by our contemporary vocabularies in our redescriptions of the past, something that seems rather easier in the breach. He wants us to have a sense of historical context, but not a historicism that can be used to diminish the emotional impact of the writing. 'A contemporary critic,' he writes, 'would produce another, and more complicated account, which would probably be influenced by the study of sciences of more recent growth. The modern account would fit in better with our mental furniture, but would not necessarily be more true for this reason.' It is the burden of the present to distract us from the past. He urges us, particularly in writing about Johnson (and Dryden), to accept that critics 'concerned with literature as literature, and not with psychology or sociology', are more likely to have what he calls 'enduring usefulness'.

'In our own day,' Eliot goes on – and he does go on – 'the influence of psychology and sociology upon literary criticism have been very noticeable'; and even though this has, he says with faint disdain, 'enlarged the field of the critic', 'this enrichment has also been an impoverishment'. For Eliot, this is not a contradiction in terms because it has been a particular kind of impoverishment: 'an impoverishment for the purely literary values, the appreciation of good writing for its own sake, have become submerged when literature is judged in the light of other considerations'. Johnson, Eliot felt, was particularly prone to this kind of impoverishing view of his work because he wrote in what Eliot calls, rather amazingly, 'a settled society' in which there was 'a definite and limited public, in the midst of which there would be a smaller number of persons of taste and discrimination, with the same background of education and manners'; whereas Eliot, who delivered these lectures in 1944, was living 'amongst the varieties of chaos in which we find ourselves immersed today'. In this light, we should value Johnson because he is not our contemporary; and we make him our contemporary, and thus radically misrecognize him, by foisting on his writing other considerations, such as the modern vocabularies of sociology and psychology (the 'literary', in this view, presumably becomes everything that is not sociology or psychology). Like Davie, Eliot implicitly acknowledges that Johnson in particular – like Coleridge, but not like Dryden or Arnold – is a poet-critic who tempts us to be, as it were, psychological about him. Johnson seems to be a writer for whom what we now think of as psychological descriptions seem particularly illuminating, or perhaps just well suited. By being so vividly a character but not a character-type – by being so observed and biographied and sustained as a culture-hero – Johnson's writing all too easily calls up in us psychological thoughts; and Freudian thoughts in those of us for whom, if there is such a thing as psychology, it is psychoanalysis.

For literature students of my generation, Walter Jackson Bate was the authority on Johnson, and Bate could not resist, four years before Norman O. Brown's *Life Against Death* (1959), seeing Johnson and Freud as essentially related. 'Few classical moralists,' he wrote in *The Achievement of Samuel Johnson*, 'are closer to Freud than Samuel Johnson, or have so uncanny a sense of what repression can mean.' So it may be worth, briefly, testing this claim, and what, if anything, it impoverishes. What is at stake, for both Johnson and Freud, is whether sanity – or rather, what kind of sanity – depends upon the acknowledgement of reality. They both give an account in their writing of what it might be not to go mad. To be interested in repression is to be interested in the necessities it serves. It is to picture what an unrepressed life might be like.

The 'Uncanny', in the sense Freud gave it in his paper on the subject, is an experience of something apparently new that is a disguised version of something from the past. If, in Bate's view, Johnson had an incomparably uncanny sense of what repression can mean, then he must have been, though clearly not an influence on Freud's thought, a precursor. Freud's picture of repression is something old disguised as something new, not simply a redescription of something that has been around one way and another, and in one place and another, for some time. 'That it is vain to shrink from what cannot be avoided, and to hide that from ourselves which must some time be found, is a truth which we all know, but which all neglect,' Johnson writes in *Idler* 41. This is not startling because it reminds us of Freud, but because of its accuracy, its realism, its precision of diction and syntax; it is vain to shrink from what cannot be avoided because it is at once futile and self-flattering, futile because self-flattering (rather than, say, self-evoking).

Freud's concept of repression was not new, according to Bate; the truth is that Johnson knew about what Freud later called repression; that is, indeed, what Bate asserts. Johnson, he claims in *The Achievement of Samuel Johnson*, 'really anticipates the psychoanalysis of the twentieth century', though not, he is keen to clarify, in terms of the kind of psychological *aperçus* that psychoanalysts have found in Johnson's writing. 'Johnson's own sense of the working of the human imagination,' he argues, 'probably provides us with the closest anticipation of Freud to be found in psychology or moral writing before the twentieth century.' Anticipation is a looking forward, a foreseeing, but not necessarily an accurate conceiving. This uncanny anticipation of Freud, he writes,

is not to be found in simple thrusts that cut through a sentimental and complacent idealism about human nature. It is to be found in Johnson's studied and sympathetic sense of the way in which the human imagination, which is blocked in its search for satisfaction, doubles back into repression, creating a 'secret discontent', or skips out diagonally into some sort of projection. The result, of course, is not a series of formal analyses.

71

Freud does, of course, write about the imagination, though it is not one of his technical terms (the word appears 174 times in James Strachey's translation of his works). And it matters that Freud does, under the aegis of science, perform a series of formal analyses – that is, writes in a quite different genre or register – and that, for Johnson, repression and projection are not key words. In Bate's account, Johnson has nothing to add to Freud; there are no revisions to Freud's account, however implicit, in Johnson. In this tacit progress myth, it is one-way traffic. Bate doesn't propose a rereading of Freud in the light of Johnson, he just encourages us to see the ways in which, to put it as crudely as possible, Johnson was years ahead of his time; Johnson's work, whatever else it is, is more good proof and illustration of the veracity of Freud's account. It is clearly part of the achievement of Samuel Johnson to anticipate Freud.

We are more likely to think now that it is the formal and historical – the cultural – differences between Johnson and Freud that are significant, even if it is the aphoristic *aperçus*, what Bate calls the 'simple thrusts that cut through a sentimental and complacent idealism about human nature', that are striking. When, for example, Johnson writes in *Rambler* 134, 'To act is far easier than to suffer,' or, in *Rambler* 32, 'The cure for the greater part of human miseries is not radical, but palliative,' the psychoanalyst will prick up her ears. Indeed, a case could be made – a tradition could be constructed – in which Johnson and Freud would figure, of writers working on a realistic account of human suffering; a genre of the 'real', so to speak, as indicated by Henry James's definition of what is real as that which it is impossible not to know. A tradition we might read for its occasional insights, and eccentric know-how (neither Johnson nor Freud, as writers and as critics of other people's writing, was interested in what Eliot calls, in an obscure phrase, 'literature as literature'). So, when Bate says of Johnson, 'Few classical moralists are closer to Freud than Samuel Johnson, or have so uncanny a sense of what repression can mean,' we might take him to be saying these writers are preoccupied by how people go about not knowing the things they know; and by how they render themselves unrealistic and, in that sense, unreal, by disavowing truths about themselves, and about the way the world is. (Both Johnson and Freud believe in a Reality Principle, even though only Freud calls it that.) People become unrealistic in the service of self-protection, and this is the most unrealistic thing about them.

Anyone interested in repression is interested in what requires repression and why. The real, in this sense, is whatever wishing and willing cannot change, whatever cannot be transformed by redescription. 'Be not too hasty,' says Imlac, 'to trust, or to admire, the teachers of morality: they discourse like angels, but they live like men.' The realism inheres in the semantic progression from one word to the next. Trust is a form of admiration, and in our eagerness to trust we are prone to admire. We know how men live but not how angels discourse. Our potential – in this case for the good – has to be bound up with what we can actually know about ourselves. The speculative can't afford to float free of experience. Both Johnson and Freud write, in quite different languages, about how the possible can only be a version of the real. As Bate wrote, in a sentence that no one could write now: 'The perennial value of Johnson's example is that the *real* issues are still not dead.' When Bate reprises *The Achievement of Samuel Johnson* in his famous biography of Johnson, the stress falls rather differently. Certain things are made rather more explicit. 'But the part of Johnson that really anticipates psychoanalysis,' he writes (omitting this time round 'and it should be stressed that it is only a part'),

is not to be found in simple thrusts that cut through a complacent sentimentalism about human nature. It is to be found in Johnson's studied and sympathetic sense of both inner 'resistance' and what in psychoanalysis are called defence-mechanisms, or, in Johnson's phrase, 'the stratagems of self-defence'. In particular he anticipates the concept of 'repression' as he turns on the way in which the human imagination when it is frustrated in its search for satisfaction, doubles

73

back into repression, creating a secret discontent, or begins to move ominously into various forms of imaginative projection. The result, of course, is not a series of formal analyses.

The 'simple thrusts that cut through a sentimental and complacent idealism about human nature' have become 'simple thrusts that cut through a complacent sentimentalism about human nature'; sentimentality, Bate intimates, is the more pernicious form of idealism. But what Bate has most notably added, or rather changed, is that Johnson's studied and sympathetic sense is no longer of the way in which the human imagination deals with frustration. It has become, more starkly, a sense of 'resistance' and 'defence-mechanisms', with Bate running the Freudian term alongside Johnson's 'the stratagems of self-defence'. This is where, for Bate, Johnson and Freud echo each other: resistance, stratagems of self-defence, repression. As in the earlier text, Bate concludes – and it is not an insignificant qualification – 'the result, of course, is not a series of formal analyses'. Of course, Freud pioneered a therapeutic method that might make us more realistic, and a model of the mind that we could use to picture our conflicts; Johnson had neither a method nor a system, but he did have religion and a way of writing and of reading. And both Johnson and Freud were obsessed by conflict, by the impossibility (and the danger) of imagining life without intractable conflict.

Freud, Bate believes, helps us with Johnson, gives us a language to redescribe Johnson's preoccupations; and Bate helps us see Johnson as a kind of phantom precursor of Freud. 'What we most value in the eighteenth century,' Bate writes in his *The Burden of the Past and the English Poet*, '[is] its recognition of fact without the surrender of the ideal.' Freud we can value for his recognition of fact and his analysis of the function of ideals. As so-called moralists, both Johnson and Freud want us to have realistic hopes, whatever that phrase might mean. But what is the problem that is being solved in reading them together? I can only see them as in some tradition of moral realism, as writers wanting to give an account of our evasiveness; and of them both being able to do this because they believe in something they both call human nature. And this, in a sense, frees us to read them each in the light of the other. So it is equally pressing to wonder what Johnson might be able to tell us about Freud; and if that question is verging on the unintelligible, why that might be so. A Freudian reading of Johnson is clearly plausible, but what would a Johnsonian reading of Freud be like? The language of certain descriptive writers — and Freud is one — can be turned into schools and movements and methods and approaches; they lend themselves to this. It is part of their intent. But there are other descriptive writers — and Johnson is one — with whom this cannot be done; writers that are useful for all the ways in which they cannot be used. 'Human experience,' Boswell quotes Johnson as saying, 'which is constantly contradicting theory, is the great test of truth'; and a theory constantly contradicted is not much of a theory, though it may be something better, or at least something else. You can train to be a Freudian, but not a Johnsonian. Everyone sounds, or can be made to sound, Freudian, but only one person, it seems, sounds Johnsonian. And that, too, is real.

Byron on the Run

I

I could not resist the first night of anything.

Byron, letter to Thomas Moore, 23 April 1815

What has always seemed so modern about Byron is the way he pits an enlightenment sensibility – empirical, sceptical, agnostic, hedonistic – against an explicitly troubled and tumultuous personal history, to see what, if anything, they might have to say about each other (once Byron got to Venice after his summer in Geneva in 1816, he purchased the ninety-two volumes of Voltaire's complete works). But what is more than modern about Byron is that he never assumes that one can be used to explain the other, or that explanation can ever be sufficient ('I look / Around a world where I seem nothing, with / Thoughts which arise within me, as if they / Could master all things', Cain says in Byron's poem of that name). He was an ironic rationalist, who – like all rationalists, ironic or otherwise – had an irrational personal history. And this unusually troubled personal history has a significant bearing on the before and after story that may be one story of Byron's life. It was the summer of 1816 in Geneva – which the critic David Ellis, in particular, makes the case for – that was a turning point in the life of the man who was the most famous European poet of his age; who, as

Wilde wrote in *De Profundis*, 'was a symbolic figure, but his relations were to the passions of his age and its weariness of passion'.

To understand what became of Byron during and after that summer we need to know something of what Byron called his 'hot youth'; Byron's 'acute unhappiness' in Geneva that summer certainly seems to have had a long history. The Byron who was born with what became a famously deformed foot was also abandoned by 'Mad Jack', his profligate father, virtually at birth; he was brought up as an only child by a violent and moody mother – who, Byron wrote later, 'cankered a heart that I believe was naturally affectionate' – and sexually molested by a Calvinist nurse-maid. When he wrote in the Preface to *Childe Harold's Pilgrimage* that he wanted to 'show that early perversion of minds and morals leads to satiety of past pleasures and disappointments in new ones', he was both pointing a (modern) moral, and more than hinting at a personal experience. He moved a lot as a child between friends and members of his extended family, never being able to settle anywhere for long, which seems to have left him with a moody restlessness that never really left him and that he found a way of making himself famous for ('My restlessness tells me,' Byron wrote in his journal, 'I have something within that "passeth show",' restlessness being a passing and a passing through). As a young adolescent at Harrow, and then at Cambridge, he quickly became actively bisexual at a time when homosexuality was a greater crime in England than incest (Childe Harold describes himself in the poem as feeling 'the fullness of satiety' and 'with pleasure drugg'd'). What Byron was to refer to many years later as 'a propensity to be governed' – '. . . set a pretty woman or a clever woman about me – with a turn for political or any other sort of intrigue – why – they would make a fool of me' – meant that getting himself governed and seeing if he could get away, preferably without being made a fool of, became one of the stories of his life.

In an early biography of Byron published in 1830, six years after the poet's death, Thomas Moore reports a conversation between the schoolboy Byron and his tutor 'Dummer' Rogers. Witnessing the agonies caused by the treatment for the club-foot Byron was born with, Rogers remarks, 'It makes me uncomfortable, my Lord, to see you sitting there in such pain as I *know* you must be suffering'; to which Byron replies, 'Never mind, you shall not see any signs of it in ME.' He could not conceal his lameness but he could conceal his feelings about it. If you have a physical disability, and when you are a child – which for some children, and Byron seems to have been one of them, is also experienced as a kind of disability – you invite descriptions that masquerade as knowledge and that you can all too easily feel trapped in. Secrecy becomes a kind of freedom; you have to find ways of making what people think they know about you not matter so much ('never mind'). Byron dealt with his propensity to be governed by never showing any signs of being governed. Not giving anything away, not letting on – both whether it was possible not to let on and how to go about doing it – was Byron's thing. Guardedness became his theme, and for this you need a talent for display, which Byron seems to have had from a very young age. He had the theatricality, and the love of theatricality, of the extremely shy (and sly); and many people were surprised and touched by just how awkward and tentative he could be on first meeting (he is a great poet of first meetings and first impressions). All his biographers seem to agree that Byron was unusually determined to perform himself as he would prefer to be seen, despite and because of his lameness.

By the time he left England for Europe in 1816 he had become famously famous overnight as the author of *Childe Harold*, and notorious over several years for his many affairs and liaisons with various servants, actresses and duchesses, culminating in the debacle with the disturbed and sometimes deranged Lady Caroline Lamb and his 'incestuous' relationship with his half-sister Augusta Leigh. He was well known as a 'regency rake' and a virulent anti-Tory in the House of Lords, a combination barely imaginable now. He was an admirer, so to speak, of the French Revolution and of Napoleon when this was a seriously unfashionable (i.e. unpatriotic) thing to be.

Always over-exposed as lame – as more vulnerable than he wanted to be – Byron was wanting, in his youth, to find out what he could get away with. But by the spring of 1816, Byron's cover had been blown. His determinedly debauched life had become a scandal. He was suffering a catastrophic disillusionment with himself – and with the corrupt hypocrisy of the English ruling class, reflected, he believed, in the way his private affairs were treated with fashionable disgust – following a very public fall from grace after the collapse of his marriage to Annabella Milbanke. He was showing all the signs of having nowhere to hide, always Byron's greatest fear. 'I have been more ravished,' he would write in a letter in 1819, 'than anybody since the Trojan war.' It was a kind of epic, and not entirely of the ironic kind that he preferred; it was terrible and he needed to get away; he was, he wrote, 'like the Stag at bay who betakes him to the waters'. He was not sure, in other words, whether it was a spa he was going to to recover, or to his death from what he called the 'envy, jealousy and all uncharitableness' of the English he had grown to hate. He went initially to Geneva and it is this first strange summer abroad, at bay but unbowed, that, at least in Ellis's view in his book *Byron in Geneva* – and, indeed, in the view of most of his modern biographers – is essential to our understanding of Byron. We don't need to minimize the bad behaviour of Byron's youth – or, at least, of the part of his youth spent in Britain – by making it more interesting; but in these few months in Geneva, Byron was more interestingly confounded and confined than, perhaps, at any other period of his life. In Geneva he wanted to see the sights rather than to be one. He wanted some respite from his notoriety. There was something he wanted to be relieved of.

Byron, unlike all the other great Romantic poets, was keen on debauchery and made no secret of what he called his 'gallivanting', his pleasure in being disreputable; and, indeed, in making women expose themselves in their desire for him. They would show all the signs and he mostly would not (in no writer is it so obvious as in Byron that when he is writing about women he is writing about himself – that is, his fears about himself). In the journals and letters of the period it is never clear to Byron whether he is resisting the many women who want him, or whether he is, and perhaps always has been, disillusioned with (and by) women and the pleasure they might bring. 'It is true from early habit,' he wrote in 1812 to his close friend Lady Melbourne, 'one must make love mechanically as one swims. I was once very fond of both, but now as I never swim unless I tumble into the water, I don't make love till almost obliged.' It was the early habits, the mechanics and the obligations, that were beginning to torment Byron and that he fled to Geneva, in 1816, to escape from, after his first attempt at escape through marriage had failed.

As, clearly in part, a pragmatic solution to what he called in a letter 'literally too much love', he had married the respectable Annabella Milbanke in 1814, with whom he had a child but who had left him because of his ill-treatment of her and his growing public reputation as a 'sodomist' and an incestuous adulterer. As the scandal of his marriage and his past emerged, he became infamous almost as quickly as he had become famous. He feared 'assassination', and was wary of going to the theatre for fear that the audience might turn on him. He was also grossly in debt – within minutes of his departure from London, bailiffs had seized all of Byron's property in his affluent residence at Piccadilly Terrace in lieu of unpaid rent owed to the Duchess of Devonshire – but needing, above all, to recover his 'name', a word that his poems obsess over and that for Byron covered everything from his family history, his personal reputation and whatever might be either unnameable or unnamed in himself.

In his flight from London Byron was on the run, in shock, and having, as they say, to turn his life around, but without wanting to explain himself, or feign regrets he did not feel, or a wish for forgiveness that he did not want (Byron's heroes nobly prefer oblivion to forgiveness). He did not leave England with the intention of writing more – with, as it were, writerly ambitions – but this is what he found himself doing with more time to himself, especially at night. 'Who would write,' he wrote with characteristic aristocratic hauteur in 1813, 'who had anything better to do?' By October 1816, after the summer in Switzerland in which he had written and published the third canto of *Childe Harold* and *The Prisoner of Chillon and Other Poems*, and begun *Manfred* and *Darkness*, among much else – the period, that is to say, in which he had written some of his most remarkable poems, and the prelude to the writing of his great poem *Don Juan* – poetry had begun to matter a bit more to him, but there were still the necessary reservations. '. . . poetry is – I fear – incurable – God help me,' he wrote to Murray in October 1816, '– if I proceed in this scribbling – I shall have frittered away my mind before I am thirty – but it is at times a relief to me'. To fritter is to waste time but, as Byron knew, it also means to break into fragments, a connection that would appeal to Byron who thought that too much time spent putting the pieces together could be futile and 'egotistic' and that the mind *was* fragmented; that this was the point that had been turned into the problem. That too much coherence was being looked for in the furious egotism of his 'poetic' contemporaries. It was the meeting and brief companionship with Shelley and his entourage that marks this summer as a transition in Byron's life, and not just more of the same. Even though there was, of course, more of the same as well.

Thinking about this summer of 1816 is a good idea partly because it makes us take seriously what happened to Byron, and what he was to make of it in his great later poetry; and also to wonder, by the same token, whether there really are turning points in people's lives, or just obscure evolutions punctured and punctuated by crises. Marchand in the abbreviated version of his monumental three-volume life of Byron, *Byron: A Portrait*, gives it only twenty pages out of nearly five hundred; and Fiona MacCarthy's more bracing recent biography, *Byron: Life and Legend*, gives the Geneva episode just over thirty pages in her slightly longer book (she entitles the section of her book about Byron's life abroad after the separation from his wife rather winningly, 'Celebrity in Exile'). Though both books, it should be said, intimate that there was something significant about this transitional moment in Byron's life, without quite knowing what to do with it. But there is a sense in which Byron is always ill-served by biography because his 'tempestuous' life seems to explain the poems in a way that the poems are always inviting us to be sceptical of; by shedding so much light on his poems, his life obscures just how cunning and clever and subtle they are.

But that summer Byron was changing, though largely through his irresolution and the narrowing of his social life, and, indeed, by his shrewd unwillingness to change at all. We get the sense that in these significant months he realized that the only change worth having was changing by staying more or less the same. But what was changing was his writing of poetry. Though Byron was to write rather caustically about Shelley and his circle after they all left Geneva, he was clearly impressed at first by the conversation of the rather more idealistic, more atheistic (and younger) Shelley. 'Through Shelley', Ellis writes, Byron 'had been introduced to that closer relationship with landscape so often evoked in the poetry of Wordsworth'. But it was the landscape, Ellis is careful to note, that was the important thing, not Wordsworth's poetry (Byron famously remarked that all the important poets of his generation were 'on a wrong revolutionary poetical system'). Byron and Shelley greatly enjoyed each other's company in these months. But what they gained and got from each other was a clearer and instructive sense of just how different they were. 'Lord Byron,' Shelley wrote to Peacock in July, 'is an exceedingly interesting person, and as such, is it not to be regretted that he is the slave to the vilest and most vulgar prejudices, & as mad as the winds?' Shelley clearly hadn't had quite the effect he had hoped. And Byron had a rather different sense of what he needed to be liberated from.

Byron, in fact, first met Shelley in Geneva that summer – though Shelley had been a long-time admirer of Byron's poetry – and not incidentally as a consequence of a previous rather half-hearted liaison in England with Claire Clairmont, the half-sister of Shelley's wife, Mary. It was because of Claire's desire to see Byron that Shelley had come to Geneva with her and his wife. Known to be libertines, atheists and political radicals, the Shelley ménage was taken to be a scandalous group, with rumours around of Shelley having 'relations' with both his wife and his sister. And their association with Byron added to their notoriety. Claire was pregnant with Byron's child, Allegra, who he would soon keep from her mother and place in a convent, where she would die of a fever. There is a book to be written, though it would be a disturbing one – and something of an antidote to the romantic invention and idealization of childhood – about both Byron and Shelley's treatment of their various children and the women with whom they had them (an interest in childhood is always also an interest in misogyny). But despite his continual ill-treatment of her, Claire had been determined to see Byron. It seemed to be too often Byron's fate that people could get to him whether he wanted them to or not. As it turned out he virtually refused to see her, and most of the socializing was done by the men without the women. What the summer of 1816 began to clarify for Byron was not what he should believe in, as Shelley clearly wished, but how he wanted to spend his time; a far more interesting thing.

In the short period Byron tried to recover and to change. He did neither, of course – and Byron would not, I imagine, have wanted or thought it possible to be radically transformed – but he did something more intriguing: 'under the influence of Shelley', Ellis writes, Byron 'tried to transform himself into a nature poet of the Wordsworthian variety' and failed. Soon acknowledging he could not 'find solace for his acute unhappiness in landscape', he began to see what kind of poet he wanted to be by realizing what kind of poetry he distrusted. This is, of course, rather different from the idea that Shelley encouraged Byron's interest in landscape. Whether or not this was the influence Shelley wanted to have, it was clearly unpromising, a radical misrecognition of the kind of poet and man Byron was. He was neither transformable, nor in any way Wordsworthian. Harold Bloom has made it impossible now not to be attentive to what influence might mean between poets – and especially between Romantic poets – and indeed to whether there really is such a thing, rather than something more akin to a kind of dream-work between poets in which they read and digest with unpredictable consequence the writing they are drawn to, and the writing they are not drawn to. It is, of course, more difficult to track the power of personal influence, but it seems likely that Byron and Shelley's keen interest in each other during these months – celebrated in Shelley's great poem *Julian and Maddalo* – was inspiring for Byron, though in unpredictable ways. Their pleasure in each other's company, though, is patent in their correspondence and recollections.

Byron was certainly acutely aware of his own propensity to be taken over by people, indeed to be undone by them. But he was not taken over by the landscape either – much of Byron's best poetry is about the dread and the draw of being taken over – and was not becoming a Wordsworthian nature poet. In that summer of 1816 Byron made, according to Ellis, 'one crucial step towards the decision he was to make later that he was not a Romantic poet after all, and that the Romantic movement as a whole, especially as it was represented by the Lake poets, was a mistake'. It has always been difficult to get the tone right in writing about Byron because his mockery is so infectious and intimidatingly intelligent that it undoes academic concepts and categories. But he did spend a lot of time, both before and during his summer in Geneva, distancing himself from contemporary poets and poetry, and particularly from their self-importance as bringers of news that was not news. Byron was interested in whether there was a good way of taking oneself seriously, and what, if anything, this had to do with the writing of poetry. In that first summer abroad Byron got more serious, without having to get serious.

The 'mistake' of the Lake poets was, in Byron's view, that they were using Nature for self-promotion and spurious reassurance (as early as 1809 Byron was writing in *English Bards and Scottish Reviewers* about Wordsworth's Idiot Boy: '. . . all who view "the idiot in his glory" / Conceive the Bard the hero of the story'). But the other mistake they had made, and that was of a piece with this – Byron saw the link between what he considered their specious nature-worship and their trimming Toryism – was to do with what might be called their knowledge claims: about Nature, about God, about Poetry, about Politics, and about themselves and other people. They wrote about Mystery, but with great authority. Their morality was sexually timid and self-aggrandizing (the two tending to go together). They were never amusing, and believed they were telling the truth. And their pleasures were not the pleasures of disguise. In Switzerland, of course, where there is a lot of nature – and Byron saw a lot of it – he found that it didn't have what he was encouraged to believe was its desired effect. 'Neither the music of the Shepherd,' he wrote to Augusta Leigh, 'nor the Torrent – the Mountain – the Glacier – the Forest – nor the Cloud – have for one moment lightened the weight upon my heart – nor enabled me to lose my own wretched identity in the majesty & the power and the Glory – around – above – & beneath me.' Identity, as Byron knew, is hard to lose; and that because identity was increasingly a problem for himself and his contemporaries nature had begun to look like a solution (or an absolution). Byron was beginning to believe that it may be our nature not to find nature reassuring; even in, or especially in, its sublimity. For Byron, it was clearly not alluring – or rather, it was a temptation to be avoided – to be somehow other or more than himself. Sexuality seemed more revealing to him than mountains and lakes. And something along these lines was crystallizing in him during the summer of 1816.

In sex, privacy is always what is at stake, and Byron was obsessed by privacy – by what people could know and expose about others and themselves; and especially by what people were doing when they gave an account of themselves. He relished concealment – he was wonderful at dressing up, as the Byron iconography makes abundantly clear – thought confession was bribery, and that most self-justification was showing-off – at best unpromising and at worst implausible – just a form of politeness (whenever he or others attempted to excuse themselves in letters, it is all too often ironized: 'your letter of excuses has arrived', he writes to his publisher Murray. 'I receive the letter but do not admit the excuses except in courtesy'). When Byron famously wrote of Coleridge in the dedication to *Don Juan*, 'Explaining metaphysics to the nation / I wish he would explain his explanation,' he was alerting his readers at the outset to the fact that explanation never ends, and that that too needs explaining. Byron is the most philosophic of poets by being the least metaphysical (and the least earnest); he lived, and his poetry lives, neither by mysteries nor by systems. And in this, as he knew, he was quite different from the other major poets of the period (like the other major poets of the period, Byron was involved in a quest romance, but to find out why people go on quest romances). What was dawning on Byron while he was in Geneva was just how important and productive these differences could be. He had come to Geneva to recover his privacy, and he found himself as a poet; not so much making sense of what had happened to him, but dramatizing a predicament. Inventing a new kind of hero.

II

I do detest everything which is not perfectly mutual.

Byron, letter to Lady Melbourne, 21 October 1813

Byronic heroes often despair of being able to explain themselves, and often seem to wonder what they might do instead. 'The Tree of

Knowledge is not that of Life,' Manfred declares alone, at midnight, in his Gothic gallery – in Byron's great poem begun in the summer of 1816 – suggesting that the first choice had been the wrong choice and that the Tree of Knowledge had been a dead end. What he asks of the Spirits is 'Oblivion, self-oblivion' because his life is unbearable to him, and because he wants us (and himself) to consider the difference, if there is one, between these two kinds of oblivion. Byronic heroes are always haunted by shameful secrets, but Byron is always as interested in whether (and how) people can hide things from themselves and others, as in what is hidden. We can be governed only by people who claim to know us, Byron seems to assume, and so we must be able to obscure ourselves; to hide things not only from other people but from ourselves. Indeed Byron sometimes intimates that perhaps the original Cain – who clearly fascinated him for obvious and unobvious reasons, as his mother's only child – may just have had to be excessively ingenious at isolating himself. That stigma can be a perverse form of privacy. That transgression is a quest for solitude. That it gives one a life (and a death) of one's own.

Fiona MacCarthy, in her wonderful biography of Byron, argued persuasively that Byron's big secret was his homosexuality. But more often than not, at least in his poetry, the secret, the sin, the shame, legitimates the hero's solitude; it is a pretext to keep him apart from other people. The problem of the Byronic hero and narrator – that makes him so modern, and that Ellis implies was beginning to become clear once Byron had left England – is sociability; not his beginning to wonder, as Byron himself was intermittently, what he was doing by spending all this time with other people, but knowing that isolation was his fate, and possibly his preference (Larkin, one could say, was in this Byronic tradition). After this summer in Geneva there were to be further loves, but fewer, and an increasingly determined commitment to radical politics, to the liberation of Greece from the Turks and from its warring factions. The more socially and personally disillusioned he became, the more politically committed he was. But to the struggles of a country that was not his own.

Byron was, at least by his own standards, rather unsociable in Switzerland, mostly avoiding large gatherings, sticking with his close friends, and dieting. He was recovering from the excesses of the previous months and years (when, for example, he dined in England with his close friend Scrope Davis, they would often drink six bottles of claret, as well as whatever else they were drinking). Even though, such was his notoriety, tourists could hire boats and telescopes to get a glimpse of Byron in his villa, sightings were rare. He had come abroad to see himself not being seen. And it made a change. When the abbot wants to see Manfred he is told that it is impossible, 'He is most private, and must not be thus / Intruded on', and the 'thus' is the point, because privacy is there to manage intrusion, to keep violation at bay. Love is always the Byronic hero's problem because it stops him keeping himself to himself. So celebrity for Byron – and possibly not only for Byron – was not simply about fame or recognition, but about testing the limits of privacy. About finding out what about him people couldn't see.

When Byron fled to Geneva in 'that summer of 1816' he was beginning to have doubts about sociability that could be cured neither by religion nor by nature – nor by Shelley's militant atheism; neither by metaphysics nor by introspection. It wasn't simply that his celebrity had caught up with him and he was feeling over-exposed, but that all the personal and cultural solutions to his more and more private predicament were failing him. He was, it seems, having a representative, peculiarly modern kind of mild nervous breakdown. But Byron's predicament that summer was, at least in retrospect, more than just personal (it had been building during that turbulent first decade of the nineteenth century when, for Byron at least, politics seemed to be about the forcing of consensus because there was no real consensus to be had). 'I only go out,' he had written in his journal in 1813, 'to get me a fresh appetite for being alone.' It was after he left England in 1816 that he was to write his greatest poetry about the appetite for being alone, and about what that could be an appetite for. Byron was beginning to realize, in other words – and the other words were his poems, letters and journals – that not only was his own privacy now being continually violated, but that the idea of privacy – of a secret inner self, like the idea of a god – was under threat; or even that it might be, to use his preferred word, 'cant'. That all life was becoming public life; that you needed something to hide in order to have somewhere to hide. That what MacCarthy called Byron's 'pathological need for privacy' was his growing acknowledgement that there may be no such thing. Or that if there was, it might need to be reinvented. Privacy might mean whatever no one, including yourself, ever knows about you.

In the summer of 1816 Byron felt not just as he had often claimed to feel – that his life was somehow doomed, an always already exhausted project – but that after the flagrant risk and catastrophe of his marriage he may not be able to restore, let alone reinvent, himself. That being on the run was running out for him; that the glamour of his bravado was unsustainable. And yet by removing himself from the scene – from the scene of his various 'crimes', and the scenes that were always being made by the various women around him but never by him – he had made what had happened to him and what he had done all the more immediate and revealing. But as inspiration not as self-knowledge. What was revealed was that poetic invention was the better alternative, indeed the antidote to the cant of so many versions of self-knowledge. That whatever else poetry could do it could complicate and ironize a sense of motive. That a conversion experience, of any sort, was what was not needed. That what Shelley called Byron's vile and vulgar prejudices turned out to have a vitality (and a resilience) that no mountains could match.

All the contemporary accounts of human nature that Byron knew about – and he was a voracious reader throughout his life – tended to make people feel less alive, or want to be less alive. For Byron, 'The great object of life,' as he had written fatefully to his future wife in 1813, 'is Sensation – to feel that we exist – even though in pain – it is this "craving void" which drives us to gaming – to Battle – to Travel . . .' By removing himself to Geneva, as is abundantly clear – and especially given Byron's acute sense of the spirit of place – Voltaire and Rousseau and Gibbon could preside over his imagination in powerful and obscure ways (as did Calvin, but as a rather more minatory presence). Byron and Shelley visited the settings for Rousseau's *Julie* and the house in Lausanne where Gibbon had once lived. And Byron's reverence for the writers that mattered to him is, as always, striking. 'I have traversed all Rousseau's ground,' he wrote to John Murray on 27 June, '– with the Heloise before me – & am struck to a degree with the force & accuracy of his descriptions – & the beauty of their reality.' Force and accuracy mattered a great deal to Byron.

In Switzerland he began to feel again that he existed. He enjoyed travelling with his oldest friend, John Cam Hobhouse, who joined him soon after he arrived; and he enjoyed meeting Madame de Staël again, whom he liked more in Switzerland than he had when he first met her in London. She made the now forever homeless Byron feel at home. But most of all it was his trips and talks with Shelley that restored Byron's spirits, if not his poetry, which didn't need restoring. Shelley's misunderstanding of him worked wonders for Byron. The famous story of the telling and the writing of *Frankenstein* happened during this summer. And, indeed, in the context of Byron's being so radically disheartened, the famous story of bringing something (or someone) to life and being persecuted by the life you have made has an added resonance.

Byron would later describe this period in his life in his journal, as one in which 'I should have blown my brains out, but for the recollection that it would have given pleasure to my mother-in-law.' Byron had more than mixed feelings about giving women pleasure, and often wondered what he would have to suffer in the process. But the summer of 1816 marked a change in his appetite for poetry, and ultimately for politics. After Geneva there would be Italy and Greece, with their liberation movements; and *Don Juan*, of which Byron would write to John Murray in 1820, 'The truth is that IT IS TOO TRUE.'

Emerson and the Impossibilities of Style

I

> If anything could stand still, it would be crushed and dissipated by
> the torrent it resisted, and if it were a mind, it would be crazed; as
> insane persons are those who hold fast to one thought, and do not
> flow with the course of nature.
>
> Ralph Waldo Emerson, 'The Method of Nature'

For Emerson, writing is beset by temptation. And even though, by
definition, he never quite tells us how we should write – because our
words are inspired by what he calls our 'genius', they are not ours for
the taking – he knows what we should avoid. Anyone who writes, he
tells us (and himself) in his various ways, will find himself, at least
to begin with, imitating other people and repeating himself (which is
imitating oneself). But imitation is fear of the future; as Emerson puts
it, 'Imitation cannot go above its model', and our models are there
only to go above and beyond. They are prompts without scripts.
Imitation, Emerson admonishes us, is a sabotaging of possibility.
Indeed, 'Imitation is suicide', he writes in 'Self-Reliance' – a standing
still when everything in nature is torrential. 'There is a time in every
man's education', Emerson writes, when he must recognize that 'the
power which resides in him is new in nature, and none but he knows

what that is which he can do, nor does he know until he has tried'. Knowing is experimental, and knowledge is of the new. The kind of trying Emerson promotes is not the trying of effort, but the trying out of the essayist. But the essayist who, as he writes in 'The Over-Soul', 'has broken our god of tradition, and ceased from our god of rhetoric'. To break a god is no mean feat. Emerson's demand on himself is exorbitant. No sentence he writes must hold him to anything.

The shock of the new may make the past alluring but only the future, Emerson believes, should be irresistible. Though there is always the risk that language links us to our losses, that in the wake of what is happening we can get dragged back, or want to get dragged back. The 'trait' we should value, Emerson writes in 'Character', 'is the notice of incessant growth'. There is incessant growth, and we should value the noticing of it – which is what Emerson wants his writing to do, what his style is for – and of what it gives notice. That we must not let ourselves try to impede our growth ('embarking', the *OED* tells us, is one of the words Emerson brought into the language). Because the 'onward trick of nature is too strong for us' we should not think our strength is in resisting it. And yet, as Emerson knew, growth is incessant but its acknowledgement isn't always possible, or bearable. The new knowledge that we grow through can be calamitous.

And so, there was, abidingly, for Emerson, also the temptation of mourning, of a writing consumed and stalled by grief. His father died when he was eight, only four of his eight siblings survived childhood; in 1828, when Emerson was twenty-five, his brother Edward went mad, dying six years later, followed by his next brother, Charles, who died in 1836; and his first wife, Ellen, whom he married in 1830, died of tuberculosis a year after their wedding. Emerson remarried, but in 1842 his favourite child, Waldo, died of scarlet fever at the age of five. Emerson would remark with shocking straightforwardness after the devastating loss of his son, 'The only thing grief has taught me, is to know how shallow it is,' as though grief gave him nothing; it was always Emerson's determination not to be set back, to make something, in William James's words, 'to be going on from' ('for everything you have missed', Emerson writes in 'Compensation', keeping all the meanings of 'missed' in play, 'you have gained something else'). After Waldo's death Emerson wrote to Carlyle, 'Well, I have come back hither to my work and my play, but he comes not back, and I must simply suffer it. Doubtless the day will come which will resolve this, as everything gets resolved into light, but not yet.' His work and his play suggest something more than grim determination – the refuge of work alone – and, though 'doubtless' reminds us of doubts kept at bay, it is no less than Emerson's faith that 'everything gets resolved into light', an image stunning in its clarity and its complication.

There is everywhere in Emerson's writing a terror of the elegiac, alongside his heartfelt and heart-rending recognitions. He represents a new American need for the new – a new version of the new – assailed on all sides by a fear of stultifying interruption. If '. . . the war of Independence', as the historian Sam Haselby writes in *The Origins of American Religious Nationalism*, 'posed rather than answered the question of American nationality' then Emerson seemed to be preaching an improbable nationalism based on the radical, ongoing independence of each of its citizens. Writing as commemoration could all too easily drain the future of its draw; and Emerson wanted a style to look forward with. So his style, whatever else it is, is an attempt to dispel grief, and so an acknowledgement of just how paralysing and pervasive grief can be (a charitable view of Emerson's initial blind spot about slavery would be that he couldn't bear the grief it entailed). 'Our life,' he writes in 'Experience', 'seems not present so much as prospective; not for the affairs on which it is wasted, but as a hint of this fast-flowing vigour.' In a New World, in what Emerson famously calls 'this new yet unapproachable America', there have to be new ways of writing that are, as it were, unprecedented; and so somehow more of a piece with this fast-flowing vigour. A style that is not a standing still nor a looking back, that neither aspires to, nor needs to ironize, the monumental, the immutable or the established ('We need change of objects,' he writes in 'Experience'; 'Dedication to one thought is quickly odious'). A style that quotes, or alludes, or refers, but with a view only to revision not to legitimation. An approach to the torrent. 'Expression is all we want,' Emerson wrote in his journal. 'Not knowledge but vent.'

Where once there was consolidation now there must be release; and new measures are required ('The way to write,' Emerson once said, 'is to throw your body at the mark when your arrows are spent'). So is there a style, then, for what Emerson calls in 'History', 'onward thinking', a way of writing, of using language, that can go with a flow; that can be of a piece with the unrelenting transitions of natural life and the new arrangements of political life that was America's evolving democracy; that can live with, and not against, impermanence; a writing of prodigal, unsuspected aims and eccentric means? A way of writing in which the means always justifies the ends? And in which the individual affirms his singularity, the uniqueness of his divinely inspired genius? 'Adhere to your own act,' he writes in 'Heroism', 'and congratulate yourself if you have done something strange and extravagant, and broken the monotony of a decorous age.'

Congratulating oneself is itself strange and extravagant; and it is Emerson's way, where he can, to enact the proposals of his sentences. It was this shedding of limitation, the limitations of tradition – and his reiteration of imitation and limitation urges on us the imitation in limitation – that Emerson craved (and which made Whitman Emerson's exemplary poet of what Whitman himself would call 'a strange, unloosened, wondrous time'). 'Rejecting as explicitly as he does all institutionalised allegiances,' Richard Poirier writes, '[Emerson] is forced to claim a place and function for himself almost wholly through his style.' And yet rejecting allegiances does not destroy them, and language itself is a form of allegiance. But Emerson's explicit allegiance was to the new, to the future, to what Whitman would call

'Democratic Vistas', and he wanted a style that could get him there, uncompromised by the past.

Can writing, then, be a way of desiring that ultimately unknowable and obscure object of desire, the future? Or is language fated, as Emerson feared, to be a relentless celebration of and mourning for the past? Reverence for the dead, great or otherwise, could be a great deadener ('Europe', Emerson writes in 'Friendship', is 'an old faded garment of dead persons: the books their ghosts'). If time will not relent, and there is no standing still now, but only the wish to stand still; if we are utterly dependent, not on each other and not on the institutions of the past, but on something quite other that generates our descriptions and that is itself beyond description, or the idea of description – and which Emerson calls, variously, Genius, Character, the Over-Soul, Nature, God – then what do we want to do now with our language? Could we, for example, give up on wanting to be understood ('To be great is to be misunderstood,' Emerson wrote in 'Self-Reliance', knowing that the opposite was not true)? How can we write in, and for, a New World? These are Emerson's questions, which, as he himself insisted, were as much questions of style as they were questions about how to live. How do you live – and write and speak as part of that living – if the project is, as Emerson writes in his essay 'Character', 'illuminating the untried and unknown'?

'Emerson's interest,' Robert D. Richardson writes, 'is in the work-shop phase, the birthing stage of art, not the museum moment, the embalming phase.' The birthing stage of art but also the birthing stage of the self; and not because Emerson conceived of the self as a work of art but because he believed that art, as one among many forms of expression, could be an integral part of the work and working-out of selves, which were themselves always untried and unknown; always, to use Emerson's word, 'unattained'. We are always different from ourselves and from others – and continually becoming so – and this, in Emerson's view, is our distinctive virtue that has become our defining fear. And even as a young man Emerson knew that to acknowledge this was to acknowledge something about style. 'A man's style is his intellectual Voice,' he wrote in his journal in 1825, when he was twenty-two, and also thinking of his own style,

> only in part under his control. It has its own proper tone & manner which when he is not thinking of it, it will always assume. He can mimic the voices of others, he can modulate it with the occasion & the passion, but it has its own individual nature.

To think about your style is to undermine it; it can be baffled or muted by your own self-consciousness and by your pleasure in mimicry (you might want to write as you think you want to write, or as you think others might want you to write). It is vulnerable, because distractions abound, because there is something about one's individual nature that one is averse to (how it might separate you from others, say, or create too great an intimacy). But your style is there with its own proper tone and manner if you will allow it, if you can be receptive to it. But, a bit like a forbidden pleasure, you are always tempted to disavow it, to dissociate yourself from it; to say it's not really you, or yours (which it is and it isn't). Your style, which is the voice of your individual nature, is you but not you as you know, or perhaps want, yourself to be (it is 'only in part under his control'). For Emerson, a person's style was the voice in themselves that they had to yield to, to accede to, without waylaying it (style is the voice in you you must resist your resistance to). It was fear of the future, fear of unpredictable consequences, fear of the torrent, Emerson believed, that made a person's relationship with their style so precarious. Style was the sustaining Voice, and anything that is sustaining is dangerous. And 'If the faith that stands on authority is not faith', as Emerson wrote in 'The Over-Soul', we need now something more sustaining than authority, and perhaps a new version of faith. If faith wasn't in authority of one kind or another, what could it be in? And what would this faith be like? This is Emerson's provocation.

If you are committed to the untried and the unknown, to birthing rather than embalming, to faith as opposed to authority, to your style and not to your mimicry, then already existing practices, including the practices of language – and of politics, of the arts and the sciences – are always only provisional, and cannot be unduly privileged. Because they are potentially confining they need to be redescribed, they need to be moved on. Because their value is only in the transitions they provide, the futures they facilitate, their status is always uncertain (where they take us to is not simply more important than what they are, it is what they are). And they always run the risk of immobilizing us, of tempting us to find ways of supposedly standing still. For Emerson the original sin is of stasis, of renewal refused, of form as fixity.

So when Emerson, in his essay 'Self-Reliance', urges on us his newly self-reliant, self-trusting man, the new teacher, who 'acts from himself' by 'tossing the laws, the books, idolatries and customs out of the window' and so 'restores the life of man to splendour', he leaves us and himself in an obvious and abiding quandary: where has he got his new language from – the grammar, the style, the rhythms of his sentences – if not from the laws, books, idolatries and customs he has tossed out of the window? And tossing them out of the window doesn't destroy them, it just puts them somewhere else. (It is a provocative image: someone else might find them and use them; he might see them the next time he looks out of the window; he might want to jump out of the window if he doesn't get rid of this stuff.) A style might also be what you are left with after a lot of good riddance.

Emerson, we should note, is not a book-burner, a destroyer of the past, he just wants – in what he helped make, and which became known as the American grain – to keep moving, to resist the temptation to be stopped in his tracks for too long. He wants, in the pragmatic way that he also partly inspired, new ways of using the past. He doesn't want to be over-impressed by what people have already done at the cost of what they might do (if to quote is to recontextualize, then to write in a quotable style, as Emerson so surely does, is to invite the using and re-using of one's words; is to give them an untellable future). He wants to use the past differently, and to see it as something one can use. This, as we will see, has consequences for the ways he writes and the ways he wants to write, a style being at once a preferred way of writing and an unavoidable way of writing, a venting of intention and helplessness. It makes his every sentence fraught with the burden of progressing towards an unknowable destination ('The maker of a sentence like the other artist,' Emerson writes in his journal, 'launches out into the infinite and builds a road into Chaos and old night'). So Emerson works one sentence at a time, without knowing, or letting the reader know, what could be coming next. As though each sentence was a leap, and he was wanting not to look before he leaped: or each sentence was a model, or a lead, that need not be followed. This was what John Morley referred to as Emerson's 'difficult staccato', the fits and starts of a style that wanted nothing more than to be always beginning.

If 'be unpredictable' like 'be spontaneous' can be a double-bind – if you do it you are not doing it – then we can see Emerson, in courting these binds (and others), making a style out of impossibility ('In these checks and impossibilities,' he wrote in 'Nature', 'we find our advantage': in them not through them). So he must, for example, try to avoid insistently repeating his terror of repetition or going on and on imitating his own fear of imitation; something, of course, he is actually unable to do, such are the paradoxes and contradictions he embroils himself in so intently. Emerson wants to believe that a man's style, his intellectual voice, never mimics itself, or shouldn't. You know it by its inexhaustible originality, by the fact that you can anticipate only that it is unanticipatable. 'Who,' after all, Emerson asks in 'Nature', 'can set bounds to the possibilities of man?' A sense of impossibility, Emerson insists, is the unwillingness to see possibility; indeed, impossibility is where possibilities flourish, if they can only be looked for. 'A man is a golden impossibility,' he writes in 'Experience', but '. . . In the thought of genius there is always a surprise . . . Every man is an impossibility until he is born; every thing impossible, until we see a success.' For Emerson there is no knowing beforehand; or rather, the only use of what we think we already know is to make surprises possible. Each person has his own genius, and it speaks the language of hope.

Throwing all that stuff out of the window – and often in his writing, in this mood, it is most of Western (not Eastern) culture that he wants to throw out of the window; and he needs a style in which he can seem to be doing this – is an act of understandable exasperation (and hope). But exasperation about what? About having to be born in his particular community, or in a human community at all? About being born into a world that pre-dated him, and made him unchosen promises? About not being able to choose his inheritance? About entrapment or the paralysis of imitation? About the death-in-life routine and ritual of repetition or the temptations of self-betrayal? About the vanishing acts of conformity or the seductions of compliance? Or about enslavement, the haunting presence in much of his writing? As is often the case with Emerson, the image of tossing these things out of the window is simple, straightforward, but the after-images, the after-effects, are prolific. We are left to wonder, when we thought we were being taught something. Emerson wants his writing to be informative only in so far as it makes it evocative.

In Emerson's writing, it should be noted, there are many questions and very few question marks, and perhaps this is because provocations, like evocations, require an answering response but not an answer. To provoke can be to incite and to excite, and Emersonian provocations are not, by definition, manipulations; they are not intended to engineer a known reaction (in that sense they are questions without answers). It is not, that is to say, Emerson's style to, however subtly, intimidate his reader. He is wanting, in his writing, an alternative to doctrine or dogma and to what we might call propaganda or ideology. That is to say, he does not know what it would be for his writing to be successful (so much of his writing is about what he does not want writing to be, or to do). So when, in a famous passage from his essay 'Self-Reliance', familiar doctrine is invoked, it is there to be waylaid; he goes in recognizable directions, but seeking indirection out:

> I shun father and mother and wife and brother, when my genius calls me. I would write on the lintels of the door-post, Whim. I hope that it is somewhat better than whim at last, but we cannot spend the day in explanation.

Emerson here refers to Jesus's words in the famous passage in Luke, 14:26 – 'If any man come to me, and hate not his father, and mother, and wife, and children, and brethren, and sisters, yea, and his own life also, he cannot be my disciple' – but he replaces Jesus with himself, with his own genius. And even though we might think it comes to the same thing Emerson makes it clear that it does not. The doctrine Jesus was preaching was not whim, and the doctrine Emerson is referring to, if that is what it is, he is not willing to explain. A whim, the *OED* tells us, is 'a fanciful or fantastic creation . . . a capricious notion or fancy . . . a fantastic or freakish idea'; perhaps, Emerson intimates, what Jesus preached was akin to a whim, and we could do 'somewhat better' than that (though we could not): and he won't inform us what would be better. Nor why his genius inspired him to write that particular word (how could he know?). We cannot spend the day in explanation – about writing whim or about anything else – because we have got better things to do. Emerson is reminding us here that there are people who spend their days in explanation, but that that is not his style. Explanation has to be plausibly coherent and intelligible, and always seeks assent; it is Emerson's 'hope in these days [that] we have heard the last of conformity and consistency'. So in any consideration of Emerson's style we have to imagine a sentence, a paragraph, an essay – not to mention a life, or a life of writing – without consistency, conforming to nothing. And we have to imagine such impossibilities as a way of talking about the unheard-of potentialities of language that Emerson longs for, and wants to call a person's style, their intellectual voice, unique in its tone and manner (Emerson doesn't mention its matter, or he intimates that tone and manner may be the matter). Language, and other people, are there to surprise us into new forms of life. We have courage and style to help us contend with what he calls 'the Lords of limit', Lords being the kind of people that America was founded to abolish.

'If you desire to arrest attention,' Emerson wrote in his journal, 'to surprise, do not give me the facts in the order of cause and effect, but drop one or two links in the chain, and give me cause and an effect two or three times removed.' Emerson here is asking someone else ('you') for something he wants from them (to be surprised, to have his attention arrested, his delirium interrupted, and so go off in a different direction). This, of course, is the writer privately calculating his effects; he wants to arrest attention and surprise but not with any prescriptive account of where attention might go after being arrested (it might be released, it might go to the expected prison). And even though cause and effect are being staged, it is worth noting that it is cause and an effect 'two or three times removed'; that is to say, other effects are acknowledged as possible. For Emerson a sense of possibility, of aliveness and its consequences comes out of verbal precision ('All writing should be selection in order to drop every dead word'); but it is an acuity that is always understated, and plainly in view. 'What seems to me signature in Emerson,' Stanley Cavell writes, 'is the weight he puts on the obvious, where the difficulty is taking him at his word.' His words are obviously there on the page, and they are more or less ordinary words, but to take him at his word we have to, as it were, give the obvious a second chance; to see how it might surprise us. So, in so far as this is possible, there will be no dead words in his writing, no element of his style that is inert. 'Do not put hinges to your work to make it cohere,' Emerson told his friend Woodbury, inviting him to imagine, say, doors and windows without hinges, and what you could do with them: 'consistency', he wrote, 'is the hobgoblin of little minds', as though there was something mischief-making about consistency. It would be cute to say that Emerson's style was mischievous, but true to say that he doesn't always want us to know where we are with him.

We are prone, Emerson suggests, to take too much for granted, which then grants us too little. The incoherent and the inconsistent wake us up. 'The most interesting writing,' he told Woodbury, 'is that which does not quite satisfy the reader. Try and leave a little thinking for him . . . A little guessing does him no harm, so I would assist him with no connections.' Assisting someone with no connections is a nice way of putting it. If you take the connections out, connections will be made. If you wrong-foot the reader it might put him on a different footing. If satisfaction kills desire we need to be kept guessing. It is Emerson's style to sustain anticipation, to keep the future alive (he wants to intrigue us without tantalizing us). Coherence and consistency in the writer can lead to inattention in the reader (and in the writer); or so Emerson intimates. What Stanley Cavell calls Emerson's 'terrible exactness' is itself exacting in the attention it requires of us. Attention to what is coming next, to the next good thing, which may or may not be the next best thing; attention to what he calls, in 'Nature', 'enhancement and sequel', the two necessarily going together for Emerson.

II

Language must be raked, the secrets of the slaughter-houses and infamous holes that cannot front the day, must be ransacked, to tell what negro slavery has been.

> Ralph Waldo Emerson, 'On Emancipation in the
> British West Indies'

If you are interested, as Emerson is, in forms of attention that have unpredictable consequences, you have to be vigilant about the good and the bad ways in which attention can be arrested and confined; and about the ways in which language forces attention, as well as doing many other things to it (organizing it, exploiting it, consoling it, distracting it, undermining it, all of which Emerson is duly attentive to in his writing). Slavery, the greatest scandal in American history and of Emerson's time, a radical arrest and confinement so tormenting and tormented that people, including Emerson himself as he eventually knew to his shame, couldn't initially engage with it, couldn't find the words to prevent it, was the prevailing issue. Language itself needed to be raked and ransacked, so hidden and obscured had the reality of slavery become; and by the language that had described and justified it (language needed to be raked by language, so obscuring and obscure had it become). People's enslavement of themselves and each other, and the costs incurred, became Emerson's theme. The narrowing of the mind that was the cause and effect of despair. The narrowing of the mind that was the old language pre-empting the new thought, the old concealments preventing the new disclosures.

Emerson always seems to have known what he feared he could get stuck with, or in (imitation, repetition, mourning, tradition, being understood; but also righteous indignation about the way the world was). His style was a way of being alert to this (his style was a kind of alarm system). So the fear of his, and other people's, attention being imprisoned – in idols, in customs, in institutions, in laws, in certain kinds of writing – made Emerson, perhaps unsurprisingly, idealize forms of transition (if transitions are what you most value, thresholds like windows and doors, and the beginnings and endings of sentences and paragraphs, are important). In a well-known passage from 'Self-Reliance' Emerson spells out the extraordinary consequences of what might be called his personal religion of transition:

> Life only avails, not the having lived. Power ceases in the instant
> of repose; it resides in the moment of transition from a past to a

new state, in the shooting of the gulf, in the darting to an aim. This one fact the world hates, that the soul *becomes*; for that for ever degrades the past, turns all riches to poverty, all reputation to a shame, confounds the saint with the rogue, shoves Jesus and Judas equally aside.

If power resides in the moment of transition – and it is power that you want: and the power Emerson wants is style, what he calls the individual's unique intellectual voice – then you will not be wanting to come to conclusions (and since you can't settle for the unsettling you have to do something else with it). And you will always need new gulfs to shoot and new aims for darting (the violence of the terms is not incidental). The one fact that the world hates, that the soul becomes, doesn't, of course, tell us what the soul becomes, only that it becomes; and the world hates this partly because what it becomes is unpredictable and partly because it makes the past largely irrelevant, merely more evidence of becoming. The past has no authority – it pushes both Jesus and his betrayer aside in a clean sweep – and is neither a source nor a foundation. 'My heart's inquiry,' Emerson wrote in his journal, 'is, whence is your power? . . . The one thing we want to know is where is power bought.' The past is only of use for the power we can get from it, the power of becoming. The power of going on being the 'volitant stabilities' he describes us as being. As though the perceived danger was in our being only stable or only volatile.

Emerson was always a writer who needed to get himself in and out of corners, who needed to insistently formulate his trap so he could spring himself (his equivocations about slavery, and his idealizing of 'Compensation' exemplify the vice of his virtues; there were certain radical injustices he couldn't spell out to himself). And because, as Richard Poirier rightly warns us in *A World Elsewhere*, 'Emerson's theories and recognitions must not, however, be confused with his performances,' we can't avoid wondering, as readers of Emerson, how he is going to pull it off; whether he can find a style that doesn't make a mockery of his proposals; a style commensurate with his principles. A style, impossible as it sounds, that can improvise itself out of repetition and out of rehearsing the past. How, that is to say, is Emerson going to write in a way that provokes people into not becoming his disciples, or not becoming disciples at all (so one question might be – a question he might have asked himself – could he find an inspiring style that was not a persuasive, or a persuading style?)? Could he write a new world out of the language of the old world? Could he write moments of transition, in a transitional style, without being too impressed by his conclusions, without having to stop?

And then, of course, there is the unanswerable question: how do you know whether it is the voice of your Genius, how do you know whether your style is your style? Emerson, in other words, as a late Romantic, both preaches and exemplifies the kinds of pressures the demand for originality put on style. As though style is nothing if not original, and as though originality was not a function of convention. But distinctively, for Emerson, style is essentially an aspiration, not an achievement. It is not deferred, but always in the making, a work in progress. For Emerson, style, like the self, is never achieved, but always unattained ('to have a self', for Emerson, Cavell writes, 'is always to be averse to one's attained self in one's so-far attained society': to have a style is to be averse to one's attained style). Style, like the soul, is always becoming, which is why the world (and oneself) might hate it; the hatred taking the form of envy, say, or mockery, or mimicry, or self-mimicry (staying with the style one has found, and is recognized by). 'The quality of the imagination is to flow and not to freeze,' Emerson writes in 'The Poet', and it is freezing with fear that is also implied. In Emerson's account, style is what the world hates about the writer, and what the writer, out of fear, might resist in himself. Emerson's jeremiad, then, is about style, and about how impossible it can be to hear it, or to let it speak. To recognize it and to back it. To affirm it as something growing, and therefore never attainable. Emerson, that is to say, believes neither in original sin nor in original virtue, but in original possibility.

III

> Who shall forbid a wise skepticism, seeing that there is no practical question on which any thing more than an approximate solution can be had?
>
> Ralph Waldo Emerson, 'Montaigne'

To approximate is to approach. And we might see Emerson's theories and performances as an ongoing series of approaches; though informed by a strong sense of what needs to be cleared away – not cleared up – to make approaches possible. And a stronger sense that the majority of his fellow-countrymen want America to be as unapproachable as possible. Writing in the only language they have, the language that they have inherited, they write to keep novelty at bay. They fear surprising themselves; they fear becoming enigmatic; they fear what might be in store for them. As though there is something about their originality, their inspiration, that they dread, that they are intimidated by (as though the strange and the extravagant is not what they are, or want, or want to be). They don't want the independence they have declared. Their conformity starves them of their gifts; they would rather fob themselves off with false satisfactions – 'fashion, custom, authority, pleasure, and money': that is, all the present objects of desire and cultural ideals available – than acknowledge what he calls 'the privilege of the immeasurable mind'. 'There are resources in us on which we have not drawn.' As though they were blind to their resources, or couldn't recognize them, or even feared and so resisted them. As though everything they thought they wanted was false measures, or that what mattered could be measured.

'Let me admonish you,' he tells the senior class at the divinity college in Cambridge in 1838, 'first of all, to go alone; to refuse the good models, even those which are sacred in the imagination of men, and dare to love God without mediator or veil . . . Imitation cannot go above its model. The imitator dooms himself to hopeless mediocrity.' Refuse the good models, but also do not presume to know which they are, or assume their sacredness, or even assume you know what a model is, which is like presuming to know God. 'Truly speaking,' he tells his audience, 'it is not instruction, but provocation, that I can receive from another soul.' Truly speaking we can only become who we are through provocation. Instruction makes us followers, provocation stirs our unsuspected (and unsuspecting) selves, which may or may not be leaders, but will have the significant contributions to make. Style provokes, instruction makes us mimics. Emerson's style continually provokes, and is inimitable. Though it is not, of course, without its own precursors and precedents.

But Emerson, who is nothing if not inconsistent – there is no provocation without inconsistency – also wants to warn us that style, too, like anything else we value, can become an end in itself, an idol, a fetish, a standing still (the Emersonian injunction would be, once you find your voice, lose it). What Emerson calls Nature won't let anything, or anyone, stay where they are; she is a torrential becoming that mocks our will to stability and conservation. 'For Nature,' Emerson writes in 'Nominalist and Realist',

who abhors mannerism, has set her heart on breaking up all styles and tricks, and it is so much easier to do what one has done before, than to do a new thing, that there is a perpetual tendency to a set mode. In every conversation, even the highest, there is a certain trick, which may be soon learned by an acute person, and then that particular style continued indefinitely. Each man, too, is a tyrant in tendency, because he would impose his idea on others; and their trick is their natural defence. Jesus would absorb the race; but Tom Paine or the coarsest blasphemer helps humanity by resisting this exuberance of power.

A style can be a trick, and the trick can be a tyranny, of repetition, of the old masquerading as the new; a trick that all too easily takes and catches on (that is, it can be taught, and Emerson distrusts anything that can be learned by being taught). Indeed the wish to create or force a consensus, to impose an idea on someone else, to create the illusion of stopping time through reiteration, is what tyranny is for Emerson (and, indeed, what irredeemably, and unsurprisingly, complicates his politics). America was to be the place, at least for Emerson, where such tyrannies, where all lords of limit, would be tossed out; even, he implies, the tyranny of Christianity ('Every thing looks permanent until its secret is known,' Emerson wrote in 'Circles'; Nietzsche, Emerson's follower, would expose what he thought was Christianity's secret – that it was a slave-religion). Indeed Christianity could be described as a style, and a trick. But then any set mode for Emerson, and any tendency to a set mode, was a coercion to be avoided. He wanted instead to promote what he called in his essay 'Compensation' 'the natural history of calamity':

> The changes which break up at short intervals the prosperity of men are advertisements of a nature whose law is growth. Every soul is by this intrinsic necessity quitting its whole system of things, its friends, and home, and laws, and faith, as the shell-fish crawls out of its beautiful but stony case, because it no longer admits of its growth, and slowly forms a new house . . . In proportion to the vigor of the individual, these revolutions are frequent, until in some happier mind they are incessant.

The necessity of incessant growth, at least in sufficiently vigorous natures – and it would be the idea of such vigorous natures that

Nietzsche would also pick up on and promote – entails a state of almost permanent revolution (despite, that is, Emerson's misgivings about permanence: he wants a language in which the incessant is not more of the same). Emerson wants natural growth, at its best, to be revolutionary – 'every soul . . . quitting its whole system of things' – and the revolutionary, in its American sense, to be total and irreversible. Again Emerson wants us to imagine the impossible – everyone 'quitting [their] whole system of things', their entire life, quit as though it were a job they no longer wanted – and he needs a way of saying things, a style, in which he can do this. It is a version of the Christian injunction to lose your life in order to find it; but, as always with Emerson, the echo is a revision. Quitting is not losing, and a whole system of things may look like a life but may not be one. Emerson could theorize this quitting, but there was a limit to how much he could perform it in his writing. Or rather, the theory awaited (and awaits) its performance.

Emerson's project was to find a style that was not a tyranny. And in doing this he was acknowledging, at its most minimal, that style, at least as we have so far conceived it, tends towards the tyrannical. Unless, that is – like the shellfish – it comes to no conclusions, and can endlessly renew itself. Vision is revisionary. Bad style consolidates, good style surprises. It is impossible to be continually surprised, but wanting to be continually surprised is full of possibility.

Clough's *Amours*

Where are the great whom thou would'st wish should praise thee?

Arthur Hugh Clough, *Dipsychus and the Spirit*

There is a consensus among critics of the last century that Clough is a poet consistently underrated and insistently misplaced. He is a greater poet than we have been able to acknowledge, and more a modern (or even modernist) poet than we take him to be. And it has been around *Amours de Voyage* – a contentious work from its initial publication in the *Atlantic Monthly* of February–May 1858 – that the claims have been made. 'To speak of Clough's modernity,' Barbara Hardy wrote, 'is understandable but misleading. Perhaps no other Victorian writer is so visibly imprisoned in his Victorianism.' Hardy overstates the case as though the case won't be properly made both for Clough as sufficiently confined, and for Clough as a man of his time. And there may be forms of imprisonment that force a broaching of the future. Isobel Armstrong sees Clough, and particularly *Amours de Voyage*, as both a sign of the times and of the times to come. Once again, as in the poem itself – which is so concerned to distinguish the imprisonings that are self-imprisonings from the imprisonings that are not – openness is the issue. '*Amours de Voyage*,' she writes, 'approaches the condition of a modernist poem, a self-reflexive poem without closure, dwelling on its self-reflexivity. It has often been compared in this respect with T. S. Eliot's *The Love Song of J. Alfred Prufrock*.' We are being warned that Clough's apparent modernity helps and hinders our reading, that the poet and the hero of his poem are caught in something – are in some way stuck as representative men of their time, or of our time – and that we are likely to get the poetry wrong if we don't read it as resolutely mid-Victorian and ineluctably modernist.

If what Philip Davis calls Clough's 'strange new realism' – 'By a strange new realism, the poetry reproduces, with honest unease, a disorientating sense of incongruously confused categories and languages and voices' – makes *Amours de Voyage* sound rather more like *The Waste Land* than *Empedocles on Etna* or *Maud*, it is because the poem seems to have been clarified by modernist poetics rather more than by the poetry (and the criticism) of its own time, as though it is a poem that has made more sense as time has gone on. And yet this has at once relegated its status, and relegated it to the status of influential precursor. 'Clough has been given a good deal of attention in recent years,' John Goode wrote in what is still the best essay on the poem, 'but most of it seems to be of the wrong kind . . . if Clough does foreshadow Eliot . . . this really entitles him to no more than a paragraph in a history of Eng. Lit.' All good roads lead to Eliot, which is one way of diminishing *Amours de Voyage* (and not only *Amours de Voyage*), and one of Eliot's contributions to the history of Eng. Lit. was famously to diminish the Victorians. The Victorian nineteenth century, Eliot wrote in a grand, dismissive sweep, 'was a time busy in keeping up to date. It had, for the most part, no hold on permanent things, on permanent truths about man and God and life and death.' Leavis was to be the academic consolidator of Eliot's charge that the 'Victorian poetic tradition' was nugatory ('It was Mr Eliot who made us fully conscious,' Leavis wrote, 'of the weakness of that tradition'). If *Amours de Voyage* has been, as Goode intimates, one of the casualties of what became a certain Lit. Crit. orthodoxy, it is also very much a poem about the difficulty of making claims, of knowing what to value and how to value it, of what the whole process of evaluation involves us in, and reveals us as. Which is why its reception – the language in which it has been redescribed and revalued – is peculiarly important.

When evaluation, and especially the self-evaluation of its hero, is a poem's abiding preoccupation – and *Amours de Voyage* is a series of inconclusive self-evaluations by Claude, the sound of whose name intimates someone being got at – the reader veers between being an antagonist and an accomplice (as one does with oneself). We need to take to heart, in other words, Clough's epigraphs to *Amours de Voyage*, and perhaps particularly the first one from *Twelfth Night*, 'Oh, you are sick of self-love, Malvolio, / And taste with a distempered appetite!'. One can be sick of self-love in two senses, and one sense can entail the other. Claude is sick of the way he loves himself – which seems to preclude loving anything and anybody else, and, indeed, of loving some of the things that might matter to him most – and sick because he loves himself. And what is being intimated is that something was wrong with the way contemporary people valued themselves – both with what they chose to value about themselves and how they did it, how they cultivated and enacted such value as they had. This, as the letters and the biographical information we have confirm, seems to have been the abiding preoccupation of Clough's adult life. In *Amours de Voyage*, Clough dramatizes the bathos and pathos of (modern) self-doubt; of the self imprisoned by the way it evaluates itself; of self-doubt as a kind of passionate and enervating self-love. The *OED*'s first cited instances in the language for 'bearableness', 'be-maddening' and 'untraitored' are in Clough's poetry (as are 'busy-ish' and 'poeticism', not unrelated to the narcissism of distraction). Claude can be a modern master of defeatedness only by finding ways of never quite knowing what matters to him.

Amours de Voyage is a poem about what became known as the value of value – a theme, so to speak, that links the Victorians with the so-called great modernists. And there is a paradoxical sense in which the claims made for the poem, both for and against, are of a piece with the preoccupations the poem explores. It is a poem, all of its critics insist in their different ways, that we are likely to get wrong, both as to its genealogy and its value. Indeed, the relationship between genealogy and value emerging in the nineteenth century was encountered as an essential perplexity. 'The claim that must be made for *Amours de Voyage*,' Goode suggests, 'is not just that it is a masterpiece, but a major masterpiece . . . the major masterpiece of high Victorian poetry.' When masterpieces have to be distinguished from major masterpieces, and major masterpieces distinguished from *the* major masterpiece, evaluation has become fraught.

We can place the writing of *Amours de Voyage* with some historical accuracy – the poem was begun in 1849 and worked on intermittently until its publication in 1858 – but it has been, as we can see, a poem otherwise notoriously difficult to place. And this was also true for its contemporary readers and reviewers, and especially for Clough's friends, friendship having been the mainstay of Clough's life until his late marriage in 1854 ('Clough,' Palgrave wrote in a memoir of his friend, 'might be said not so much to trust his friends, as to trust himself to them'). When his friends were not despairing – 'I would cast it behind me and the spirit from which it emanates,' Clough's friend John Shairp wrote to him, 'and to higher, more healthful, more hopeful things purely aspire . . . on the whole I regard Les Amours as your nature ridding itself of long-gathered bile' – they were baffled and dismayed. And yet in their misgivings they are strikingly engaged in the poem even when they are not engaged by it. As though it was the effect of the poem to inspire pertinent doubt in its readers, doubt about what became known as the foundations of knowledge and belief, in which it is newly assumed that nothing is but naming makes it so, or as Claude writes, in ironic allusion, 'that which I name them they are'. As though convictions are replaced by impressions, and appearances can be compared only with each other and not with anything beneath them or beyond them. In a straightforward unrhymed couplet – about how shadows no longer have anything to rhyme with – Claude makes an ordinary language dismissal of Platonism and Christianity: 'What our shadows seem, forsooth, we will ourselves be. / Do I look like that? you think me that: then I AM that.' 'Forsooth', for the Victorians an antiquated term, a faux medievalism, is an affectation about speaking truly. The correspondence theory of truth, in which words are suited to reality, is the first casualty of this poem that takes the form of a correspondence. But the astounding verbal precision of this poem about failure, narrated by someone who, in his own words, has 'always failed', failed two of Clough's closest friends, Matthew Arnold and Ralph Waldo Emerson, in the most revealing of ways. For both men the poem lacked substance.

Arnold was famously dismissive of *Amours de Voyage* in a letter to Clough, though his misgivings about Clough's poem were known, of course, only after the publication in 1932 of *The Letters of Matthew Arnold to Arthur Hugh Clough*. 'We will not discuss what is past anymore,' Arnold writes, 'as to the Italian poem, if I forbore to comment it was that I had nothing special to say – what is to be said when a thing does not suit you – suiting and not suiting is a subjective affair and only time determines, by the colour a thing takes with years, whether it ought to have suited or no.' How long does it take before we know whether we value something? We know things and people can come, in time, to matter to us, but how can we include this acknowledgement in our judgements? This is worth wondering about, and worth wondering about a poem so troubled by deferral as at once a necessity, an alibi and a failing. Being unengaged is recognition of a kind – to disidentify with something (or someone) is to have first identified something – but what Arnold doesn't have to say about 'the Italian poem' is remarkable in the eloquence of its equivocations. We do not know now what the past is that Arnold doesn't want to discuss in the letter, but we do know just how much being in Rome makes Claude wonder what about the past is worth discussing, and what we might be doing by discussing the past – what Nietzsche was to call in the 1870s the question of 'History in the service and the disservice of life', and what Claude poses as a slightly camp demand, 'Utter, O some one, the word that shall reconcile Ancient and Modern!' As Clough and Arnold as accomplished classicists would know, the 'calling together' of ancient and modern that is the Latin origin of 'reconcile' was not going to be the work of a word, or the Word.

The poem is not in Italian – 'the Italian poem' – and you can't help but hear the bore in Arnold's 'forbore'. It is, though, very much a poem about Italy and what Italy, and especially Rome and Roman republicanism, had become to the English by the mid-nineteenth century. 'If I forbore to comment' keeps Arnold's options open – and he does go on to comment – but to forbore is to 'tolerate, endure . . . do without . . . to part with or from . . . to avoid, shun . . . abstain or desist from' (*OED*), and these are the very things that Claude, the hero of the poem, does both to Rome and to the woman he desires, and indeed to his own desires. And then there is the reiterated 'suiting', a word Arnold picks up, wittingly or unwittingly, from the beginning and the end of Clough's poem. In the first section of the first canto Claude sets what will become the distinctive tone of the poem, and of his own voice within it: 'Rome disappoints me much; I hardly as yet understand but / *RUBBISHY* seems the word that most exactly would suit it.' *Amours de Voyage* is a poem in which nothing really works for Claude (it 'seems' the word but it may not be; and suits have seams that hold them together). But finding the word that suits at least reveals why Rome doesn't suit him. Clough is interested, among many other things, in how it might suit Claude to see Rome as 'rubbishy' – full of the rubbish of the past, full of the least beautiful things that need to be got rid of – and why Rome doesn't suit him, and won't. 'Rome will not suit me,' Claude begins his last letter in the poem, '. . . the priests and soldiers possess it'. Whether things and people are defined by who possesses them will also exercise Claude – as will the cumulative disappointment he is heir to as *Amours de Voyage* becomes an elegy for the modern self's quest for an accuracy about itself. That exacting modern self-consciousness seems to produce no more than a vaunted sense of failure, one that is endlessly ashamed of feeling such shame. 'I am ashamed my own self', Claude declares, and the odd syntax breathes shock and disbelief. Rome, that will all too briefly liberate Claude – 'for the first time in life I am living and moving with freedom' – will expose his shamefully inadequate sense of who he is, and what he might be capable of wanting. It is pointedly not his life he refers to but life, and the wording suggests that living with freedom – as an idea in one's mind? – is not enough. One must move with it as well.

Rome 'not suiting' more obliquely refers also, at least for contemporary readers of the poem, to the Oxford Movement that Clough flirted briefly with at Oxford, and to Newman's ultimately finding that Roman Catholicism suited him. Once again in this context, the word is used, allusively, to ironize certain gravities. Claude, like his author it seems, is a character for whom conversion, to anything, would be part of the problem rather than part of the solution. When, in 1842, Clough had to subscribe to the Thirty-Nine Articles of the Church of England in order to take up his fellowship at Oriel (where Newman was one of his colleagues), he wrote to his friend John Gell, 'It is not so much from any objection to this or that point as general dislike to [*sic*] subscription and strong feeling of its being after all . . . a bondage and a very heavy one, and one that may cramp one and cripple one for life.' In the 1840s Clough was progressively subscribing to the idea that he must not subscribe to anything or to anyone, and to wondering what kind of success this might be, and what kind of failure. If the moral (and professional) life organizes itself around states of conviction, and states of conviction are a bondage, a cramping and a crippling for life, what kind of violence or violation is belief, religious or otherwise? *Amours de Voyage*, that is to say, is a mid-nineteenth-century poem with what turned out to be startlingly modern preoccupations. Is some form of belief to be found, or is what William James called the will to believe itself the problem? *Amours de Voyage* was to be a poem vexed by subscription and its terrors – subscription that is itself a form of writing that is also a form of commitment, a self-declaration that is also a form of assent.

The poem tells a story of thwarted commitments, of a failed love affair between Claude and Mary Trevellyn, and of Claude's unplanned witnessing of the failed defence by Mazzini and Garibaldi of a new Roman republic. It is very much about the difficulty Claude has in finding or knowing what suits him – socially or politically, as a tourist or as a lover – and of being able to act on such knowledge (whether the words suit the things, and whether the words and the things suit the people). Claude is the suitor who is never quite sure what will suit him. As Arnold implicitly acknowledges in his letter, the word itself, in all it entails – in its multiple and significant contemporary meanings – requires a certain forbearance, partly because it juxtaposes, to use another of the poem's key words, the overlapping preoccupations of Clough's capacious poem itself, which pays attention to evolution and to manners, to marriage and to miracles. The *OED* has for the verb 'suit': 'To pay court to a woman . . . to set in due order, sort out . . . To make appropriate or agreeable to; to adapt or accommodate in style or manner . . . to be agreeable or convenient to . . . To be good for, to agree with' – all things Claude tries and fails to do and is confounded by in the poem.

Amours de Voyage is a poem about the hero's inconclusive attempts to love, to be politically engaged, to be 'open' to what is going on around and inside him; but it also houses a more radical uncertainty about what it would be to change, and to change for the better. The poem is riddled with images and vocabularies of change – and disclaimers: 'let us not talk of growth' – but with Clough leaving us feeling that Claude has travelled without knowing, or indeed finding out, what it would be to arrive. R. H. Hutton wrote of Clough: 'the stronger the desire, he teaches, the greater is the danger of illegitimately satisfying the desire by persuading ourselves that what we wish to believe is true'. In a melancholic parody of a quest romance, the traditional theme of the self defined by its dissatisfaction with itself – with its search for something essential that is missing – is replaced by a sense of the insufficiency of the self's desire, and the insufficiency of its objects of desire. All that is left for Claude is the pursuit of a rather nebulous knowledge. By the end of the poem Claude has neither solved nor resolved any of his problems; he has not answered his questions, nor clarified them; he has not taken refuge in paradox, or irony or the delights of indeterminacy, in the modern way. He has dispensed with Love, Scripture, Faith and Art ('I have no heart, however, for any marble or fresco'; the line wanting us to hear the 'art' in 'heart'). The only thing he believes in now is the quest for Knowledge, something we were told in the second canto of the poem that women, and indeed Claude himself, have no appetite for: 'woman', he writes to Eustace, '. . . has no heart for the timid, the sensitive soul; and for knowledge, – / Knowledge, O ye Gods! – when did they appreciate knowledge? / Wherefore should they, either? I am sure I do not desire it.' Neither women, nor the Gods – and the phrasing makes them indistinguishable – nor Claude 'desire' it, so what is it for? Is it merely a refuge from the real objects of desire, from the essential aspirations? The only real knowledge Claude has so far acquired, from what the poem has told us – and if what the drama of the poem tells us is anything to go by – seems to be the knowledge that he is not suited to his life; or, if Claude is taken to be one kind of representative Victorian man, 'we' are not suited to our lives as we have thus far conceived of them: the dawning realization that haunted the nineteenth century. But the knowledge Claude seeks, if not actually redemptive, will bring some kind of value to his life – though he makes a characteristically rather vague assertion, a conclusion in which little is concluded. It has a rousing and resounding blandness in its half-hearted and clichéd description of the conventionally rigorous life: 'Let us seek Knowledge; – the rest may come and go as it happens. / Knowledge is hard to seek, and harder yet to adhere to. / Knowledge is painful often; and yet when we know we are happy.' Claude notably doesn't tell us what we should seek knowledge of but that, perhaps ominously, he is going to seek it 'Eastward' in Egypt (not, in other words, in the West: as though the West no longer had the knowledge he needed). But he does tell us, oddly, that this knowledge is the only thing that can make us happy. We are not convinced by this invoking, at the last minute, of the great utilitarian term, nor by this vague Orientalism – is it the antiquarian, the scholarly, the mystical, the scientific that Claude is now promoting? – and we are not supposed to be. It was this that made Clough's other friend Ralph Waldo Emerson take against the poem in yet another letter.

For Emerson in 'Self-Reliance' – and Clough was a keen reader of Emerson's essays – 'Power . . . resides in the moment of transition . . . in the darting to an aim.' *Amours de Voyage*, Emerson intimated, seemed (like Claude, like Rome) to be going somewhere – the paramount transcendentalist and pragmatic criterion – and then it misfired. Perhaps it even betrayed itself, and its readers. Just as Arnold did, Emerson takes in the poem, takes on the poem, by voicing his disappointment; as though the poem about things not really working or working out works, in an uncanny way, by not working for people. It seems to be about the way it disappoints, or fails to engage, or confounds, while being itself a poem about a character who disappoints and is disappointed, and fails to engage, and is confounded by himself. It is as though the poem is somehow contagious: it can't ultimately be celebrated because it doubts celebration. It can't ultimately succeed because success has become an unknown quantity. It can't aim because it doesn't have a target – as though Claude's (and Clough's) failure was that they had no picture of their satisfaction. This, at least, is what Emerson suggests in his letter of 1858. 'When we began to build securely on the triumph of our poet over all gainsayers,' Emerson writes,

suddenly his wing flags, or his whim appears, and he plunges to a conclusion, like the ending of the Chancery suit in *Bleak House*, or like the denouement of Tennyson's *Princess*. How can you waste such power on a broken dream? Why lead us up to the tower to tumble us down? There is a statute of Parnassus, that the author shall keep faith with the reader; but you choose to trifle with him. It is true a few persons compassionately tell me, that the piece is all right, and that they like this veracity of much preparation to no result. But I hold tis bad enough in life and inadmissible in poetry. And I think you owe us a retribution of music, and to a musical argument.

We should perhaps remember that Emerson would write 'Whim' on the lintel of his study, being a great believer in having the confidence of one's whims and one's genius ('I shun father and mother and wife and brother, when my genius calls me. I would write on the lintels of the door-post, Whim'). And we should also note that there is another 'suit' referred to here, in the context of a discussion – and Emerson allows the alternative view in – about how well suited the end of the poem is to the gist of the poem. The images are of failed agreements, broken promises, misleadings, tantalizations and violent punishment. Something has gone badly wrong in a poem about things going badly wrong. 'He may be right and I wrong,' Clough commented in a letter on Emerson's verdict, sounding rather like Claude, 'and all my defence can only be that I always meant it to be so and began it with the full intention of its ending so – but very likely I was wrong all the same.' Right but wrong, wrong but right; both of them. That intentions are incommensurate with consequences is another thing that exercises Claude in *Amours de Voyage*. And also how wrong he is always likely to be, and the shame of not being able to be right. What are the cultural conditions, what are the inherited traditions, that might have created this peculiarly modern kind of shame, and that might make knowledge, or the seeking of knowledge, seem like the self-cure? Claude describes the Christian faith in the first canto as involving 'Aspirations from something most shameful here upon earth', and 'shame', as we have seen, is a key word in the poem. Emerson wanted

Claude's travails to have inspired him, transformed him, given him more life, more self-reliance. But all he has gained are losses, loss of love and loss of confidence in love, loss of religious faith and loss of that belief in culture that Arnold hoped would replace and better the religious faith of previous generations.

Arnold was not, he claimed, disappointed by the poem (as if he had had no expectations of it); he just had 'nothing special to say' because the poem didn't suit him. This sets aside the rivalry that is everywhere in Arnold's engaged disengagement with 'the Italian poem' (it is an interesting principle that when a poem works for a reader he has something special to say about it, something that seems special if only to himself). Emerson, though, felt betrayed, at least by the end of the poem, and felt that Clough had betrayed himself by concluding the poem in the way he did. And the parallels that come to mind are Dickens in *Bleak House* and Tennyson in *The Princess*. For Emerson, that is to say, the poem is evasive, and about evasion (another key word in *Amours de Voyage*), about spurious resolutions and failures of nerve. For Arnold, it is about something not suiting. It is easy to feel that there is something evasive in Arnold's insistent reiteration of 'suiting' as the suitable word, and in his question that is not entirely a question because it doesn't have a question mark to identify it – 'what is to be said when a thing does not suit you' (*Amours de Voyage* is what might be said, or rather written, when a thing doesn't suit you: the poem is, in this sense, an answer to his question). And it is not difficult to feel that, for Clough, in *Amours de Voyage* the satisfactions sought by Emerson were no longer possible, neither availing nor available. And that this too was the subject of the poem.

When Clough wrote to Matthew Arnold's brother Tom, in 1848, about Emerson he was, in a sense, setting out his own project in *Amours de Voyage*; and giving us an important clue about the civilization and its discontents that he was to explore in the poem. 'He is much less Emersonian than his Essays,' Clough wrote. 'There is no dogmatism, or arbitrariness or positiveness about him.' Clough wanted to write in the way Emerson performed himself when he was not writing (Emerson's essays are dogmatic, arbitrary and positive, and it is part of their artful originality, as Clough knew, to reveal the links between these terms). He wanted to find out if there was a form of virtue, a version of the religious, or the political or the moral life – and a style, a kind of writing – that was neither dogmatic, nor arbitrary nor speciously optimistic. So if, as has often been noted, Goethe's *Roman Elegies* are in ironic juxtaposition to Clough's *Amours* in their unequivocal commitment to sexual love – in their positive worship of Eros and the Priapic – Emerson's *Essays* are the writings that *Amours de Voyage* most corresponds and argues with. *Amours de Voyage* is, among many other things, a counter-life to the life proposed and supposed by Emerson's *Essays* – the counter-life of a poetry that, as Clough wrote in a review of recent English poetry in 1853, need not 'content itself merely with talking of what may be better elsewhere, but seek also to deal with what *is* here'.

What is there for Claude in Rome is the accumulated past of Paganism and Christianity that he sees, in his casual dismissal of Western culture, as 'rubbishy': 'All the incongruous things of past incompatible ages / Seem to be treasured up here to make fools of present and future.' It was, of course, Emerson's view that we must not let the past diminish the present and the future, or not use it to do so; and that, as he wrote in his essay 'The Poet', it was the poet's vocation to 'ensure' his 'fidelity to his office of announcement and affirming'. But through Claude, Clough announces the difficulty he has in affirming anything, and the difficulties inherent in affirmation itself (fidelity to an office of affirming is possibly what Clough meant by Emerson's 'positivism'). One of the difficulties inherent in affirmation is that it requires something to affirm; and *Amours de Voyage* begins by doubting what it proposes, by inviting us to go on a journey while warning us that travel is futile. *Amours de Voyage*, in its quest to deal with what is here, begins by wondering where here should be, so it begins with an urge to travel that is at the same time a scepticism about the lure of travel:

> Come, let us go; though withal a voice whisper, 'The world that we live in,
>   Withersoever we turn, still is the same narrow crib;
> 'Tis but to prove limitation, and measure a cord, that we travel;
> Let who would 'scape and be free go to his chamber and think;
> 'Tis but to change idle fancies for memories wilfully falser;
> 'Tis but to go and have been'.

In 'Come, let us go' we hear the beginning of 'Prufrock'. But there also may be an allusion in this prologue to *Macbeth* in his 'fit', before the banquet, referring to himself as 'cabined, cribbed, confined, bound in / To saucy doubts and fears'. Macbeth has suffered from his ambition for change, and for changing places; and Claude will suffer from saucy doubts and fears (the *OED* has for saucy, 'insolent towards superiors . . . smart, stylish'). But there is a stronger echo – not unrelated to this moment in *Macbeth* when the consequences of decisive actions begin to be fully felt – in Emerson's essay 'Self-Reliance', in which we are being encouraged to stay put if we want to get anywhere, and being grandly reassured that there is more to life than either idle fancies or memories wilfully falser. It is integral to the drama of the poem that at the very outset the enemy of promise – the voice that whispers, not unlike Milton's Satan in *Paradise Lost*, and insinuates that the only freedom is freedom of thought – invokes the always promising Emerson:

> It is for want of self-culture that the superstition of Travelling, whose idols are Italy, England, Egypt, retains its fascination for all educated Americans. They who made England, Italy, or Greece venerable in the imagination, did so by sticking fast where they were, like an axis of the earth. The soul is no traveller, the wise man stays at home . . . He who travels to be amused, or to get somewhat which he doesn't carry,

travels away from himself, and grows old even in youth among old things . . . He carries ruins to ruins.

Italy has been Claude's destination after leaving England, and Egypt is to be his next destination. 'Rubbishy' is Claude's word for the ruins, and Clough shows us the ruins Claude brings to these ruins: the ruination of a mid-nineteenth-century scepticism in which everything can be doubted because nothing can be affirmed, and in which an obsession with failure is the secret sharer of the age of Empire and progress. What Emerson's Transcendentalism can't or won't quite countenance – and this is part of its strength as well as of its weakness – is that a person (or a culture) might actually *be* ruined. What Millicent Bell calls 'the transcendentalist illusion that the disengaged spirit can keep itself free from constraining conditions, free from a design of life dictated by causes outside the sovereign self' is the illusion, or the true belief, that Claude can neither sustain nor wholly dispense with. *Amours de Voyage* was Clough's attempt to straddle, or failing that to explore, this contradiction between Emerson's infinitely self-reliant self and the self conditioned by circumstance, situated by its history.

For Emerson in 'Self-Reliance' the risk of travel is imitation; the engaged travelling spirit simply has more to imitate. 'What is imitation but the travelling mind?' Emerson asks. 'Insist on yourself, never imitate.' And Claude, significantly, is in two minds in *Amours de Voyage* about his seemingly infinite capacity for imitation which he sees, characteristically, as both an escape and a return: 'I can be and become anything that I meet with or look at.' And yet, Claude feels, there is something evasive or regressive about this 'faint . . . but faithful assurance' that he can lose himself in anything:

E'en from the stones of the street, as from rocks or trees of the forest,
Something of kindred, a common, though latent vitality, greets me;
And to escape from our strivings, mistakings, misgrowths, and
    perversions,

> Fain could demand to return to that perfect and primitive silence,
> Fain be enfolded and fixed, as of old, in their rigid embraces.

Claude, taking Emerson's injunction to its logical conclusion, as it were, sees his ability to imitate and identify with others – the non-human and, by implication, the human – as a death wish. But he sees as the alternative to this death wish – in an implicit critique of Emerson's injunction – 'strivings, mistakings, misgrowths, and perversions'. We should hear the two misses in the line, and the dread of desire and aspiration. At the end of the poem Claude's quest is to rationalize his fear of wanting a woman. In his distress in the final canto at having lost Mary, Claude speaks a line that sounds rehearsed, and sounds like Prufrock, 'I have had pain, it is true: I have wept; and so have the actors.' Imitation, and invoking the imitators, is now the only way. Claude began by apparently insisting on himself – which means asserting a mixture of Oxford-educated intellectual doubts and upper-middle-class English prejudices – but concludes by imitating. Apart from his grief he imitates (and by imitating attempts to affirm) a pale version of pagan belief. There is nothing else but imitation, it seems, and yet we can only imitate the past, that which already exists and is available to be imitated. These are Claude's tacit conclusions, and they are, whatever else they are, an argument with Emerson and his Transcendentalist conceptions that opened up the future by not revering the past, that wanted the future to be an open invitation.

For Claude, in the first two cantos of the poem, falling in love and political engagement are forms of imitation, conventions he can disdain and do without. His questions are always – and they could be lines from one of Emerson's essays – 'Is it an idol I bow to, or is it a god that I worship? / Do I sink back on the old, or do I soar from the mean?' If we can't tell the difference there may not be one. One answer to the first question is that an idol won't tell us, and a god won't need to. But if gods and idols are similar, then we are never quite sure what we are valuing, and worship may be merely servility (and perhaps it is our abasement, our servility that matters most to us?). Claude is all too conscious that how we value what we value exposes us, and that uncertainty about values is radically depleting: 'but guessing is tiresome, very. / Weary of wondering, watching, and guessing, and gossiping idly, / Down I go . . .' The half-rhymes of 'very' and 'weary' and 'idly' and 'I go' make the necessary links. Clough is clearly worrying away here about liberalism, about whether we can have beliefs without believing in them too much, and if we can't what we can do instead of believe, or have instead of beliefs. As Claude falls for the appropriately named Mary, and begins to be moved and involved by the republican struggle in Rome – that is, stops guessing, wondering, watching and gossiping – he gains not, as Emerson would have wished, a renewed sense of power, but suffers further disillusionment. 'The Fates, it is clear, are against us,' he concludes, but with a marvellous phrase of blighted resignation, 'I will go where I am led, and will not dictate to the chances.' Claude's question has always been: what will I have to submit to? Marriage and family, political commitment, the class mobility of liberal democracy, art, learning, religious faith? And now he knows (Mary will find out what she has to submit to at the very end of the poem). If the Fates are against us then our projects count for nothing in the world as it is.

And yet, 'Do I sink back on the old, or do I soar from the mean?' is Emerson's question – his continual warning about the tyranny of the past, about our regressive wearying drive to imitate the past, our using the past to diminish and disqualify ourselves. The pun on 'mean' reinforces the point, and by knowingly referring us back to Aristotle's 'mean' in the *Nichomachean Ethics*, it is another sinking back on the old. Soaring is what Satan does in *Paradise Lost*, and the old as the mean – that which has become average, the costive and ungenerous – is an Emersonian affirmation (whether or not Milton was of the Devil's party, Emerson certainly was). For Emerson we believe simply by imitating believers. And as Claude (and Clough) knew, to submit to the Fates is to sink back on the old, to endorse (i.e. imitate) an ancient belief about the cosmos. The Bible may be what Claude at one point in the poem calls, in another arch archaism, 'the olden-time inspiration', but so, from Emerson's point of view, is the wisdom of the ancients. 'And when we begin to build securely on the triumph of our poet over all gainsayers,' Emerson wrote, 'suddenly his wing flags . . . and he plunges to a conclusion.' The end of *Amours de Voyage* was not uplifting in the Emerson way. It was not a journey with an unexpected, desirable outcome.

Just as Claude and Mary fail to rendezvous – keep, in both senses, missing each other – so Emerson too, like many of Clough's contemporary readers, has a missed encounter with *Amours de Voyage*. He misreads Clough as having taken flight in the wrong sense. He sees the poem as, finally, a failure of nerve on Clough's part, when the poem is rather a study of a man's failure of nerve. Clough was speaking up in *Amours de Voyage* – as he was in many of his finest poems, most notably in *Adam and Eve, Dipsychus and the Spirit*, and some of the shorter lyrics – for the impossibility of whole-heartedness and the implications of this for relations between the sexes and for political engagement. New forms of self-division were appearing – new pictures of what was dividing the self, and of what it was divided into – and the sign of these self-divisions was a haunting sense of uncompleted or uncompletable actions, of desires spoiled by the conflicts they entailed, of beliefs undone by what the will to believe exposed.

What Claude articulates in *Amours de Voyage* is the narcissism of self-doubt, scepticism as a form of self-obsession. But this narcissism, this self-obsession, is the province of a certain kind of man, wherever he travels, and whenever he advises against it. It is this that makes Claude's incredible ignorance about women in *Amours de Voyage* such an essential part of the poem. Claude is at his least convincing – is, that is to say, at his most starkly defensive – in his pronouncements upon women and what they want, and this too is something about the poem that has become more legible over time. Claude's object of desire is his own unconvincing self; he is fascinated by his own gloomy uncertainty. Unlike Goethe's *Roman Elegies*, with their spellbound erotic attentiveness to the loved and desired woman, *Amours de Voyage* is an elegy for a love affair that never happened – and, on a larger scale, an elegy for a culture's failed love affair with love itself. Claude, Clough wants us to see – like Goethe, but in a quite different way, an opposite way – couldn't make the woman he desired real enough for long enough. And so, Clough suggests, he couldn't make his desires real enough to himself. His own failings were more alluring than Mary was.

Incredible ignorance about women presumes, of course, a credible knowledge elsewhere. But I think Clough was impressing upon us, wittingly or unwittingly, both by his inclusion of women's voices in the poem – notably minimized by Claude's volubility – and through Claude's clichéd musings about women, a picture of Victorian masculinity, one version of it, in which an obsessive, cultivated (in both senses) self-preoccupation is organized to preclude exchange with women. Cultural ideals may be self-obsession by other means. It is not incidental that after the first two sections of Canto I, in which Claude pontificates interestingly but in rather self-important ways about Rome, Christianity and the history of the West – what it was and what it should have been – the first words in the poem by a woman are Georgina Trevellyn's to Louisa, 'At last'; at last, an opportunity to speak (write), and at last, the reader might feel, a different kind of voice, a voice more exactly the kind of poetic voice that Clough was promoting in his review quoted earlier, a voice dealing with 'what is here', and not with what is, in the abstract, better and elsewhere. Claude writes of Roman history; Georgina writes of the practical actualities of travelling and family life.

We first hear Mary's voice in a postscript to one of Georgina's letters at the very end of Canto I in which we are given a description of Claude that is easy to assent to, both in its subtlety and its straightforwardness: 'I do not like him much, though I do not dislike being with him. / He is what people call, I suppose, a superior man, and / Certainly seems so to me; but I think he is terribly selfish.' The first line is what the reader tends to feel about Claude, but it is the casual suggestion that superiority in men is just a form of terrible selfishness that is arresting. It had been a culture of superior men that Clough had grown up in (though he notably devoted the last years of his life to a superior woman, Florence Nightingale). And it was as a critique of the idea of the superior man that he wrote *Amours de Voyage*. The second epigraph to the poem, from an unspecified but pointedly 'French Novel', 'Il doutait de tout, même de l'amour,' is implicitly revised if not reversed by the end of the poem that has 'amour' in its title – to doubt love is to doubt everything.

Because Claude can't deal with the obstacles to love – with love as an obstacle-course, in which resistance is the point and not the problem – he cannot love, and Mary sees this clearly. The women in the poem, as Clough surely intended, are more clear-sighted though less 'cultured' than the men: more clear-sighted, that is to say, as Clough intimates, by being less cultured, less educated in the masculine way. As though the men, and particularly the superior men, have been hugely distracted – and in Claude's case paralysed – by an education in self-love. Mary, Clough wants us to see, is much more exact, and therefore less speciously exacting than Claude. 'Oh, and you see I know so exactly how he would take it,' she writes,

> Finding the chances prevail against meeting again, he would banish
> Forthwith every thought of the poor little possible hope, which
> I myself could not help, perhaps, thinking only too much of;
> He would resign himself, and go. I see it exactly.
> So I also submit, although in a different manner.

'Banish', with its Shakespearean echoes – the word is used most often in *Romeo and Juliet* – is what the man does, to thought and possibility and hope, all implicitly linked. Claude's resignation is a self-banishing, a refuge from his desire for Mary. Both Claude and Mary have to submit to the vagaries of Claude's character but, as Mary writes, in a different manner.

In a review of Clough's poetry in the *Atlantic Monthly* in April 1862, Clough's friend Charles Eliot Norton wrote of *Amours de Voyage* that it was 'at once established in the admiration of readers capable of appreciating its rare and refined excellence. The spirit of the poem is thoroughly characteristic of its author, and the speculative, analytic turn of his mind is represented in many passages of the letters of the imaginary hero.' There were, we are reminded, readers not capable of such appreciation. And the speculative, analytic turn of the imaginary hero is taken, by his author, to be at best a mixed (and ironized) blessing. But there was another part of the author's mind represented by his imaginary heroine, and she would have seen exactly the force of her author's final epigraph to the poem, from Horace, about Anacreon – that is, about Claude – who 'in simple metres deplored his love' (to deplore being to grieve and to disparage). Or perhaps even more she would have known so exactly the truth of Thucydides, who provided an epigraph to *Amours de Voyage* from *The Peloponnesian War* that Clough ultimately discarded. Though it is, perhaps, a final word about Claude and, indeed, something Mary herself might have said: 'What you are looking for all the time is something that is, I should say, outside the range of ordinary experience, and yet you cannot even think straight about the facts of life that are before you.'

T. S. Eliot and the Soul of
Man under Psychoanalysis

I

One walks about the street with one's desires, and one's refinement
rises up like a wall whenever opportunity approaches.

T. S. Eliot to Conrad Aiken, 31 December 1914

Writing a 'London Letter' for the *Dial* in August 1922, Eliot suggested
that there were 'at present . . . three main types of English novel'. There
was the 'old narrative method', the traditional tale, represented by Wells,
Bennett and Compton Mackenzie. And at the other end of this contemporary spectrum was the 'dangerous' Dostoyevskyan novel in which
the writer has what Eliot calls 'the gift, a sign of genius in itself, for
utilizing his weaknesses'. Dostoyevsky, in Eliot's view, has a relationship
to his own pathology that is a form of artistic vocation. 'Epilepsy
and hysteria,' Eliot writes, 'cease to be the defects of an individual and
become – as a fundamental weakness can, given the ability to face it
and study it – the entrance to a genuine and personal universe.' The idea
that what one is suffering from, that what one experiences in oneself as
weakness or defect or shame, might be 'the entrance to a genuine and
personal universe' sounds, of course, like the kind of thing Freud and
his various inheritors were saying at around this time. That symptoms

of illness were signs of meaning, that personal vulnerability was an opening – an 'entrance' to use Eliot's word – that where people were vulnerable was where they had once made room for other people. For Eliot, 'the most interesting novelist in England' is D. H. Lawrence, who has, in his view, been 'affected' by Dostoyevsky.

And yet sandwiched between the conventional and the Dostoyev-skyan novel there is what Eliot calls 'another interesting type, but of a very short ancestry . . . the psychoanalytic type'. Ancestry was, as we know, very important to Eliot. Psychoanalysis itself – a 'scientific method', Eliot writes, '[that] rests upon a dubious and contentious branch of science' – was very new at this time (the British Psycho-analytic Society was set up in 1919). So the whole notion of a psychoanalytic novel was of an unprecedented type. This type of novel, 'most notably illustrated' by May Sinclair's *Life and Death of Harriett Frean*, was not, in Eliot's view, promising. 'The conclusion of Miss Sinclair's book', he writes,

> . . . extracts as much pity and terror as can be extracted from the materials: but because the material is so clearly defined (the soul of man under psychoanalysis) there is no possibility of tapping the atmosphere of unknown terror and mystery in which our life is passed and which psychoanalysis has not yet analysed.

Extracting pity and terror in obedience to Aristotle suggests something at once willed and formulaic about Sinclair's novel. But the allusion to Wilde's *The Soul of Man under Socialism* is perhaps more telling in this context. Neither Wilde nor Freud, for quite different reasons, were ever Eliot's cup of tea. Indeed they both seem to represent for Eliot false solutions to a similar problem, the problem of evil. Psychoanalysis and socialism, not to mention Wilde's particular brand of flagrant theatricality, were for Eliot a patently inadequate response to Original Sin. 'For . . . the men of the nineties,' Eliot wrote (in 'For Lancelot Andrewes'), evil was very good fun. Experience, as a sequence of outward events, is nothing in itself; it is possible to pass through the most terrible experiences protected by histrionic vanity; Wilde, through the whole experience of his life, remained a little Eyas, a child-actor.

It is that something is being treated with insufficient seriousness; whether it is the excessive clarity of Sinclair's psychoanalytic novel – 'the material is so clearly defined' – or the excessive, hedonistic self-regard of Wilde's 'histrionic vanity', some fundamental experience is being alluded to, in Eliot's view, without the appropriate gravity. It is what he calls 'the most terrible experiences', 'the atmosphere of unknown terror and mystery in which our life is passed', that he needs to find the language for. And clearly it cannot be found in the dubious science of psychoanalysis, and was evaded in Wilde's amused child-acting. 'On the other hand,' Eliot adds to his uneven-handed appraisal of Wilde, 'even to act an important thing is to acknowledge it'; but it was the important thing that mattered to Eliot, and the important thing was Sin. Eliot predicts that 'Miss Sinclair will find herself forced to proceed from psychotherapy even to the supernatural'; because, presumably, you can't get at – through psychoanalysis, in the language of psychoanalysis – the important thing that Sinclair is deemed to be gesturing at.

The phrase 'the soul of man under psychoanalysis' tells us, perhaps better than any elaborated critique, where Eliot stood in relation to the ambitions of psychoanalysis; both what he saw these ambitions as being, and how he saw them as operating. Where once, from a theological point of view, there was Sin, there was now, from a socialist point of view, exploitation and class war; and from a psychoanalytic point of view, instincts and incest. The soul of man under psychoanalysis, in other words, was deemed to be suffering from a secular form of self-division. What Eliot calls in *Notes Towards the Definition of Culture* 'higher religion', 'imposes a conflict, a division, torment and struggle within the individual'. 'In the higher religion,' he writes, 'it is more difficult to make behaviour conform to the moral laws of the religion.' For Freud, it is one's instinctual nature in its definition by culture that creates 'a conflict, a division, torment and struggle within the individual'. It is notable that the language of the experience is the same – conflict, division and struggle (torment perhaps has a rather different inflection) – but the source is relocated, and the conflicting agencies and forces are redescribed by Freud in secular, quasi-scientific terms. Where Eliot describes his 'higher religion' as 'imposing' this conflict, this division for the redemption of the soul, Freud found that his patients were the casualties of imposed ideals; that higher religions – in their various modern secular and sacred guises – were what people were now suffering from. Their supposed nature was irredeemably at odds with their cultural ambitions for themselves. They couldn't, in Eliot's words, make their behaviour conform to their moral laws. Their symptoms were the sign – the attempted self-cure – for the impossibility of this project.

The 'fundamental weakness' that Eliot saw Dostoyevsky as so successfully transforming into great art was sinfulness; for Freud the source of Dostoyevsky's great art is captured in the title of his paper of 1927, 'Dostoyevsky and Parricide'. This, one could say, would be a kind of glib shorthand for the differences between them. And yet Freud and Eliot, with their quite disparate personal and cultural histories – Freud a godless European Jew and Eliot a gradually aspiring American Anglo-Catholic – have what might be called a shared perplexity, an anguished scepticism about the self. They are both preoccupied by how modern people render what is unacceptable about themselves intelligible; the preconditions for recognizing something as unacceptable, and the nature of an adequate response to it. That we are divided souls – if not actually divided selves – is not in question for either of them. What is in question is finding the suitable, the sufficient, language for this conflict, this division, this torment and struggle within the modern individual.

When Harold Bloom writes with his useful (and usual) fervour about

Eliot that 'To have been born in 1888, and to have died in 1965, is to have flourished in the Age of Freud, hardly a time when Anglo-Catholic theology, social thought and morality were central to the main movement of mind,' he is writing with unnecessary triumphalism. The whole idea of 'the main movement of mind' is, after all, as precious to Eliot as it is to Bloom. If in some spurious, putative cultural competition the language of Freud has won over Eliot's language of Anglo-Catholic theology; if some or many or most of us are more likely to talk about sexuality, violence and childhood than about the soul, original sin and redemption when we talk about people now, it is surely worth remembering just what this transition from the language of sin to the language of unconscious, incestuous desire entails. It is naive to believe – as both Eliot and Freud showed us in their different ways – that languages could ever be anything other than the traces of their own histories. We would be right to assume that there were continuities and evolutions where there seemed to be ruptures and revolutions. That in speaking (and writing) a language we enunciate our histories. And both Freud and Eliot write out of a history of descriptions of self-division; of the individual in conflict, riven in one way or another. It is no accident, so to speak, that Laing took his title *The Divided Self* from William James's *The Varieties of Religious Experience*.

It is one thing to suffer from a sense of unease or anguish, but it is quite another thing to organize it into a conflict. The whole notion of conflict implies powers of discrimination; the ability to judge, for example, just what it is about one's nature that is sinful. For there to be a conflict of any sort there has to be a separating out of forces, recognizable differences. You can't have a war if you don't know who the enemy is. In other words, conflict and self-division – as descriptions of what is going on inside ourselves, and between ourselves and others – depend upon a high level of intelligibility. When I identify a thought or a feeling or a gesture as sexual, when I feel bad about my unkindness, it is as though I have understood myself. To be ashamed of oneself is to be in a state of total conviction, a state of conviction so absolute that it would seem impossible and silly to wonder just how one had acquired such certainty about the nature of one's actions. It is shocking to realize just how opportunistic one's scepticism can be. Our scepticism seems to be no match for our self-punishment, or indeed our punishing of others.

If, as seems to be the case, we take self-division, we take conflict for granted – as Freud and Eliot clearly do – and if we take seriously the problem, and not merely the progress, of secularizing a language, then the question becomes, is this division, this conflict we experience in ourselves, a revealing of our sinfulness, and if not, what is it revealing of? It may be revealing just of the fact of division or conflict itself – the setting up of oppositions, the sorting out into adversarial or competing positions – or it may be a self-cure for excess, the excess of feeling and desire; and yet so much depends upon the way in which we assign moral status to the combatants. In this agnostic picture of ourselves – by which we are clearly compelled if not actually bewitched – there is an anxiety about the division of the moral spoils. Once we relinquish the reassuring but sparse intelligibility of a world of goodies and baddies we begin to experience the vertigo, the disarray of what is politely called moral complexity.

When we don't understand something – and especially when we have taken understanding to be our currency – we are prone to coerce and oversimplify. 'It is human,' Eliot writes, using the difficult word,

> when we do not understand another human being, and cannot ignore him, to exert an unconscious pressure on that person to turn him into something that we *can* understand: many husbands and wives exert this pressure on each other. The effect on the person so influenced is liable to be the repression and distortion, rather than the improvement, of the personality; and no man is good enough to have the right to make another over in his own image.

Perhaps it is too Freudian to say that Eliot's stated dislike of Freud was an inverted affinity; but the language here – unconscious pressure, repression and distortion of the personality – and elsewhere in Eliot's prose, is more than merely allusive. And running the psychological account into the overtly religious, 'no *man* is good enough to have the right to make another over in his own image', dramatizes the collision and collaboration of languages that is integral to my subject. But more importantly for my purposes here, I want to read Eliot's description from what could be called a psychoanalytic point of view, and say that it is also an account of the unconscious pressure people put on themselves when they don't understand themselves. That what Eliot thinks of here as an inter-psychic pressure – something going on between people, and perhaps couples in particular – is also an intra-psychic pressure; something we do to ourselves when our unintelligibility to ourselves makes us suffer. We make ourselves apparently familiar to ourselves. And what else, we might wonder, could we possibly do? This, I take it, is one of the dilemmas that psychoanalysis sets out to explore. People come for psychoanalysis because there is something about themselves that baffles them and that they cannot ignore (to use Eliot's word). This is the quotation from Eliot, rewritten:

> It is human when we do not understand ourselves, and cannot ignore ourselves, to exert an unconscious pressure on ourselves to turn us into something that we *can* understand: many husbands and wives exert this pressure on each other. The effect on the person so influenced (oneself, that is) is liable to be the repression and distortion, rather than the improvement, of the personality; and no man is good enough to have the right to make another over in his own image.

Eliot is writing of the human fear of not understanding something or someone that is human. He is saying – in his version and in mine – that when we cannot understand another person or ourselves we put pressure on them, one way or another, to become something we can understand; and that this pressure is the kind of influence that represses and distorts. As though there can be an anxiety about not understanding those people – including oneself – that one cannot ignore. And not being able to ignore someone – or not being able to ignore something about oneself – is itself a kind of revelation of character. In a sense, we are what we are unable to ignore. And what we do with what we cannot ignore is, of course, at the heart of psychoanalysis.

Eliot is a writer fascinated by what he cannot understand, by the limits of intelligibility, by the obscurity of experience. 'The world, as we have seen,' he writes in the Conclusion to his Harvard dissertation on F. H. Bradley, 'exists only as it is found in the experiences of finite centres, experiences so mad and strange that they will be boiled away before you boil them down to one homogeneous mass.' This acknowledges both the recondite eccentricity of personal experience, and its irreducibility to a system. There is something, even the young Eliot believed, about experiences so mad and strange that by definition, as it were, resist explanation. So when he writes of May Sinclair's novel that 'the material is so clearly defined (the soul of man under psychoanalysis) there is no possibility of tapping the atmosphere of unknown terror and mystery in which our life is passed and which psychoanalysis has not yet analysed', it is more than implied that psychoanalysis has not yet analysed this atmosphere, and will never be able to. Because this unknown terror and mystery, these experiences so mad and strange, are not subject to anything we can call analysis. As he writes tartly in his dissertation, 'For a metaphysics to be accepted, good-will is essential.' Assent is generous bad faith.

Experiences so mad and strange, unknown terror and mystery, can be addressed and described in both secular and religious terms. What Harold Bloom calls so tendentiously the Age of Freud is better known as the period in which more and more people in Europe were moving over to a secular, at least quasi-scientific account of what had been traditionally religious concerns. Previously, what was unintelligible in experience had been referred to God. For Freud, among many other people of the time, the unintelligible was referred to materialism, and more specifically to the body in culture; and to what bodies could do to each other, and why they did it (Darwin, of course, is one of the central figures here). What couldn't be understood in human experience found a new set of referents. Freud was not talking to his patients (or to his colleagues) about their souls and their relationship to God, he was talking to them about their bodies and their relationships with their parents; and above all, about their relationship to their spoken (and unspoken) words. In this medical context, experiences so mad and strange were called symptoms; and the therapeutic project was to find forms of understanding that made a difference. The psychoanalytic conversation, such as it was, was about personal history rather than religious observance. What Bloom refers to, with perhaps a bleak irony, as flourishing in the Age of Freud, meant no longer seeking religious solutions for the problems people saw in life. But it is the fate of the unintelligible – of that which cannot be ignored and cannot be understood – that preoccupies Eliot and Freud, among others, at this time. The mystery in life either needed a new referent, or people needed to be reminded, in no uncertain terms, of its traditional, sacred referent.

II

Act in such a way that I can speak to you.

Maurice Blanchot, *Awaiting Oblivion*

There is a dramatic moment in Eliot's essay of 1951, 'Virgil and the Christian World', when it is as though Eliot is looking both ways at once. He is in the process of discussing the question of whether Virgil's fourth Eclogue was in fact a prophetic text; prophesying the coming of Christ, as some later commentators were to insist. 'Whether we consider Virgil a Christian prophet', Eliot writes, will depend upon our interpretation of the word 'prophecy'. That Virgil himself was consciously concerned only with domestic affairs or Roman politics I feel sure: I think that he would have been very much astonished by the career which his fourth Eclogue was to have. If a prophet were by definition a man who understood the full meaning of what he was saying, this for me would be the end of the matter. But if the word 'inspiration' is to have any meaning, it must mean just this, that the speaker or writer is uttering something which he does not wholly understand – or which he may even misinterpret when the inspiration has departed from him. This is certainly true of poetic inspiration.

The question is how we understand the meaning Eliot gives to the word 'inspiration', a word he uses very sparingly in his prose, as one might expect (there are only eight references cited in his other writing, and they are all in his plays). If poetic inspiration comes from God, from Eliot's Christian God, so to speak, then it is as though Virgil, in this case, may not understand what he is writing but God did and does, as do Virgil's later Christian commentators. Prophecy, after all, is not so much to predict the future, but to foretell it, to know what will be called history in advance. The mystery would be that the poet, Virgil, could write at once so knowingly and so unknowingly.

And yet if we take Eliot's definition of the word 'inspiration' away from Virgil's pagan (or proto-Christian) world and Eliot's Christian world, we get an astonishingly precise account of what Freud was to call free association, and that became the Golden Rule, the distinctive thing, about his psychoanalytic method. 'The speaker or writer is uttering something which he does not wholly understand – or which he may even misinterpret when the inspiration has departed.' If God is no longer deemed to be in some sense the source of these unwitting words, then what or who is? It is not too extreme to say that Eliot's description of poetic inspiration is at its most minimal an account of what happens to the patient when he free-associates in analysis; and may, from a certain psychoanalytic point of view, be simply an account of what happens when we speak and write. We never wholly understand our words, we never wholly understand the word 'understand'; and we are never in a position to authoritatively interpret them. Because of the unconscious, one could say crudely, we never quite know what we are on about. And it is perhaps incidentally of interest that Freud claimed to have got his idea of free association as a therapeutic method from one of the favourite authors of his youth, Ludwig Borne. In 1823 Borne had written an essay entitled 'The Art of Becoming an Original Writer in Three Days', in which he wrote:

> Take a few sheets of paper and for three days in succession write down, without any falsification or hypocrisy, everything that comes into your head. Write what you think of yourself, of your women, of the Turkish War, of Goethe . . . of the Last Judgement, of those senior to you in authority – and when the three days are over you will be amazed at what novel and startling thoughts have welled up in you. That is the art of becoming an original writer in three days.

Borne's list of what comes into one's mind is in itself revealing; free association is always a period piece (and largely class-bound). This is the attempted democratization of inspiration; inspiration and originality for everyone. From inspiration to free association as the route to, or the sign of, originality (for Freud, what is original about oneself is one's history: which is not entirely to one's credit). Not trying to understand what you are writing – indeed, not being able to understand what you are writing – as the way to write. The way to speak is not to choose (or over-choose) your words.

The method of free association is about what happens when people don't try to understand each other; or rather, when understanding is deferred. If, as Borne suggests, you write down 'without any falsification or hypocrisy, everything that comes into your head', you are simply following wherever your words take you. And the implication is that this is something we do not usually do, indeed that we might work quite hard to avoid doing. As though to follow our words wherever they may go is surprisingly dangerous. And that the ordinary act of trying to understand what we are saying – the wish for discernible meaning – may be a kind of anxious vigilance. That – at least sometimes – we interrupt ourselves with what we call understanding; that understanding is the way we foreclose curiosity. So when Eliot writes, appropriately in *Notes Towards the Definition of Culture*, 'It is human, when we do not understand another human being, and cannot ignore him, to exert an unconscious pressure on that person to turn him into something that we *can* understand,' and that 'The effect on the person so influenced is liable to be the repression and distortion, rather than the improvement, of the personality', we cannot help but wonder what we fear will happen if we do not exert this pressure. What else might we do with someone – and the someone who is ourselves – that we cannot understand and cannot ignore? If we lost faith, or even interest in the understanding project, what else might we do with each other? Though Freud never quite goes this far, he does invent a form of therapy that might be described as an interim measure. He says, in effect, if you as the analyst listen to another person and suspend your will to understanding; and if you as the patient defer your appetite for understanding and just let yourself speak, something else will come through in your words. And sometimes it will even seem as if something else – something quite other – is speaking through you.

And this, of course, has consequences for what used to be called the moral life. When Eliot writes, in his great essay on Baudelaire of 1930, that 'so far as we are human, what we do must be either good or evil', we may or may not agree, and yet still wonder how we go about making such decisions, how we know just how to assess our actions. It is one thing to say that our actions are either good or evil, it is quite another to be jumping to conclusions about which is which. In the project of suspending internal censorship and saying what comes into one's mind, Freud is encouraging us to play for time, morally. He is not saying our words are not good or evil, he is saying that when we speak we censor ourselves too knowingly. It is as if we live as though there is something inside us – call it a figure, or a voice – who already knows the difference between good and evil, and intervenes accordingly. That we are moralists wanting to be, and fearing to become, more morally complex and subtle. What happens, Freud asks, what do you find yourself saying if you hold on to not understanding, if you hold at bay all your forms of moral judgement that are ordinarily called understanding? Is the idea of Original Sin, for example – or even Freud's idea of a death-instinct, some unavoidable internal badness – something that turns up when understanding can no longer be deferred; when it is intolerable not to seem to know what is happening?

I want to suggest that if we de-Christianize Eliot's definition of inspiration – if we take it out of the context that most interests him – it becomes something akin to an alternative to Original Sin. Or, to put it the other way round – to put it perhaps the Freudian way round – a sense of sinfulness could be seen as a pre-emptive strike against inspiration; against 'the speaker or writer uttering something which he does not wholly understand'. That sin, in short, can be used as a form of understanding; part of the unconscious pressure we put on our experience to make it bearable. The idea of sin tells us beforehand that there is such a thing as sin: it settles an issue.

III

Thought asks too much and words tell too much; because to ask anything is to ask everything, and to say anything is to ask more.

R. P. Blackmur, *Henry Adams*

What Freud and Eliot are saying, in their different ways, is that the pressures we live under seem to put pressure on us to make them intelligible. That to be human in the best sense is to have some understanding – to be able to give some kind of account – of what we are suffering from. Whether the appeal is made to Original Sin, or personal history and unconscious impersonal instinct, these are gestures towards an understanding of something, and of an acknowledgement of the limits or of the constraints upon such understanding as we have. And yet both Eliot's account of inspiration and Freud's therapeutic Golden Rule of free association point us in two directions at once. At their most reassuring they tell us that not wholly understanding what we utter – in psychoanalytic terms, deferring one's concern to make sense of oneself – can lead us, in the fullness of time, to a deeper understanding, to a more profound apprehension of what is ultimately only a concealed intelligibility. Sense-making, in other words, is not abrogated as a project, it's just that a more illuminating way of making sense has been found. You have to, as Eliot wrote in 'Little Gidding', with a different intent, 'put off / Sense and notion. You are not here to verify, / Instruct yourself, or inform curiosity / Or carry report . . .'; the next words are 'You are here to kneel / Where prayer has been valid', but this is also a meticulous description of what Freud encourages the psychoanalytic patient to do, but with a view to something essentially secular and deemed to be therapeutic. Their intentions (if that is the right word) may be radically at odds with each other, but both Freud and Eliot – whatever they may think about the soul of man under psychoanalysis – have a sense of direction. They may not be able to fulfil their wishes, to meet the obligation of their ambitions, but they have, to put it crudely, aims and objectives. Indeed their writings are an attempt to describe the good that they seek.

But there is another direction which they, or their words, point out – even if to call it a direction is in itself misleading. And this is the possibility that through inspiration or free association, understanding will never emerge; or rather, that what is revealed in inspiration or free association doesn't so much challenge or stimulate our sense-making capacities as baffle them, or endlessly defer them.

That all we can do is interrupt a bewildering delirium. The more outlandish implication is that Eliot's inspired poet, like Freud's free-associating patient, has injected something irreducibly enigmatic into the culture, something no one quite knows what to do with. These irruptions might get assimilated, they seem to suggest, but we need to be mindful what is at stake in the act of assimilation. What Eliot called the 'unconscious pressure on that person to turn him into something we can understand' – which could be redescribed as our consoling myth of interpretation – was understood by him to be, in all likelihood, a distortion and a repression. But what else are we supposed to do, what else can we do, with whatever compels our attention, but eludes our grasp?

Eliot's inspired 'speaker or writer' (it is worth noting that it is both), and Freud's ideal patient who has agreed to set aside all his misgivings about what he has to say, have been released in some way from the need to be intelligible to themselves. The pressure to turn themselves into something someone can understand is off, at least for the time being. It is assumed by both writers that the pressure to make sense – to be recognizable as something other than enigmatic – is considerable; that we live under the tyranny of not being too puzzling, both to ourselves and others (it was surrealism that programmatically exploited the irony of assuming that there was less dream-work in the interpretation of the dream than in the dream itself). But above all it is when the pressure to understand is taken off that the most valuable words are spoken or written; the act, the struggle to make oneself intelligible, must therefore be some kind of distraction; in psychoanalytic terms, some kind of defence. The words that matter most are the words we don't understand. If previously we have believed that words can matter only when we, at least to some extent, understand them, in what way might they matter to us when we don't? We are, after all, rightly wary of the cultivation of mystery, of the curators of secrecy.

What Eliot took to be characteristic of the soul of man under psychoanalysis – 'the material is so clearly defined . . . there is no possibility of tapping the atmosphere of unknown terror and mystery in which our life is passed' – was that this soul was too knowingly organized; it was clearly defined; the rules or principles governing this particular soul's behaviour were, by definition, intelligible. And it's worth nothing that his alternative to this is a novel in which this atmosphere of unknown terror and mystery is 'tapped'; not known, or explained, or assimilated, but presented as such. So on at least one of its versions – and I think Eliot is right about this – psychoanalysis is too rational an account of irrationality. It displaces that atmosphere of unknown terror and mystery that is so precious to Eliot. If for Eliot the soul of man under socialism is unrealistically reasonable – social engineering as a cure for original sin; by the same token, the soul of man under psychoanalysis – paradoxically, one might think – is too sure of itself, too complacent about its own descriptions. It puts human authority where, in Eliot's view, there is something else. And this something else – this other source – we may remember, he found in the novels of Dostoyevsky and D. H. Lawrence.

My paraphrase of Eliot's remarks is: people who are psychoanalytically informed – people who have been convinced (if not converted) by Freudian explanations – are likely to understand things in a certain way, are likely to phrase their accounts in a particular language. They will bring a kind of confident assurance to whatever it is they find to be enigmatic; and when this kind of conviction turns up in fiction it will make the fiction too knowing. It will be as though the language in which the fiction is written has fixed referents. Whereas the only conviction a Christian writer will bring to his work will be a conviction of mystery. As Augustine says in one of his sermons, 'Since it is God we are speaking of, you do not understand it. If you could understand it it would not be God.' So the question in secular terms is – and this would be a preposterous, presumptuous question to the Christian believer – how will our lives be better if we entrust ourselves to mystery, rather than to intelligibility, to understanding? God is presumably not a mystery to himself; so if God works in mysterious ways, at least

God is there running his mystery. Someone, as it were, knows what's going on, even if, by definition, we can't be party to this knowledge.

If we were to put this in psychoanalytic terms, to redescribe this crudely, we might be asking, is it better to believe in your mother, or to understand her? And the answer would be, you begin to do what we call understand your mother only when your belief in her has been shaken (as it must be). Or we might be asking: should we simply abide by the incest taboo, or should we be enquiring into it, enhancing our understanding of it so we might have a different apprehension of it? And the answer would be, in this case I think, merely another question: how does one go about being curious about the forbidden? From a psychoanalytic point of view, in other words, it is trauma that turns belief (or obedience, or faith) into a need for understanding. Or at least into a need for what William Empson called 'truth-feelings'. Both Freud and Eliot are trying to work out, in their different ways, where understanding comes in. And of course, like everyone else, neither Freud nor Eliot had fixed, formulated beliefs about the nature of understanding; their views evolved. But staging them – if not framing them – as antagonists allows us to review our options. Freud can be too narrowly knowing, too rhetorically persuasive in his explanations and in his belief in the value of understanding our lives (understanding our lives, that is, in the psychoanalytic way). Eliot, as a Christian, can perhaps be too knowing in his distrust of explanations, in his scepticism about our all-too-human accounts.

Both Freud and Eliot, of course, appeal to non-human forms of authority to make the human world intelligible. For Eliot there is the mystery of God, and the curse of Original Sin, 'the atmosphere of unknown terror and mystery in which our life is passed, and which psychoanalysis has not yet analysed'. For Freud there is instinctual life (the drives) and incest. The soul of man under psychoanalysis – and the phrase itself is odd because, even though Freud uses the word 'soul', it is not obvious what a psychoanalytic soul would be like – is a transgressive soul. What Freudian man and woman want is not to be saved, but to satisfy their forbidden desire. Which means to put their lives in mortal danger. For Eliot, for Eliot's Christian, there is, one might say, a destination, even if it is not within a person's gift to secure it; for Freud, for Freudian souls, it is not clear whether there is a destination or only a direction.

IV

... what is meant by defending one's goods is one and the same thing as forbidding oneself from enjoying them.

Jacques Lacan, *The Ethics of Psychoanalysis*

Eliot, as Christopher Ricks among others has shown, was always shrewdly allusive; so it is perhaps worth wondering, by way of conclusion, why he might have yoked Wilde and Freud together – and indeed psychoanalysis and socialism – in his throwaway phrase 'the soul of man under psychoanalysis'. Wilde's famous essay of 1891 does not in any obvious way bear any kind of family resemblance to the psychoanalytic writing Eliot was referring to. There is, in 'The Soul of Man under Socialism', a radical critique of altruism and a paganizing of Christ; 'What Jesus meant was this,' Wilde writes. 'He said to man, "You have a wonderful personality. Develop it. Be yourself." ' This, of course, would not be Eliot's version of Christ, this would be Eliot's version of play-acting with religion ('Disobedience,' Wilde writes, '. . . is man's original virtue'). Nor would the young Eliot have been overly impressed by Wilde's ceding of all authority to the individual; 'The true artist,' he writes, 'is a man who believes absolutely in himself, because he is absolutely himself.' 'All authority,' he writes, 'is quite degrading. It degrades those who exercise it, and degrades those over whom it is exercised.'

Wilde's promotion of the flagrantly self-invented individual – his new religion of Individualism – might, one imagines, have amused Freud (and even interested him); but the soul of man under psychoanalysis – the individual as Freud described him – was more driven than self-fashioned, more riven than whole; had indeed dispensed with the whole notion of what Wilde calls 'perfect harmony'. Man may have, as Wilde says, 'sought to live intensely, fully, perfectly', but, Freud adds, he is too frightened of his own nature, of his own desire to do so. What man seeks, Freud says, is not the Sovereign Good of traditional moral philosophy; nor indeed of God's love, or grace, or redemption. What man (as Freud still calls us) seeks is the forbidden object of incestuous desire. We seek, that is to say, a pleasure we cannot bear, not a moral or religious ideal that, were we to achieve it, would complete us. And because what we desire is forbidden – because we as it were recognize the object of desire in our sense of mortal risk – we need to obscure it, to conceal it from ourselves. In brief, Wilde's proposed new individual under socialism is – from both Freud and Eliot's point of view – too jaunty in his freedom. He really seems to believe that his life is his own, and if he is sufficiently gifted he can make of it what he will. He is a man on his own terms. His descriptions of himself can be referred to no higher or lower authority. Answerable to no one else, he is to his own taste (or he is nothing).

And yet despite all this Eliot, as usual, has picked something up, has heard something in psychoanalysis that even psychoanalysts themselves may not have wanted to hear. 'Happiness,' Freud wrote in *Civilization and Its Discontents*, 'is something entirely subjective.' Not only is our pleasure idiosyncratic, it is revealing of our idiosyncracy. If you want to find out who you are, recognize what makes you happy. Your subjectivity, Freud suggests, is in your happiness. Freud, in other words, is not saying – to adapt Tolstoy's infamous beginning – that all happy individuals are the same. In connecting the soul of man under psychoanalysis with *The Soul of Man under* (Wilde's) *Socialism*, Eliot was, I think, locating something that troubled him, and that Freud and Wilde were preoccupied by. And this was the possibility that the individual realizes himself – reveals himself – through his pleasure. 'It is,' Wilde writes, 'mentally and morally injurious to man to do anything in which he does not find pleasure.' Wilde is quite clear – or rather, quite insistent – in his essay that suffering is bad for us.

The Christ of medieval Christianity was, Wilde writes, 'realising his perfection through pain . . . The injustice of men is great. It was necessary that pain should be put forward as a mode of self-realisation.' But, he writes, this is all wrong; this is utterly misleading; 'Pain is not the ultimate mode of perfection. It is merely provisional, and a protest . . . Pleasure is Nature's test, her sign of approval.' Suffering as a fascination, as a vocation, is just what Wilde wants to provoke us out of. It is not our suffering we need to understand, it is our happiness; we need only understand our pain so we can get to our pleasure. Pain is a 'protest' against the absence of pleasure. Like Freud, Wilde has no truck with sin; it is through pleasure that what he calls 'Individualism' becomes possible. The aim, in his view, of both socialism and science is 'Individualism expressing itself through joy'; and the artist is the exemplary individualist. 'Art is individualism,' Wilde writes, 'and individualism is a disturbing and disintegrating force'; and if the artist 'does not do it [art] solely for his own pleasure, he is not an artist at all'. This is not, of course, worlds apart from the view Freud was to take thirteen years later in his paper 'Creative Writers and Daydreaming' (1908), in which he celebrates, indeed privileges, the artist because he is a more tenacious hedonist than what Freud calls the ordinary person. For Freud, as for Wilde in *The Soul of Man under Socialism*, what is to be understood, what is to be sponsored, is how modern people – as 'clever animals' – safeguard and sustain their pleasure-seeking; and how it is that this pleasure-seeking is their lifeline to everything that matters in life.

Wilde's writing was a problem to Eliot – and particularly perhaps Wilde's writing in *The Soul of Man under Socialism* – because it is an experiment in making no appeal to a non-human authority. You can neither, as it were, ask God why you are unhappy, nor can you start explaining and understanding your unhappiness by telling a story about human nature and its instinctual vicissitudes. Wilde says, in effect: we have nothing but our own ingenuity (which we might call wit), and it doesn't much matter where, if anywhere, it comes from. For Eliot, this would be play-acting as though one was writing the play oneself; for Freud, it would be the apotheosis of egotism, of the ego's illusion of autonomy. For both Freud and Eliot, it is a question of where you locate, how you describe, the non-human authority which, in their view, we cannot help but abide by. For Eliot, there was what his biographer Lyndall Gordon called 'a consuming search for salvation'; for Freud, there was no salvation, no redemptive myth, but the secular alternative: a realistic apprehension of one's nature.

The soul of man under psychoanalysis wants, knows what he wants, and doesn't want to know that he knows what he wants. As Eliot intimates, we could live under psychoanalysis in the way we might experience ourselves as living under socialism; that is, under an imposed regime of descriptions of what we want, what we like, and what we are like. And we may feel similarly oppressed living under psychoanalysis as we might if we were ever to live under socialism. Eliot's distaste for both systems is resonant in his phrasing of the question. Yet Freud and Wilde and Eliot would all agree that we are inherently transgressive creatures; for Wilde this is the point, for Eliot this is the problem, and for Freud it is the point and the problem. And this is why – if there is a soul, and if it has to be under anything – I prefer the soul of men and women under psychoanalysis. Because psychoanalysis tells us a story about ourselves that both consoles and confounds us. It gives us a myth and a mystery, a coherent narrative and a disturbing incoherence simultaneously; at one fell swoop our lives seem to make perfect sense, and are perfectly senseless.

Psychoanalysis can tell us a reassuringly normative story; we begin by desiring (and wanting to murder) the parents; registering the horror, not to mention the impossibility of this project, we more or less relinquish it. We renounce our first desires and wait; and eventually, if all goes well, we will as adults find people who are sufficiently reminiscent of the parents to be exciting, but sufficiently different so we can consummate our desire. We want something; we realize the dangerous error of our ways; and we find the substitutes that can satisfy us. We can, in a sense, have what we want because it isn't what we really want, which we could never have anyway. This is a story about human development as both possible and potentially satisfying. Good-enough mothers and fathers facilitating good-enough lives for their children.

But then there is the parallel text to this story – the other life that makes our lives double – and that is more akin to Eliot's atmosphere of mystery and terror. In this life our desire is ineluctably, undistractedly, transgressive; in this life we are driven to always approach and avoid the objects of desire, and what makes us feel most alive makes us feel we are risking our lives. In this life the good-enough mother is always a bad-enough tantalization. In this life uncanniness is way in excess of our canniness; our actions feel at once inevitable and unintelligible (and so as shorthand we say we are in love, or we are tragic heroes, or we have made a Freudian slip). We do not know what we are doing, and yet we feel ineluctably involved in our lives. Where once there were security operations, now there is risk; where once safety was the be-all and end-all, now fear is preferred. A sense of aliveness displaces a sense of certainty as a paramount consideration. Surprise and dread are the order of the day. In our transgressive life it is as though there is something – or someone – we seem to value more than our lives, more than life itself.

'Life is impoverished,' Freud wrote in 1915, 'it loses in interest, when the highest stake in the game of living, life itself, may not be risked.' The essay from which this comes is entitled 'Thoughts for the Times on War and Death', but the analogy Freud uses to illustrate his point makes a comparison with relations between the sexes. Life, he writes, 'becomes as shallow and empty as, let us say, an American flirtation, in which it is understood from the first that nothing is to happen, as contrasted with a Continental love affair in which both partners must constantly bear its serious consequences in mind'. The soul of man under psychoanalysis is about nothing more and nothing less than the relation between the sexes, about what it is to live with nothing to love and hate but each other. For the soul of man under psychoanalysis the 'atmosphere of unknown terror and mystery' emanates from nowhere but ourselves. And all we can go on doing is describing what it is like, in all its unlikeness.

Isaac Rosenberg's English

I

It's the man with impudence who has more experience than anybody. He not only varies his own, but makes other people's his own.

Isaac Rosenberg, *Collected Works*

In 1911, at the age of twenty-one, Isaac Rosenberg decided, despite
the poverty of his working-class immigrant family, to become an artist
and so to leave his demoralizing job working for a firm of engravers.
'Free,' as he wrote, 'to do anything, hang myself or anything except
work,' he spent a lot of time copying the Great Masters in the National
Gallery. One morning he was copying Velázquez's *Philip IV* when
King George was due to come to the gallery to open some new
rooms. When it was known that the King had arrived, the other
students left their easels and lined the corridors to see him. 'Whether
out of shyness, disdain, absorption or ignorance of protocol,' his biographer Joseph Cohen writes, 'Rosenberg did not stop painting to
acknowledge his presence, even though the king paused for a moment
to watch him paint.' Cohen, quite understandably, wants to give
Rosenberg several options. But nevertheless, here was a young Jewish
man – whether to be defiant or to gain his regard – ignoring the King
of England, and painting a Catholic king under his very eye.

Five years later, having enlisted for the war effort and joined the Bantam Brigade because of his height, Rosenberg wrote 'jokingly' to his friend the publisher Edward Marsh from his barracks: 'The King inspected us Thurday. I believe it's the first Bantam Brigade been inspected. He must have waited for us to stand up a good while. At a distance we look like soldiers sitting down, you know, legs so short.' Once again, but for a different reason, Rosenberg considers the possibility of not standing up for the King of England; of doing, at least in his mind, the impudent thing. For a son of Russian immigrants who had to teach themselves English, the war – like the struggle to accommodate himself to a culture so alien to his family – complicated, as we shall see, the always problematic question of his allegiances: who he chose to identify with, whose language he was going to write in, who or what he was prepared to stand up for. 'I never joined the army,' he would write, 'for patriotic reasons'; nor, of course, did his family come to Britain, or learn English for what could be described as patriotic reasons. Having escaped from Eastern Europe – and it is not incidental that Rosenberg's father may have come to Britain to escape conscription in the Russian army – learning English was a contingent necessity. Rosenberg's uneasy relationship with the English language as a poet was to mark him, for the owners of English poetry, as an unassimilable presence; at once deferential and an eager parricide. 'This is not the first time,' he writes in 1910 to the writer Israel Zangwill, 'I have wearied you with my specimens of desperate attempts to murder and mutilate King's English beyond all shape of recognition.'

Rosenberg's earliest-known poem, 'Ode to David's Harp', written when he was fifteen, does not involve much dramatic disfiguring of the King's English. But he chooses both an interesting subject – a Jewish king, the 'monarch minstrel' David, a warrior and a poet – and an interesting model to imitate, the aspiring warrior and great poet Byron, a most unrighteous and eloquent champion of the oppressed. 'You mustn't forget the circumstances I have been brought up in,' Rosenberg wrote to a friend in 1911, the little education I have had. Nobody ever told me what to read, or ever put poetry in my way. I don't think I knew what real poetry was till I read Keats a couple of years ago. True, I galloped through Byron when I was about fourteen, but I fancy I read him more for the story than for the poetry. I used to try to imitate him.

Byron, famously, was the poet one read for the story – both the narrative adventures of the poems and the scandalous story of his life which the poems were assumed to reflect. It is not amazing that an impoverished and culturally disaffected Jewish boy of Rosenberg's generation might find Byron an object of emulation. Byron's life as an inspired aristocrat, socially mobile and irreverent, was the vivid antithesis of Rosenberg's life – 'deadened', as he then wrote of it with a lugubrious adolescent allusion to Hamlet, 'by the fiendish persistence of the coil of circumstance'.

In the 'Ode to David's Harp' – based on Byron's *Hebrew Melodies* – Rosenberg promotes a revival of the Jewish spirit through the inspiration of poetry. The poem, it should be noted, is to the harp and not to David, just as Rosenberg's first and apparently whimsical prose piece was about a door-knocker. He was preoccupied, from the beginning of his poetic life, with instruments of transition – what you need to get from one state of mind to another, from outside to inside the door. The poem begins with a prophetic invocation, reminiscent of Blake, that in the poet's view is of more than historical significance:

> Awake! ye joyful strains, awake!
> In silence sleep no more;
> Disperse the gloom that ever lies
> O'er Judah's barren shore.

Rosenberg, even at fifteen, is announcing a big programme. The gloom that 'ever' lies over the Jews – 'ever' meaning 'always', not just 'then' – may be, as the pun suggests, a lie: the lie, he will come to believe, born of a certain kind of submission to a certain kind of God – a God, he will come to believe, that one needs to rid oneself of. It was David's harp that lifted Saul's gloom, and David, the great Jewish folk-hero – 'the sweet singer of Israel' – who would displace Saul. In Rosenberg's poem David's potency lies in his music, his 'melody'; and the man he begins by serving is the man whose position he will take. The guest became the host. 'Fate is weaving / Other bonds than slavery's chains,' he wrote in lines he eventually cut from the poem.

Rosenberg was to be preoccupied in his writing by the complicity – the repertoire of complicities – between hosts and guests. And a host could be, for example, a God, a family, a country or a language. And there could also be a sense in which the past – or ideas about the past – could be seen as the host of the future. Like all great self-inventors and visionaries, he wanted to create his own genealogy, to make his own connections; reinventing the past to make possible a new kind of future. Redoing the past in this way means, among other things, being able to tell the hosts from the guests. And there is an early and ingenuously revealing story on this theme, called 'Rudolph', that Rosenberg wrote when he was twenty-one.

Rudolph is a young artist, 'God's castaway', merely 'his ancestors' remains'. 'I am the first,' he announces grandly, 'to scandalize the family with a difference . . . They consider it perfectly immoral to talk and think unlike them.' One day, yearningly despondent about himself as a failing artist, he 'strays' into the National Gallery and suddenly finds himself being asked by an unknown person to remain seated: 'He was awakened from his reverie by hearing a feminine voice saying, "O! please don't rise, oblige me."' The sexual innuendo – the double-message, so to speak – turns out to be prophetic. Quite unwittingly Rudolph has become part of this woman's painting; he finds himself in somebody else's picture – being painted into her frame. And it is this very involuntary inclusion that gets him, as it were, further into the picture; into the larger picture of this woman's social world, the high bohemian society that has always excluded him.

Discovering that Rudolph is an artist with remarkable views about painting, she asks him to what he calls 'a wealthy supper' with her brother the famous poet Leonard Harris, whom Rudolph has always admired, and other important and cultured people. But Rudolph soon realizes that he doesn't know the form, that he is not equipped for the occasion; he doesn't have the right clothes. But, as luck would have it, his friend Dave is having an affair with a landlady whose husband – 'a man with mysterious connections with 'igh Society' – has a proper suit, which is secretly borrowed by Dave for the occasion. Virtually everything going on in the story is illegitimate; everyone is an impostor of one kind or another. 'The suit was laid out,' the author writes, 'and Rudolph proceeded to make his entrance into the uniform of a gentleman, into which he completely disappeared.' 'I feel somehow I am lost in it,' he says to Dave; 'but don't you think it will make me look bigger?' He feels 'transformed, transfigured', goes to the grand dinner and performs rather well, expounding some remarkable views on aesthetics that we will come back to. But when the butler serves the coffee he drops the tray in shock, recognizing his suit on Rudolph. His host, the distinguished poet, resolves the problem by telling Henry the butler that Rudolph had thought he was going to a 'fancy-dress ball' and so borrowed the suit from Henry's wife. Everyone is therefore implicitly insulted by the gracious host, but as usual in High Society nobody appears to be ruffled or even to notice. Certainly, High Society might look like a fancy-dress ball to an outsider like Rudolph. Having already begun 'to curse inwardly the artificialities of convention, the forms that bound each man to be a mechanical demonstration of its monotony', Rudolph leaves with a sense both of dismay and of possibility. But he has experienced his performance at the dinner as some kind of betrayal of his heritage. 'His mind was in a whirl. His past – what a horrible waste of God's faculties – unused.'

Rudolph is presented in the story not so much as a Jew in particular but as an *arriviste* – the word 'rude' is barely concealed in the name Rudolph. With the lightest and shrewdest of touches this story condenses a number of Rosenberg's pressing concerns. But for the purposes of this essay I just want to emphasize the fact that Rudolph is wearing the butler's clothes. Rosenberg uses this familiar device to formulate Rudolph's dilemma as an *arriviste* and an artist; is he a guest or a servant of the host? Or, to put it another way: in a fancy-dress ball, who is the joke on? A fancy-dress ball is as good a picture as any of an alien or unmanageable culture.

In a commentary on Sartre's account of another unplaceable, displaced artist, Jean Genet, Arthur Danto wrote:

> Calling the young Genet a thief, for instance, not merely identified him as having stolen, but gave him, according to Sartre's treatment in *Saint Genet*, an identity and a project; it caused him to be a thief, since it was through the network of associations with this term that he henceforth saw himself; and as he believed himself to be, so did he act, and the power of the name consisted in causing the fact it did not neutrally merely designate.

Genet, like an extreme version of Rudolph and Rosenberg himself, is the artist as disreputable outsider. By calling himself an artist – painter and more gradually poet – Rosenberg conferred upon himself a destiny/project. Calling himself a poet – which he did against much internal and external resistance – was like promising himself the life of a poet. It was as though he made himself an invitation, one that was rarely forthcoming from anyone else (in his letters there are many pieces of fervent gratitude for any recognition or praise of his talent). But the network of associations to the notion of a Jewish English poet – as opposed to a Jewish English painter, of which there were several among his friends – was not available as a web he could catch himself in. That is to say, the pressures of self-invention on Rosenberg were considerable. And it is not surprising, then, that he should be so drawn to the American writer Ralph Waldo Emerson – the great self- and country-inventor – and that he should write of Emerson's poems: 'We have here no tradition – no tricks of the trade.' It is a revealing definition of what constitutes a tradition; or rather, of what a tradition can feel like to an outsider.

'In literature,' Rosenberg wrote to Edward Marsh in 1914, 'I have no judgement – at least for style. If in reading a thought has expressed itself to me, in beautiful words; my ignorance of grammar etc. makes me accept that.' Confronted by an established culture, or in the absence of a sustaining group, different judgement might begin to feel like no judgement; 'grammar etc.' becomes another country. For Rosenberg there were Jewish poets who did not write in English, and English poets who were not Jews. And he had no formal education in the tradition to which he aspired, primarily the Romantics, Blake, Keats, Shelley and Byron, and through them to Rossetti, Swinburne and Francis Thompson. Like Rosenberg himself, the English Romantic poets thought of themselves as reviving a tradition, the true English tradition of poetry, lost after Milton. Rosenberg was in the paradoxical position of reviving a tradition that did not exist, a tradition of Jewish English poetry; he wanted to 'wake the zeal in Israel's breast', but in a language foreign to the origins he wanted to redeem.

By all accounts, including his own, always an outsider, Rosenberg also felt estranged within his own family. Isolated and unconnected, he could, a contemporary of his wrote, 'sit from morning to evening without uttering a word'. 'He never had anything in common with any of the family,' his youngest sister, Ray, said of him, 'we were not sufficiently artistic for him.' He was known, as a young man, for his 'ungainly appearance, inarticulateness and self-effacing shyness'. In fact his biographers, Cohen and Jean Moorcroft-Wilson, the sources of this information, convey a curious impression of Rosenberg, as though he coupled a kind of slapstick inattention – absentmindedly dropping all his paintings into Cape Town harbour, forgetting to address envelopes – with an intense visionary, poetic vocation. A schoolfriend, Joseph Leftwich, wrote of him in his diary: 'His people are very unsympathetic to him. They insist on treating him as a little out of his mind. They consider him as an invalid . . . he says his taste is very poor and he enjoys boys' magazines and his sisters' novelettes. It is only in poetry that he fills himself with something.' Rosenberg began to think of poetry, and not the orthodox Judaism of his parents and their contemporaries, as redemptive, as really filling; and of the artist as the true provider. In the attempt to realize his vision he had to reject much that he had been given and much that was expected of him, both by his family and by the arbiters of taste in contemporary British poetry.

'My circumstances have not been very favourable,' he wrote in 1910, 'for artistic production.' So what did Rosenberg have to reject, or relinquish, to create the circumstances he needed? There are, of course, many ways to describe the project of a life; but one useful way of talking about a life – and Rosenberg's life in particular, I think – is to ask the question: what does a person believe he has to get rid of to have the life he wants? Because in these disposals a person can be, often unconsciously, creating a space in which something else can happen (so Rosenberg could have been at risk if he had gone for a certain kind of psychoanalysis in which he would have been encouraged to reappropriate what he needed to get rid of). By deciding to be an artist, I think, and then by enlisting, he was creating the circumstances, however unpleasant, in which he could become the man he wanted to be. 'I think the safest place is at the front,' he wrote in 1914, '– we'll starve or die of suspense anywhere else.'

II

A poet's words and rhythms are not his utterance so much as his resistance.

Geoffrey Hill, *The Enemy's Country*

Drawing a curious parallel, in 1911 Rosenberg writes facetiously to another Jewish writer, Ruth Löwy, of 'the wickedness of the times (with suffragettes throwing hatchets at kings – and poets compelling people to read their poems)'. If poets are like suffragettes and poems are like hatchets thrown at kings, then poetry, despite the odd joke, is a serious, indeed a violent, threat to the established order. The suffragettes, like the poets, refuse to comply with the order of things.

The woman in the National Gallery who painted Rudolph confessed to him that she thought 'Van Eyck the greatest artist who ever lived. I adore him because he makes the commonplace so delightfully precious.' 'I think a picture should be something more,' protested Rudolph. 'Van Eyck is interesting to me just as a pool reflecting the clouds is interesting, or a landscape seen through a mirror. But it is only a faithful transcript of what we see. My ideal of a picture is to paint what we cannot see. To create, to imagine.' To paint the world as you see it may be to comply with the commonplace. Simple mimesis is the antithesis, for an outsider like Rudolph, of the visionary transfiguration of reality that he aspires to. Mimesis has to be rejected because it signifies – or might represent – assimilation; it is an implicit form of consent to the way things are supposed to look. But if straightforward imitation – however skilled – compromises vision, if Rosenberg was critical of Velázquez, in a striking sentence, because 'his truth was more the practical truth of the mirror', then what kind of aesthetic was Rosenberg, or rather Rudolph, prepared to promote?

Showing his portfolio of drawings to the dinner party,

> [Rudolph] stood by to explain and elucidate where elucidation was necessary, which was not seldom; for he painted on the principle that the art of painting was the art of leaving out, and the pleasure in beholding a picture was the pleasure of finding out. Where he had not left out the whole picture, sometimes it was successful.

What the painter leaves out – what he disposes of – becomes the invitation that constitutes his art; an invitation to curiosity, to the pleasure of finding out. And by implication strictly mimetic art might create the illusion that everything is already there, that what you see is what there is. It is not unusual – despite Rosenberg's disavowal of any polemical or ideological allegiances (he never joined a group or signed a manifesto) – that he should, as the child of immigrants, be suspicious of, or dismayed by, the available versions of reality. And often, I think, and sometimes unwittingly, his poetry was a form of resistance; a way of joining a culture by not joining in.

Rosenberg was always keen in his writing to emphasize the differences between the arts. But this art of leaving out that he ascribes here to painting was remarkably prescient both of the way he would come – not programmatically, but by inclination – to write poetry and of the way his poetry would be judged, even by some of his most sympathetic critics. From the judgement of the first poetry competition that he entered at the age of sixteen – 'original but rather vague in parts' – to Frank Kermode's and John Hollander's comment in the 1973 *Oxford Anthology of English Literature* about 'Rosenberg's visionary fragments', there is a striking consensus: that his poetry is patchy and obscure – intermittently vivid – but leaving out too many connections.

In his opening speech for the Memorial Exhibition of Rosenberg's Paintings and Drawings in 1937 Edward Marsh described Rosenberg inappositely as 'an Aladdin whose lamp was a strong but slender searchlight which lit up now and then, but only for a moment, some jewel in the cave of darkness in which he groped'. More visceral, but no less critical of the apparent absence of structure in his poems, Laurence Binyon wrote to tell Rosenberg that his poetry came out in 'clotted gushes and spasms'. Clearly, the art of leaving out does not always lead to the pleasure of finding out; abortions and momentary illuminations can spell the failure of the artist to those who supposedly know what they are talking about. As the reviewer of Rosenberg's posthumously published *Poems* of 1922 wrote in the *Times Literary Supplement* with supercilious condescension: 'he had a genius for the vivid phrase, for illumination in flashes; if he could have learned coordination, and calmness, the broad handling of the texture of his art, he must surely have won a lasting place in the annals of our literature'. If only Rosenberg could have been what he should have been. He failed to meet the available criteria.

Rosenberg's correspondence provides a gloomy record of his bemused accommodation – his bowing to *and* resisting – to what felt like the alien aesthetic standards offered to him by the guardians of what the *TLS* reviewer called '*our literature*'. 'People are always telling me my work is promising,' he wrote to the poet Gordon Bottomley from France in 1916, 'incomprehensible but promising, and all that sort of thing, and my meekness subsides before the patronising knowingness.' Such patronizing knowingness can only come from those who recognize 'our literature' when they see it. 'Most people find them difficult,' Rosenberg wrote of his poems in 1915, 'and won't be bothered to read into them.'

But Rosenberg as a kind of double agent between cultures – in a no-man's-land of aspiration and resistance – felt that there was something inside him that he couldn't define, and that seemed to sabotage the versions of intelligibility – of poetic form – that he was constantly being judged by. 'There is always behind or through my object,' he wrote from the army in 1915, 'some pressing sense of foreign matter, immediate and not personal, which hinders and disjoints what would otherwise have coherence and perhaps weight.' There is, of course, on the one hand the foreign matter of the war, doubly foreign for Rosenberg because he was fighting for and against countries he did not belong to. But there is also the perhaps inevitable equivocation here of the resident alien, the difficulty of valuing the 'foreign matter'; of articulating what was foreign about him without making it seem disabling. If one rejects allegiances, is one thereby compelled to experience oneself as either a saboteur or a parasite? What other positions can one take, apart from the always ambiguous position of self-promoted failure? Modesty Rosenberg referred to, when he was twenty-two, as 'that most heinous crime'. Though one finds genuine abjection in his letters, in his poetry one finds an enquiry into the tactic of abjection.

Criticizing his poems consistently for the lack of connections in them – for their fragmentariness – none of his critics realized the sense in which his poetry was always about, intensely preoccupied by, the very question of connections; the question of what might link people or things without destroying their integrity. Drawn to define explicitly the kind of poetry that he valued and aspired to produce, he wrote to Gordon Bottomley: 'Simple poetry – that is where an interesting complexity of thought is kept in tone and right value to the dominating idea so that it is understandable and still ungraspable.' If something is understandable but ungraspable it eludes possession; you can have access to it but you cannot take it. To grasp a poem might be to assume a comprehension of it that makes it redundant. The poem is subsumed by one's apparent knowledge of, or competence in, what Rosenberg called 'grammar etc.'. The art of leaving out leads to the pleasure of finding out; but the pleasure of finding out depends upon there always being something ungraspable; or what Moses will call in Rosenberg's verse-play *Moses*, 'ineffable and usable'. His poems, not incidentally, are full of images of hands unable, or unwilling, to grasp. His formulation is suggestive of the sense in which language is understandable and ungraspable; the sense in which – and this may be particularly obvious to an immigrant – a language can be used but not mastered or owned. The poet and the immigrant can be the people who release a language from its proprietors.

The Scottish poet Edwin Muir touched on something very important about Rosenberg, not least because it reflects some affinity with Rosenberg's own expressed intentions. 'He used language,' Muir wrote, 'as only the great poets have used it; as if he were not merely making it serve his own ends; but ends of its own as well, of which it had not known.' This acknowledges both the possibility of creating something new and the sense in which language might use the poet if, as a virtual émigré in Rosenberg's case, he has not already been converted to the culture by assimilation – if he has not, that is to say, over-internalized the proprieties as a kind of second nature. Relatively uneducated, and so without the official grammar of association, Rosenberg did not always make the obvious connections. But the impudent man, as he once wrote, has more experience; he brings some foreign matter to the occasion.

'[C]ould a miracle destroy the dawn,' Moses says in the play, 'night would be mixed with light / No night or light would be, but a new thing.' If you refuse the obvious connections, leave out the transitions – 'destroy the dawn' – you may create a new thing. The art of leaving out is the pleasure of finding out. Or alternatively, you might be so promiscuous in the making of connections – like the lice and the bullets, the worms and the bees, the rats and the death that haunt his poems – as to be without any discernible allegiances at all. Or to put it another way: as a Jewish English poet, was he merely a go-between, an anonymous opportunist, or potentially a new kind of man, a visionary poet? Or were they different versions of the same thing?

III

. . . who knows what we miss through not having spoken.

Isaac Rosenberg, *Collected Works*

In Rosenberg's poetry, as I have said, there is a refusal of the kinds of competence that would have successfully assimilated him by compromising what he had to say. And this is because what he had to say was sometimes so strange – so close to the limits of language – that it involved him in what was often a covert critique of available forms. Even on a cursory reading, the poems are strikingly variable in both metre and rhythm. But it is clear, from what Rosenberg was himself compelled – often under pressure from others – to describe as a 'clumsiness' of technique, that he found it difficult to fit himself into the poetic forms and languages he was familiar with. One of his earliest 'war poems', 'The Troop Ship', alludes, at one level, to precisely this problem:

> Grotesque and queerly huddled
> Contortionists to twist
> The sleepy soul to a sleep,
> We lie all sorts of ways
> And cannot sleep.
> The wet wind is so cold,
> And the lurching men so careless,
> That, should you drop to a doze,
> Winds' fumble or men's feet
> Are on your face.

I don't want to do the kind of reading of this poem that in any way obviates the sense in which it is about a terrible and physically imme-diate predicament. But I think in addition to this fact it can be read as a parable of Rosenberg's poetic struggle. It is a lurid description of people trying to fit themselves in; people being turned into con-tortionists, into grotesque shapes because there is no room to do what they most want. And what they most want – and have to 'lie all sorts of ways' to do – is in this case that most natural thing, to sleep. But if they succeed in doing what they most desire, dozing off in this cramped space, they are damaged: 'should you drop to a doze, / Winds' fumble or men's feet / Are on your face'. If you succeed – which in my reading means, express your deepest desire in this imposed form – then you are subject to violation, 'feet are on your face'.

For Rosenberg – the most unpromising-sounding soldier, losing his socks, failing to oil his boots, falling over on parade – to enlist was to make vivid in a peculiarly literal way the dilemmas that constituted the struggle of his life. Because in the British army his life as a working-class Jew and an artist consisted of having alien forms imposed upon him against which he could struggle and with which he could cooperate. 'Believe me,' he wrote to Lascelles Abercrombie in 1916, in a partial allusion to his *Moses*, 'the army is the most detestable invention on this earth, and nobody but a private in the army knows what it is to be a slave.'

Anti-Semitism in the army, as Rosenberg's letters testify, was rife; and his notorious inattention was continually getting him into trouble. 'I have the morning to sleep in,' he writes in his deadpan way from the front, 'unless I happen to be doing some punishment for my forgetfulness.' But in this terrifying war – 'we spend most of our time,' he reports in 1917, 'pulling each other out of the mud' – in which he is at least nominally on the British side, he begins to write some of his most extraordinary and ungraspable poems. And in these inexhaustible, visionary works he seems to be drawn to those creatures I have mentioned – the lice and the rats, for example, that by being on neither side are everywhere, resilient in their opportunism – 'The Immortals', as he entitles a poem about the lice (the Immortals, of course, being both the pagan gods and the great poets). And alongside these inspiring and dispiriting figures there are his more elusive but characteristic images of absence, of non-differentiation, of blendings – like the famous description of the war dead, 'joined to the great sunk silences', in 'Dead Man's Dump'. As we shall see, it is these images of paradoxical connection that take Rosenberg to the limits of description.

In 'Dead Man's Dump' he refers to the young soldiers being shot as the moment when 'the swift iron burning bee / Drained the wild honey of their youth'. In this inversion of the spring the bullets are like bees, passing freely between the warring sides, and when they connect they don't pollinate, they kill; they don't suck honey, they drain blood. Like the 'mixed hoofs of the mules' later in the poem that pull the carts for the dead, they are, as it were, the product of two different sides. The most resilient creatures in the war seem, from Rosenberg's point of view, the most indiscriminate, like the lice in 'The Immortals'. It is a terrible and pertinent irony for him that the enemy is potentially everywhere. Even the titles of the two famous poems about the lice that infected their clothes ironize the predicament. In the first, calling such parasites 'The Immortals' is itself suggestive (and it is perhaps worth remembering that Rosenberg wrote an early poem entitled 'Tess', and that the last paragraph of Hardy's novel ends with the famous sentence: ' "Justice" was done, and the President of the Immortals, in Aeschylean phrase, had ended his sport with Tess'). 'I killed them but they would not die,' Rosenberg writes, likening the lice to devils, Satan, Beelzebub; and in the second stanza: 'for faster than I slew / They rose more cruel than before'. In a characteristic paradox just like Satan's party in *Paradise Lost* (Rosenberg reports reading Milton in 1912), the more you try to kill them the more you inspire them with life. And calling the second poem 'Louse Hunting' is to suggest that it is not clear who is hunting whom. The 'wizard vermin', as he calls them, have magical powers, creating an anarchic rage in the soldiers; and once again everything is inverted, the tiny creatures making a mockery of the men's power:

> See gargantuan hooked fingers
> Pluck in supreme flesh
> To smutch supreme littleness.

The question of supremacy arises again in 'Break of Day in the Trenches' when a rat – who knows no treachery because he has no allegiances – jumps out in front of the poet. And the poet is struck by the rat's curious privilege, that by being on neither side in the war he can be on both.

> Droll rat, they would shoot you if they knew
> Your cosmopolitan sympathies.

Now you have touched this English hand
You will do the same to a German
Soon, no doubt, if it be your pleasure
To cross the sleeping green between.
It seems you inwardly grin as you pass
Strong eyes, fine limbs, haughty athletes,
Less chanced than you for life,
Bonds to the whims of murder,
Sprawled in the bowels of the earth,
The torn fields of France.
What do you see in our eyes
At the shrieking iron and flame
Hurled through still heavens?
What quaver – what heart aghast?

It is the rat's 'cosmopolitan sympathies', his grand promiscuous pleasure, that free him possibly – perhaps, Rosenberg writes – to mock the soldiers on both sides, 'haughty athletes / Less chanced than you for life'. The rat has no kind of Olympian view, but sees things on the ground, so to speak. It was, of course, current anti-Semitic jargon to refer disparagingly to Jews as 'cosmopolitan' and, of course, as vermin and parasites; but it is the very opportunism of the rat's mobility – his ability, if it is his pleasure, 'To cross the sleeping green between' – that Rosenberg promotes here as a strength. But 'touching' both sides, the rat belongs to neither, and Rosenberg, I think, is genuinely perplexed about such a point of view. The questions he addresses to the 'queer sardonic rat' (and there is an implication that the rat might be a kind of dandy) are ambiguous in their implications: 'What do you see in our eyes / At the shrieking iron and flame / Hurled through still heavens? / What quaver – what heart aghast?' Perhaps the rat is so free because he sees and feels nothing, identifies with no one, is simply a figure for Death, or the kind of supreme nonchalance that Rosenberg, given his circumstances, may have aspired to.

The worm in one of his finest poems, 'A Worm Fed on the Heart of Corinth', is also, like the droll rat – and like Moses, as we shall see – a go-between of sorts, and an opportunist. But unlike Moses, he is not a visionary, though he is a paradoxical source of inspiration.

> A worm fed on the heart of Corinth,
> Babylon and Rome.
> Not Paris raped tall Helen,
> But this incestuous worm,
> Who lured her vivid beauty
> To his amorphous sleep.
> England! famous as Helen
> Is thy betrothal sung.
> To him the shadowless,
> More amorous than Solomon.

Here we have, as it were, the parasite of Western culture; eating hearts, it inspires to act. Incestuous, shadowless and amorous, it knows neither boundary nor taboo, connecting and collecting disparate powerful cultures, cosmopolitan in its appetite, and reducing their extraordinary forms – Helen's 'vivid beauty' – to formlessness, to 'amorphous sleep' (and in 'amorphous' one can hear the buried pun of being a-Morpheus, without Morpheus the god of sleep and dreams, and so in a sleepless sleep). The worm is the triumphant hero, seducer, bridegroom and lover, the figure of desire as desire for death. But the final four lines of the poem are particularly revealing of Rosenberg's confused and ironized patriotism during the war in which he died. England is described as 'famous as Helen', and Helen is famous for being desirable and divisive; and for being forced to move from one side to another. Rosenberg connects England to the great imperial cultures of the past; and yet England's betrothal – sung perhaps wishfully in this poem – is to Death. All these imperial pretensions are as nothing against the worm (Jewish imperialism was, of course, only ever the fantasy of anti-Semites). And, as we saw in the 'droll' rat, there is a grandeur and a mockery in the worm, and in the poem.

And there is also, in this extraordinarily impacted poem, a juxtaposing of the great structures of empire – Corinth, Babylon, Rome, Greece, Troy – and the great heroic figures – Helen, Paris, Solomon – against images of formlessness, of dissipation, 'amorphous sleep' and the 'shadowless' worm. It is a poem about the precariousness of structures (it's worth noting that phrases crop up in Rosenberg's poetry suggestive of a kind of eroticization of disorder, like 'gorgeous disarray' and 'promiscuous bewilderment'). But in trying to describe death – that which, by definition, eludes representation – he has to use the structure of language to evoke its imagined dissolution. If something is shadowless it does not cast a shadow; but worms are shadowless because they are mostly underground, because they do not sufficiently differentiate themselves from their environment (in one sense they are images of compliant assimilation, close to the earth). There is no space between themselves and their world. Something, one could say, that happens in sleep – another of Rosenberg's recurrent poetic preoccupations – except that in sleep the shadows cast are dreams, and they are shadows inside. Indeed, in his poem 'Returning We Hear the Larks' he describes the doubly effaced image of 'a blind man's dreams on the sand / By dangerous tides'.

Rosenberg returns again and again in his poetry to images of things joined or connected invisibly, like a dream and its dreamer. It is, of course, profoundly difficult to imagine the connection between things assumed to be identical, something one cannot represent in painting or music. In the line 'joined to the great sunk silences' ('Dead Man's Dump'), for example, where is the join and what is being joined? Where does one silence end and another begin? For there to be a discernible connection, there has to be a difference. In his poetry Rosenberg entertains the idea of people being joined in, or by, their absence. 'Untuned air shall lap the stillness / In the old space for your voice,' he writes of a dead soldier in a poem called 'In War'. Air lapping the stillness is a relationship between two invisible 'things'; the phrase 'the old space for your voice' formulates something more terrifying for its lack of limit. The space of a person's voice is an extraordinary thing to imagine, and points to the infinity of loss. 'Invisibly – branches break / From invisible trees', Rosenberg begins the final stanza of his poem 'Chagrin', confronting us again with the illogicality – the affront to logic – of absence. Whether they be family trees or the trees of tradition, words are being used to evoke what we cannot otherwise imagine, something invisible happening to – breaking a connection with – the invisible. And yet, as in the penultimate line of 'August 1914', 'A burnt space through ripe fields', absence can make of something a revelation.

Rudolph, we may remember, expounding ironically on the 'art of leaving out', had explained how 'Where he had not left out the whole picture, sometimes it was successful.' Rosenberg was experimenting in language with the possibility of leaving out the whole picture, something he couldn't do in the same way with painting; a white page is very different from a white canvas. 'Snow is a strange white word,' he begins his poem 'On Receiving News of the War'.

This preoccupation with connections and absences, and so with forms and structures – the virtual obsession of his poetry – was the product in Rosenberg of an overlap of apparently disparate phenomena: a whole spectrum, from the death of his twin brother at birth to his ambiguous position both as the rejector of his family ethos and tradition, and as a first-generation working-class Jew aspiring to be an artist in the language of his host country, but not of his parents (it is striking indeed how many of his best poems sound like translations). The war, in the very confusion of loyalties it revealed, in the midst of so much death, offered terrifying images of assimilation: what he referred to from the trenches as 'The huge and terrible sensations of sinking in the mud'. But it also produced in

Rosenberg's mind, in anticipation, the great visionary figure of Moses: Moses before the exodus and before the covenant, and subject to Rosenberg's dramatic and heretical transfiguration; the arch-liberator of his vision.

IV

I am rough now, and new, and will have no tailor.

Isaac Rosenberg, *Moses*

He has something in him, horribly rough, but then 'Stepney East' . . .

Ezra Pound to Harriet Munro, 1915

As a kind of coda to this essay I want to make a few brief remarks about Rosenberg's finest poem, the verse-drama *Moses* – mindful of the fact that it was also the Romantic poets who had tried, unsuccessfully, to revive the verse-drama in the first two decades of the previous century. 'Moses,' he wrote to the poet R. C. Trevelyan, 'symbolises the fierce desire for virility and original action in contrast to slavery of the most abject kind.' This is clearly a dramatic redescription of the Moses of the Old Testament, carrying with it as it does an emphasis on sexual as opposed to ethical potency, and the suggestion that Moses might have forfeited 'original action' by becoming the abject slave of God. The God whom Moses – disguised as a minstrel, reminding us of the 'Ode to David's Harp' – sings of in the poem, as a kind of anti-visionary poet; 'God's unthinkable imagination,' he sings in disguise, 'invents new tortures for nature.' 'The idea in Moses's brain,' Jon Silkin has written in the best essay on Rosenberg, 'is the creative impulse which tears up the old dead idea that the Jews must bear perpetual slavery.' But Rosenberg's Moses claims, like Marlowe's Tamburlaine, that he will 'ride the dizzy beast of the world / My road – my way'. His voice is one of megalomaniac rupture and release: 'Voices thunder,' he says, 'voices of deeds undone . . . Virgin silences waiting a breaking voice.' 'Who has made of the forest a park?' he asks; 'Who has changed the wolf to a dog? / and put the horse in harness? / And man's mind in a groove?' In Moses's language there is an insistent idealization of masculine energy, a pagan identification with the energies of a potentially Dionysiac nature. That is to say, Rosenberg is not presenting us with a man who will be freed, so to speak, by the Ten Commandments. This is a visionary poet in whom, as he says, 'Startled to life starved hopes slink out / Cowering incredulous.' The play ends with Moses being arrested for killing his slave Abinoah, whom he ironically refers to as his 'father'.

In a review of an exhibition of Jewish painters published in the *Jewish Chronicle* in 1912 Rosenberg wrote: 'The travail and sorrow of centuries have given life a more poignant and intense interpretation, while the strength of the desire of ages has fashioned an ideal which colours all our expression of existence.' He wanted, I think, to reject not everything that interfered with achieving the ideal itself, but anything that interfered with the fashioning of it, with its articulation. And *Moses* is, among other things, a statement of this rejection, because for the Jews God had, through the covenant with Moses, fashioned the ideal already; and it was fashioned as something to submit to, or comply with, in a way that from Rosenberg's point of view pre-empted any further articulation of alternative ideals. The paradox he used *Moses* to fashion was that to be a great visionary Jewish poet who could 'wake the zeal in Israel's breast' was to challenge God; and to succeed, to win, would be to break the convenant and cease to be a Jew.

The only extended quotation from Shakespeare, the 'father of English poets', to be found in Rosenberg's writing is, appropriately, in his piece on Emerson. It is from *The Tempest*, and it is about the death of fathers:

Full fathom five thy father lies;
    Of his bones are coral made;
Those are pearls that were his eyes:
    Nothing of him that doth fade,
But doth suffer a sea-change
Into something rich and strange.

Zeno Falls Short

I

He philosophized on the danger an animal risked because of its appetite.

Italo Svevo, *Zeno's Conscience*

In 1907, Ettore Schmitz was a novelist manqué, working for his wife's family's paint firm in Trieste, when he hired James Joyce to tutor him in English. Joyce admired Schmitz's writing, self-published under the pseudonym Italo Svevo, and found his student's character compelling (he may have been one of the models for Leopold Bloom). Years later, in 1923, when Svevo published *La coscienza di Zeno*, Joyce found him a publisher in Paris. The book became a sensation in avant-garde circles and has preserved an idiosyncratic fascination ever since.

One reason for the persistent appeal of *Zeno's Conscience* (title of the most recent English translation) is its unusual engagement with psychoanalysis. It is the story, in effect, of a failed analysis, told by Zeno Cosini. Zeno is a Trieste businessman in his fifties who has spent his life seeking remedies for mysterious ailments (insomnia, fevers, muscle pains) for which doctors can find no organic cause. He is convinced, for a time, that his illnesses are traceable to his addiction to smoking, which he cannot break because he loves the repeated but fleeting moments of exhilaration that quitting brings every time he tries it. After decades of hypochondria and other maladies of self-absorption, he has turned to psychoanalysis for a cure, and his analyst has asked him to write an autobiography as part of that therapeutic regime. On nearly every page, Zeno's narrative reveals his failure to achieve the self-knowledge that psychoanalysis claims to foster and provide. Zeno tries to tell the truth about himself, but only fitfully, and rarely succeeds. 'One of the great jokes of Svevo's novel,' writes James Wood, 'is that Zeno thinks he is psychoanalysing himself while busily resisting formal psychoanalysis.'

But Svevo's purpose is not to dismiss psychoanalysis. Instead he suggests that its therapeutic consequences can be more complex than even its subtlest defenders (including Freud) acknowledged. *Zeno's Conscience* points to the fundamental tension between Freud's desire to make psychoanalysis a medical science, rational and intelligible, and his deep distrust of anything that claimed to be common sense. It is not easy – or ultimately even possible – to dismiss clarity of understanding as a therapeutic aim. Yet understanding is always undermined, as Freud knew, by the unpredictable perversities of unconscious mental life, which unavoidably afflict the analyst as well as the patient. Addressing these ambiguities, Svevo suggests that psychoanalytic practice can proceed by misunderstanding as well as by understanding, by getting it wrong as well as by getting it right. At its best, Svevo implies, psychoanalysis may lead not to knowledge but to inspiration – including the inspiration to write novels while working in the family paint business. The question Svevo wanted ultimately to ask of a psychoanalytic treatment was not what had been understood, but what had it inspired? And that question leads us to *Zeno's Conscience*.

'Driven by boredom' one evening, Zeno goes fishing with his business partner and brother-in-law Guido, Guido's mistress Carmen and an employee. He couldn't at first decide whether he would go until he found out whether his wife Augusta would 'allow' him to stay out so late at night. But he was, he says, 'finally driven out of the house' by his baby Antonia's screams. He had tried his 'system' of 'shouting insults into that tiny ear of the yelling monkey'; when that didn't work he wanted to, as he puts it, 'try another system a bit more vigorous', prompting his wife to usher him out to his fishing trip. There is, he tells us,

> a little divergence of opinion between me and Augusta – our only one – about how to treat troublesome babies; it seems to me that the baby's suffering is less important than ours and that it is worth letting the infant endure it in order to spare the adult greater distress; she, on the contrary, feels that since we made the children, we must also put up with them.

We know, from what we have already read, that this is not the only divergence of opinion between Zeno and his wife; and we know from his descriptions of her that she is a much more loving mother than his description of her suggests, as someone who merely puts up with her child. This is misrepresentation, this is deliberately getting it wrong; these are the kinds of self-serving descriptions that we are by this point in the book more than familiar with. On his way to the fishing trip Zeno finds himself both looking at other women and 'devising a mechanism for a child', a chair which, at the flick of a switch, 'would send chair and screaming baby off, at top speed, toward the most remote point of the house, whence its voice, muted by the distance, would actually seem pleasant'. This device, we should note, doesn't merely remove the screaming child, it aestheticizes her distress, muting her voice so that it sounds 'pleasant'. Svevo is here, we might think, giving us a clue. Once Zeno goes on the boat he becomes irritated by whatever Guido and his mistress are up to, so he gets them to drop him off, using as an excuse 'the scene my little girl had made that evening, and my desire now to make sure she wasn't sick'. As it happens, when he gets back she is sick, which Zeno interprets as a 'divine punishment' for, as he puts it, 'feigning for Guido a concern for her health that I didn't feel'. He has a sleepless night – it is, as they say, all about him; he believes he caused his daughter's illness – but after 'confessing' his misdeeds to his wife, 'he immediately felt better and fell sound asleep'.

In this catalogue of lies and alibis, of callousness and calculation, it is, of course, Zeno's opportunistic hedonism, his passion to relieve himself of his suffering, that is so striking; though we may wonder in this vignette – and the book is a series of such anecdotal encounters – whether Zeno is seeking pleasure or avoiding pain, and what the difference is. And, of course, we are made to wonder about this difference as we suffer and enjoy in the reading of this book what Freud called 'the laughter of unease'. Does Zeno want anything more than to suffer and to not suffer; and to get as much pleasure as he can from both? And isn't Svevo dramatizing the compulsive narcissistic self-deception of an absurdly driven and buffeted modern man; a man who, as he says, 'For all my efforts . . . achieved the result of that marksman who hit the bulls-eye, but of the target next to his'; a man never meeting his own targets, a man brilliant at displacement. A man who wants to want what he wants but also to maintain what he calls 'great serenity of conscience'. An animal who is never as clever as he wants to be.

It is not surprising, in retrospect, that Svevo was a man drawn in the first instance to Schopenhauer and then to psychoanalysis, which is a story and a therapy about the alleviation of suffering, and of the pleasure in suffering; a story about how there is nothing less desirable than an object of desire (targets are made to be missed); and about how pleasure and self-destruction – and indeed, the pleasure of self-destructiveness – can override the necessity of survival. (Darwin, we need to note, is also referred to by name in *Zeno*, usually to remind us what it is to be an animal, and of the absurdity of being an animal that doesn't want to be one.) Clearly psychoanalysis, as the very first words of the novel ('Review my childhood?') impress upon us, is always supposed to be on our minds as readers of *Zeno's Conscience*. What we think of as the novel, after all, is supposedly both instigated by and written for the narrator's analyst. The analyst is Zeno's first and only reader, so we are reminded to read the book as an analyst might, keeping in mind the conflicted mission of psychoanalysis – clarifying self-knowledge and creative misunderstanding.

We are used to novels telling us how to read them now; and Zeno is himself quite explicit about how certain stories by or about individuals take us over, however briefly:

> I believe that many people, like me, go through periods of time when certain ideas occupy, even cram, the whole brain, shutting out all others. Why, the same thing happens to society! It lives on Darwin, after having lived on Robespierre and Napoleon, and then Leibig and perhaps Leopardi, when Bismarck doesn't reign over the whole cosmos!

It won't be long in the novel before Zeno will complain about his analyst's 'presumption that allows him to collect all the phenomena of this world within his great new theory'; and by the triumphant end of the book he will claim that, 'like all strong people, I had in my head a sole idea, and by that I lived and it made my fortune'. But Zeno wants us to see contradictions as paradoxes; he wants to have it both ways, to take his pleasure wherever possible. So he gives us an interesting list in an interesting order – Darwin, Robespierre, Napoleon, Leibig, Leopardi and Bismarck – but one thing is quite clear. The ideas of such men – imperialist, even in their desire to free people of illusion and oppression – are akin, for Zeno, to the symptoms of illness that obsess him. Such ideas, by occupying the mind and excluding all others, become like the experience of addiction to smoking (Zeno's pleasure at the prospect of the Last Cigarette keeps him smoking; seeing ideas as addictive doesn't make them any less addictive). It is as though what we are driven by is a wish to narrow our minds, as though what we are seeking a self-cure for, what we are disturbed by, is the unintelligible complexity of ourselves. 'Life is neither ugly nor beautiful, but it's original,' Zeno proclaims, in a subtle revision of the Nietszchean idea of beyond good and evil. Beauty and ugliness, good and evil, we can, to some extent, describe; originality is more difficult to come to terms with.

So at the heart of this novel – a novel that incorporates with such extraordinary wit and lightness of touch all these late nineteenth-century and early twentieth-century accounts and assumptions about Nature and human nature – there is a simple question, a question that exercised Freud and Svevo among many others, and that is an essential perplexity in and on *Zeno's Conscience* – what, if anything, has self-knowledge got to do with all this? Is self-knowledge the answer to suffering, or to pleasure-seeking, or indeed to survival itself? Is life a problem of knowledge? And what exactly would self-knowledge be knowledge about? Or has 'know thyself' been replaced by 'exploit thyself', for pleasure? Is self-knowledge another device, like Zeno's mechanism, to distance suffering and turn it into pleasure? 'Through studying myself,' Zeno declares at one point, 'I arrived at more and more rational resolutions,' resolutions that of course failed – unlike confessions, after which he sleeps soundly.

My own confession is that I can read neither Italian nor German, but I am writing on Svevo and Freud. It is a predicament that Svevo might have enjoyed. Zeno can't, he says, give a 'complete' or 'sincere' account to his analyst because they don't speak the same dialect; and the analysis doesn't work as an analysis but does work as a novel because Zeno and Dr S. don't speak the same language. There is, in other words, a very real sense in which I don't know what I am talking about; which raises the question of what you do know when you think you know what you are talking about; when, for example, you know a language (and its literature); or when, like a doctor or a psychoanalyst, you think you understand people and know what is good for them, know what they need. Or when, indeed, you claim to know something about yourself. There is, Freud suggests, a language of the unconscious that we all speak and pretend that we don't know. Indeed one of the many exhilarating things about Svevo's novel and Freud's work is that they are both, among many other things, ways of wondering in what sense we ever know what we are talking about. If our word is our bond, what kind of bond is it? In every age people have different ways of not knowing what they are talking about. Freud wants to persuade us that the acknowledgement that we don't know what we are talking about is the precondition for talking; something we might want our poets to admit but not our doctors. *Zeno's Conscience* is a book riddled with suspect doctors – and unreliable narrators.

From a psychoanalytic point of view, all narrators are unreliable narrators. This doesn't mean we don't and can't rely on them; it just means we have to redescribe the whole notion of relying and reliability. And this is something Svevo knowingly exploits in *Zeno's Conscience*, something he sees rightly as full of amusing fictional possibilities. What's an unreliable narrator if there is no such thing as a reliable narrator? This is Svevo's implicit question in Zeno. When Zeno's father tells him he thinks his son is mad, Zeno says that he has a certificate from his doctor saying he is sane, to which his father replies, 'Ah! Then you really are mad!' Mad, that is, to believe that a doctor can certify one's sanity, and mad for a doctor to believe that he could do such a thing (madness, the psychoanalyst Winnicott remarked, is the need to be believed). Describing is one of the ways we do our desiring; and Svevo is clearly very interested in the opportunism of description and in the comedy of contesting descriptions. The father, of course, certifies the son as mad like the doctor he mocks. You don't need psychoanalysis to make this joke, but psychoanalysis is about this joke, and about jokes in general.

It is not simply that both Svevo and Freud share the modernist scepticism about the referentiality of language and the foundations of belief. Rather, for both Svevo in *Zeno's Conscience* and Freud in his extensive confession called psychoanalysis, misunderstanding is a form of revelation, even if it is not always entirely clear what is being revealed. And illness and desire are taken to be, among other things, ways of organizing misunderstanding. But misunderstanding understood, so to speak, as motivated – as intent; as a form of pleasure-seeking, however baffled and baffling. For Svevo and Freud (not to mention Harold Bloom), how we mislead ourselves and others is among our most useful and revealing cultural practices, of a piece with the arts. Misleadings, misreadings and misunderstandings are artefacts; and *Zeno's Conscience* is a peculiarly artful and ruthless cataloguing of such mischiefs and misdemeanours, recounted by the apparently 'shameless' Zeno. Freud and Svevo, in other words, are part of the same modern cultural conversation about illness as a way of living, about the inextricability of pleasure and self-deception, about the complicity of authority and self-knowledge – and about the sense in which our primary relationship with ourselves is one of misunderstanding.

Consider the ironies involved in thinking of oneself as a modern, self-authorizing individual: people assuming an authority that they could never have; people misleading themselves and others; people not doing what they say, and people not doing what they say they are doing; the self-importance of hedonism, and the hedonism of self-importance; people unwittingly telling themselves lies by lying strategically; the satisfactions of failure and the ironies of success; pleasure preferred to truth; people one way or another getting it wrong; and by getting something wrong getting something else secretly right. This is what Svevo wants to tell us about in what his biographer P. N. Furbank called his 'supremely shameless way'. That is why *Zeno's Conscience* contains, emblematically, a story of a man who proposes to three sisters only to end up happily marrying the one he doesn't desire – just the kind of thing that Freud wants to tell us a rational modern story about.

Still, Freud's project, we need to remember, was explanation, ideally in the service of a treatment and a cure. There was something

Freud wanted to get right, which was his account of why people were as they were, why they suffered as they did; he wanted to make psychoanalysis a branch of medical science. But psychoanalysis was intrinsically self-ironizing, as Svevo and Zeno seem to know; the psychoanalyst's account, like the psychoanalyst himself, can never be exempt from the interference of unconscious desire. Psychoanalysts suffer from what they think they can explain. Psychoanalysts were once children too; they too are unconsciously pushed and pulled along. Freud has merely described something that by definition cannot be mastered: we are unconscious, there's no cure for that. How could the analyst be less driven than the patient? The patient may be addicted to smoking, but the analyst may be addicted to psychoanalysis (Freud was addicted to both). An analyst, for example, might take revenge on his patient by publishing his secrets, as Zeno's does. Why not, if a psychoanalyst is the person described by Freud? There is no reason why psychoanalysts should be the outright winners of what Philip Roth once called 'the moral beauty contest'.

II

When one has no character one has to have a method.

Albert Camus, *The Fall*

What the theory proposes informs the theory-making; there is a joke here that might be on the analyst. There is a comedy here that may be pretending to be a tragedy, the comedy of someone, of anyone, knowing what is best for anyone, even themselves; of knowing, by the same token, what a cure would be.

Psychoanalysis may be, as Karl Krauss suggested, the disease purporting to be the cure: health, Zeno remarks, 'is only a matter of comparisons' (*Zeno's Conscience* is a book obsessed by the notion of cure; with how you tell the difference between illness and health). The patient may just be given a dose of the analyst's unconscious ('Life has poisons, but also some other poisons that serve as antidotes,' as Zeno remarks). Svevo was right to think that *Zeno's Conscience* was a contribution to psychoanalysis, but probably wrong to think that Freud would think so. (Svevo sent him a copy; Freud never replied.)

So what does Zeno add to psychoanalysis, and what could it be about Zeno that Freud couldn't or didn't respond to? To begin to answer these questions we need to begin at the beginning of the book. But first I want to look at what Svevo wrote more explicitly about the virtues of misunderstanding. About what you know when you don't know the language. About how getting things wrong can sometimes be the best thing we do. Freud called it dream-work – Svevo, not incidentally, began a translation of Freud's *On Dreams* towards the end of the war – and Svevo calls it not fully understanding. Freud called it making a slip, when intention misfires; Svevo calls it inspiration when we get something right by getting something wrong. 'We novelists have a habit of playing with philosophic ideas, without really being in a position to expound them,' Svevo wrote in *Saggi*,

> We falsify them but we also humanize them. The Superman when he reached Italy, was no longer exactly Nietzsche's Superman . . . It's a law of destiny that the artist is inspired by philosophers he doesn't understand fully, and the philosophers in turn don't understand the artists they inspire. You know the story of Wagner and Schopenhauer. Wagner sent Schopenhauer his music with protestations of gratitude to the man he regarded as his master. Schopenhauer wrote back saying that in his view the composer who gave the best reflection of his philosophy was Rossini.

We should bear in mind here Furbank's description of Svevo's reading of Freud. Svevo, Furbank writes, 'never wholeheartedly accepted or rejected Freud, and in fact read him, as he read most things, in a thoroughly amateur manner' (what Freud showed us, to his credit, is that we are all thoroughly amateur, however professional we may be). And we should bear in mind Zeno's stricture that 'inventing is a creation and not a lie'. And we should take Svevo's examples seriously here, as well, even if what he is describing is by now a version of a familiar idea (it is, for example, a version of strong reading and poetic inspiration as misreading promoted by Harold Bloom, in the tradition of Pater and Wilde; and of course, for Bloom, underwritten by Freud). Though read in an amateur manner – not, that is to say, in a professional manner, for money – Svevo refers to one of the traditions that influenced Freud's work, even though Freud tellingly disavowed the influence of Nietzsche. Schopenhauer, though, was a significant and acknowledged influence on both Freud and Svevo ('It was not psychoanalysis,' Freud wrote, that 'first took this step' of recognizing unconscious mental processes; it was 'above all, the great thinker Schopenhauer'). When Svevo says, 'The artist is inspired by philosophers he doesn't understand fully, and the philosophers in turn don't understand the artists they inspire,' Svevo leaves it open as to whether not fully to understand is to misunderstand; as though he doesn't want us fully to understand his sentence.

But cultural transmission is not, in this account, about knowing something properly. If misunderstanding, or not properly understanding, or not fully understanding, is something to avoid and something to wonder about, what might make you believe, or want to believe, that you had fully understood something or someone? Sometimes to understand something or someone may be to diminish their value. Indeed, Svevo suggests here, the value of an object – an idea, a work of art, even possibly a person – depends on what we can turn it into, what we can make out of it, through not understanding; what we can use it to do. It may be only as good as what it can inspire. It is the right kind of misunderstanding that we should be promoting, and even teaching ('Basically,' Zeno writes, 'the pedagogue is more enchained than the pupil'). The worst thing we can sometimes do to other people is to try to stop them misunderstanding us, because the wish to understand can be the wish not to be inspired. The aim of psychoanalysis may be to provide useful understanding, but useful understanding may be a contradiction in terms. Indeed what psychoanalysis might suffer from is that psychoanalysts think they understand it and can expound it. If we think of the psychoanalytic goal as inspiration rather than understanding, then a novel question arises: has there been enough productive misunderstanding, enough enlivening misrecognition? Not: what have we learned? But: how have we been inspired? We need to remember that Svevo made a great novel out of a failed analysis; or rather the story of one.

And of course both Svevo's examples are about powerful figures of authority, Nietzsche's Superman and Schopenhauer as Wagner's 'master'. As Svevo writes, 'We falsify them but we also humanize them' by not fully understanding them; we play with their ideas 'without really being in a position to expound them'. This suggests that the precondition for being able to play with an idea is not being in a position to expound it; or that expounding is what we do when we can't play. The most dangerous ideas are the ones we are not allowed to falsify, the ones we are not encouraged to misread (and this has obvious political implications, as does the idea of Nietzsche's Superman reaching Italy; Svevo wrote to Valerio Jahier that *Zeno* was 'a deliberate counterblast to the cult of Superman'). It is not news now that the capacity to play is taken to be a moral (and emotional) good; but the ideas that understanding can be the enemy of play (or art), that knowing can be the saboteur of inspiration, and that inspiration was born of misunderstanding – or not quite understanding – were and are essential perplexities in psychoanalysis. Svevo enjoys playing with them.

And his version of playing provokes a series of questions. What if psychoanalysis was itself there to be misunderstood, to be played with, to be the inspiration for quite other things, rather than to be expounded or fully understood? As indeed it is in *Zeno's Conscience*; and by the end of the novel Zeno, in the last chapter pointedly entitled 'Psychoanalysis', is disillusioned by psychoanalysis despite the ironic fact that it has inspired his book. What if psychoanalysis – with its account of the unconscious – was unwittingly a theory about the absurdity, the futility, the masquerade, of understanding, let alone fully understanding? *Zeno's Conscience* is full of the wildest and most woeful and wonderful misunderstandings. The pathos (and bathos) of misunderstanding – the poignant violence of getting it wrong, the artfulness of saying and doing the wrong thing, of being, as we say, in the wrong – is Svevo's theme. So by implication it might be part of Svevo's contribution to psychoanalysis to suggest that psychoanalysis is there to be misunderstood; to inspire but not to cure; not to cram the mind to the exclusion of everything else, or at least not for too long.

Zeno's Conscience begins with two wrongs not making a right; with an analyst breaking the rules by asking the patient for a written rather than a spoken, freely associating account of his life, and with a declaration of revenge on the patient – doing professionally the wrong thing by publishing his patient's material; meanwhile the patient is doing the wrong thing by sabotaging the analysis. Zeno is a master of the pleasures of self-sabotage. Both the analyst and the patient are, in each other's eyes, getting it wrong, doing the wrong thing. And then there is, of course, the right that the two wrongs do make, which is the novel *Zeno's Conscience*. And you don't need to be Freud, so to speak, to notice that the analyst is Dr S., the initial of Svevo, and of Svevo's real name Schmitz.

Svevo, clearly, was inspired by Freud's psychoanalysis to write *Zeno's Conscience*; though there was, of course, more to it than that. As Furbank reminds us, towards the end of the war Svevo 'began to nurse the ambition of introducing Freud into Italian literature. It was this ambition, combined with his excitement at becoming an Italian in 1918 . . . that finally turned him to fiction again,' and to the writing of *Zeno*. Svevo wanted Freud, perhaps like Nietzsche's Superman, to 'reach' Italy. And we should take seriously Furbank's phrasing, that

Svevo wanted to introduce Freud into Italian literature, because he did this not, ultimately, by translating Freud but by writing a novel both inspired by his work and in which Freud's work became part of Italian literature. Furbank does not suggest that Svevo wanted to introduce Freud to the Italians with a view to enlightening their mind-doctors or improving their mental health. But if we say that Zeno was inspired, in Svevo's sense of the word, by Freud, we need to qualify this by remembering T. S. Eliot's account of Joyce's *Ulysses*, which Svevo revered and emulated by celebrating a bourgeois hero with a classical title. 'Mr. Joyce's parallel use of the *Odyssey* . . . has the importance of a scientific discovery,' Eliot wrote in his influential review '*Ulysses*, Order, and Myth'.

> No one else has built a novel upon such a foundation before . . . In using the myth, in manipulating a continuous parallel between contemporaneity and antiquity, Mr. Joyce [has discovered] a way of controlling, of ordering, of giving a shape and a significance to the immense panorama of futility and anarchy which is contemporary history . . . Instead of narrative method, we may now use the mythical method.

Svevo's calling his hero Zeno, after the paradoxical Stoic philosopher – whose work, not incidentally, is known at all only through secondary sources – is itself a link of the kind Eliot is making to help us understand Joyce's 'mythical method'. And yet what Svevo was doing in *Zeno's Conscience*, we might say, was building a novel on a parallel but significantly different foundation; that is, by using not a classical myth but the myth of psychoanalysis (which itself, of course, is built on the foundation of a classical myth, the Oedipus of the so-called Oedipus Complex that Zeno refers to ironically – 'An illustrious sickness, whose ancestors dated back to the mythological era!'). And in using the myth Svevo manipulates a continuous parallel between two versions of contemporaneity; and one of these versions, psychoanalysis, itself draws continuous parallels between the adult patient's contemporary life and the antiquity of his childhood ('Review my childhood?' Zeno's first astounded written words of muted hilarity suggest the possible futility and anarchy of such an enterprise). The other version, the contemporary novel, in its more or less realist modernist form – i.e., not *Ulysses* – can wonder what, if anything, psychoanalysis has got to do with contemporary life and with contemporary novel-writing. What use psychoanalysis might be for the novel, not merely as a psychology to import, but as another contemporary form of fiction-making. If Freud and Svevo are both writers, if psychoanalysis and the novel are both fictions, what is the difference? And if psychoanalysis is not a fiction, what is it? ('Review my childhood?' in William Weaver's translation suggests that giving an account of one's childhood is like reviewing a book, but without there being a book to review.)

Svevo, though, doesn't have Eliot's *Waste Land* mentality; for him, or rather for Zeno, there are many pleasures, not least being the intense pleasure, the relish, he takes in his foibles and failings (illness, one might say, is the hero of Svevo's book, and doctors are anti-heroes). Svevo, like Freud – but unlike Eliot – doesn't only see futility and anarchy in contemporary history; indeed neither of them has the dispirited grandiosity that such formulations suggest. They both believe that there is something about pleasure that is worth having, or even believing in ('True slavery is being condemned to abstinence: Tantalus not Hercules,' Zeno remarks). They both believe that pleasure can be perverted by the rage for order; that pleasure might be about not being as good as we should be; that in certain situations – perhaps in certain historical moments – pleasure has more to do with getting it wrong than getting it right; or more to do with self-harm than well-being. Or even, that for modern people self-harm, self-sabotage, ironic self-consciousness could be among the forms their pleasure-seeking takes.

Without psychoanalysis there would be no *Zeno*, just as without the *Odyssey* there would be no *Ulysses*. But it is not simply or solely a question of what Freud and Svevo supposedly had in common, but of what Svevo used psychoanalysis to do; what, in Svevo's terms, it inspired in him. And in what sense this might be described, as Svevo saw it, as a contribution to psychoanalysis. Indeed it has always been contentious – and this is the point of the book, and not its problem – what Svevo was doing with psychoanalysis, both wittingly and unwittingly, in *Zeno's Conscience*; what Svevo is doing with psychoanalysis, and what the analyst is doing with it, according to Zeno and Svevo. And this is where Eliot's formulation about *Ulysses* – 'Mr. Joyce's parallel use of the *Odyssey* . . . has the importance of a scientific discovery' – is too formulaic when applied to *Zeno's Conscience*. Svevo was not mapping one thing on to another; he is not that kind of methodical writer, but rather a writer fascinated by the ironies of method (in *Zeno*, by the methods of medicine, of accounting, of investing, of domesticity, of music, of writing and of psychoanalysis). What he is doing in *Zeno*, though, is playing off psychoanalysis against (one version of) the modernist novel. But it has been instructively difficult to get clear what Svevo might have been up to. 'Renato Poggioli,' the critic James Wood writes,

> once wrote that in *Zeno* Svevo psychoanalyses psychoanalysis itself. But one might equally say that he forces it to confess itself. The idea of life as a disease, after all, is the logical conclusion of psychoanalysis's famous difficulty with how and when to end a patient's treatment; if the patient's sessions have to continue for years and years, for as long as life itself, then life is indeed a long sickness. This might be seen as the unwanted religious or metaphysical implication of psychoanalysis's resistance to religion, its determination to be a therapy rather than a faith. In that sense Zeno does not merely psychoanalyse psychoanalysis, but sees it as another religion, and hence merely a modern fraudulence.

In *Zeno's Conscience* psychoanalysis either psychoanalyses itself, or, in Wood's words, it 'confesses itself'; that is to say, it is exposed as 'another religion, and hence merely a modern fraudulence'. Wood goes on to talk about Zeno, then, 'as a darker book than it has sometimes seemed', a parody of 'the hypocrisy of religious ailments'. Svevo, Wood concludes, 'the atheist Jew who converted to nominal Catholicism only in order to marry his wife, is consumed by confession'. Svevo is the guilty betrayer of two great religions; and the psychoanalysis in the book, in other words, is a way of talking about profounder, 'darker' religious preoccupations. You can psychoanalyse psychoanalysis, turn it against itself, give it a dose of its own medicine; you can expose it as a substitute for religion, or as a fraudulent, ersatz religion, or indeed, as a fraudulent medical practice, unending because life is a long illness (and by implication endlessly lucrative for the exploitative analyst).

But what if Svevo has even larger ambitions, if that is possible, in *Zeno*? Not merely exposing the pretensions and contradictions of psychoanalysis but exposing the idea of self-knowledge, psychoanalysis representing the modern incarnation of the quest for self-knowledge; the quest for self-knowledge that might be a perverse quest romance, of the self in search of its horribly alluring and elusive other. Nearly three quarters of the way through the book – having found it so difficult to give up smoking, give up being in love with Ada, and give up his mistress Carla – Zeno wants to give up working with Guido; and in trying to do this, as he puts it, learns something curious about himself. 'I was unable to abandon that activity of mine, even though I had decided to. I was amazed!' And the reader too is amazed, amazed that Zeno is amazed by this, and amazed that it is something of a revelation to him, something 'curious', that he is unable to abandon an activity merely by deciding to do so. Perhaps, Svevo intimates, the only self-knowledge available is one's resistance to self-knowledge? A point Freud would be able to acknowledge, but not explain. That what we really know about ourselves is how little we want to know about ourselves. The pragmatic question – that psychoanalysis claims to answer – is what has made Zeno so unself-knowing that he is 'amazed' by his inability to do what he prefers? It is as though if Zeno had the requisite self-knowledge it would just make him more efficient at doing what he had decided to do. One wonders what we want the idea of self-knowledge to do for us, and what we would be like if we were as self-knowing as we suppose we would like to be. This is a version, from Zeno's point of view, of the question: what would our lives be like if we were as healthy as we think we want to be?

And this question raises other, fundamental questions about the therapeutic dimensions of the psychoanalytic enterprise. What kind of business is the analyst in? What is he buying and selling on, at a profit? Zeno makes us wonder – especially if, as Zeno says, in one of many intriguing throwaway moments in the book, 'sickness' and 'great goodness' are 'two qualities that are very closely related'. Svevo makes it clear as the novel goes on that it is to Zeno's credit that he is unable, or unwilling, to abandon his loutish partner Guido. Vice is its own reward.

The relationship that produces Zeno's remark linking sickness and goodness is his business partnership with Guido. It is not clear exactly what business they are in or whether they are really doing anything, and Zeno tells us that he is writing of this relationship because he wants to free himself from his 'attachment' to Guido, which 'seems to me a clear manifestation of my sickness'. He sees the whole relationship as built on false premises and duplicity. 'Why should I feel good in that position,' he asks himself, 'simply because I believed my great friendship for Guido signified a great indifference toward Ada?' – Guido's wife and the first sister Zeno courted. He has helped Guido for all the wrong reasons; all his self-justifications seem spurious (Svevo exposes in Zeno the dogmatism of self-doubt). But as always with Zeno there is a twist in the tale. 'For a long time I offered him the sacrifice of my freedom, and I allowed him to drag me into the most hateful situations only to assist him! Genuine outright evidence of sickness or of great goodness, two qualities that are very closely related.' His goodness is his capacity for self-sacrifice, which is a sickness. We may have art, as Nietzsche wrote, that we may not perish of the truth; but we have illness, Zeno intimates, that we may not perish of egotism. And yet, of course, in this deliberately self-contradictory novel, Zeno's wife, the appropriately named Augusta, is a paragon of health, and endlessly kind to Zeno and her family. But then *Zeno's Conscience*, like Freud's psychoanalysis, can also be read as a study of male narcissism. Self-knowledge can be narcissism by other means.

'Many in this world,' Zeno remarks – and it is a comment addressed to his analyst, the reader – 'learn only by listening to themselves; in any case they are unable to learn by listening to anyone else.' This, as usual with Zeno, is a subtle distinction, making us wonder if reading is a way of listening and suggesting as it does, among other things, that no one can learn anything by listening to themselves or to others. This is a troubling proposition, not least in relation to doctors and patients; and something of a message, clearly, to his own analyst who is reading this, along with us. We hope our doctors have learned something by listening to other people – both their teachers and patients – and that patients can take something in from their doctors. Medicine is by definition a knowledge of self and others. It is part of Zeno's unassailable capacity of self-justification as rationalization to distrust doctors. The first doctor we meet, his analyst, is immediately and obviously untrustworthy. But so too is the next doctor, the doctor who tries to cure him of his addiction to cigarettes.

Zeno conceives a 'mad, bitter jealousy of the young doctor [Muli]. Handsome he was, and free!' – unlike Zeno, now cooped up in a clinic while he imagines, falsely, that his doctor is having an affair with his wife. It is not merely that the doctor can't help him, but that the doctor is using his clinical skills to confine him in order to seduce his wife. By outwitting the doctor and his team, escaping from the clinic and returning home, Zeno, as he says, has plenty of time now to cure himself 'slowly', which, of course, he never does. Zeno assumes that the doctor is exactly like him, an opportunistic exploiter and seducer.

And someone with no effective cures (another message to his analyst). What is striking about Zeno is the certainty of his scepticism. He knows exactly what the doctor is like, and he knows how to cure himself, and both of these assumptions are untrue. Zeno is a man in an almost continual state of conviction, even though many of his convictions are of the prophetic kind, the wishful kind, called resolutions. As his analyst ruefully exclaims in the Preface, 'He seemed so curious about himself!' So when Zeno says, early in the novel, 'for me time is not that inconceivable thing that never stops. For me, and only for me, it retraces its steps,' we know he is telling us both that he is Time's Chosen One – 'for me, and only for me' – and that he is omniscient; there is no unknown unfolding future, but relentless repetition. He is, as they say, living in his mind, where you can have things as you want them, even Time.

Zeno, in other words, has to be one of the incurables, somebody apparently unswayed, undeflected, uninformed, unchanged by other people. This ironized self-isolation that is a self-insulation is a lot of work; it is not surprising that Zeno finds it difficult to have a job. He has had to make a robustness out of his abjection – as Svevo has had to make an extraordinary character out of an addict. And yet from another point of view – one without therapeutic presumption, one without ideas of pathology or progress – we might say Zeno has had the courage of who he happens to be; and the courage, if that is the right word, to tell us who that is; to tell us what, in his own view, he is really like. And he has shown us that we are the animals who want to be different, but that we can't be different from animals. That modern identity is wanting to be different and doing everything one can to sabotage change; it means living in the magic circle of one's rationalizations while remaining, if possible, sufficiently lovable, desirable and desirous (it is not incidental that *Zeno's Conscience* is a book full of affection, not least Svevo's affection – not without its misgivings – for the character he has created). So-called identity is a hideout in which one is constantly self-consciously monitoring the effect on oneself of other people, and vice versa; it is the obstacle Freud turned into an instrument in his invention of psychoanalytic treatment. So, for example, when Zeno is trying to get what he wants from his mistress Carla, as he puts it – in one of those theological niceties that Svevo threads through the text – 'Good Devil that I am, I let myself be touched by [her] tears,' it is by definition ambiguous as to whether he was touched and allowed himself to feel it, or contrived his being touched as useful in the circumstances. And Svevo, I think, wants to have it both ways, wants it to be seen as a paradox and not a contradiction that virtue might be both heartfelt sympathy and pragmatic calculation. Fellow-feeling, sympathy or even so-called empathy are, perhaps, just some of the things we can do – part of the cultural repertoire – to get what we want. Good devils are good only opportunistically for bad ends; or they are good in the sense that they are fallen angels and were indeed once good, and may occasionally recover their original virtue. They might be nostalgic for the goodness they were willing to sacrifice. And sacrifice, as Zeno knows, is also a kind of deal.

Celebrating Sebald

There is always hope except when there isn't – it is everywhere.

Frederick Seidel, 'Sunlight'

'Is literary greatness still possible?' Susan Sontag asked in 2000. 'Given the implacable devolution of literary ambition, and the concurrent ascendancy of the tepid, the glib, and the senselessly cruel as normative fictional subjects, what would a noble literary enterprise look like now? One of the few answers available to English-language readers is the work of W. G. Sebald.' 'When *The Emigrants* appeared in English in 1996,' her encomium continued, 'the acclaim bordered on awe . . . what seemed foreign and most persuasive was the preternatural authority of Sebald's voice; its gravity, its sinuosity, its precision, its freedom from all undermining or undignified self-consciousness or irony.' There was palpable relief – among many people of similar educations – that great literature could still be written. A voice of 'preternatural authority' seems a little scary, and possibly a little ill-judged given the period of European history that preoccupied Sebald. But Sontag was clearly voicing something that was widely felt; the reviews of Sebald's books as they came out in the 1990s were, even by contemporary standards, unusually enthusiastic.

Indeed, it is difficult to remember a contemporary writer celebrated on quite this scale. There was a virtual consensus: *The Emigrants*,

Cynthia Ozick wrote in the *New Republic*, was 'sublime'; for the reviewer in the *Chicago Tribune* it was 'a unique masterpiece', for the *Spectator* 'an unconsoling masterpiece' and for Sontag 'an astonishing masterpiece'. It was clearly not enough for the book to be just a masterpiece. *The Rings of Saturn*, to give one more example, was greeted by James Wood in the *Guardian* as 'a great, strange and moving work'. 'Sebald is surely a major European author,' John Murray wrote in the *Independent on Sunday*, who 'reaches the heights of epiphanic beauty only encountered normally in the likes of Proust'. It is perhaps more difficult to be eloquently celebratory than eloquently critical, which is itself interesting, and Sebald's books, as we shall see, have something to say about this. But these blurbs suggest also that Sebald's remarkable books made people want to celebrate his writing in quite extraordinary ways.

There were, of course, dissenting voices: 'One of the most striking developments in English-language publishing in the last five years,' the poet and translator Michael Hoffman wrote in a piece in *Prospect* magazine entitled 'A Chilly Extravagance', 'has been the extraordinary success of the books of W. G. Sebald.' 'The complete absence of humour, charm, grace, touch is startling,' he wrote, 'as startling as the fact that books written without them could enjoy any sort of success in England.' Sebald's writing, Hoffman claimed, had been 'more often praised than accurately described', and he attempted to remedy the situation by going on about Sebald's 'chilly extravagance . . . numbed obsessiveness . . . the complacency and lack of urgency in Sebald's academic sleuthing and the pedantic rosters of his prose catalogues'. Clearly what disturbs Hoffman is the blizzard of praise that met Sebald's work. And even if one disagrees with the content of Hoffman's criticism – and it is surely startlingly wrong to find Sebald's writing humourless or charmless – he does pick up on an interesting question: why exactly is Sebald's writing praised in such effusive ways, and what exactly is being celebrated? What kind of pleasure do we get from Sebald's often grim, always melancholic books? When Bob Dylan was asked on American radio if he had been surprised by the success of *Blood on the Tracks*, he said, after a pause, that he didn't know how people got so much pleasure from so much pain. It is not news that people get pleasure from pain, but how they do it is worth considering. And one of the tasks that such consideration might involve is finding better descriptions of what it is to celebrate or to praise.

At the heart of this essay is a simple observation: Sebald's much celebrated writing has itself very interesting things to say about celebration. Sebald's writing is indeed obsessed with greetings and welcomes, with festivities and the difficulties that attend them, and with celebration as a kind of remembering. In this regard, the responses, our responses, to Sebald's writing appear as puzzling, in their way, as the books themselves. And the puzzle, I think, has partly to do with celebration. 'Surely one of the things that makes it so difficult to write about Sebald,' the critic Eric Santner writes,

> to say anything new or genuinely revelatory about his work, is that he has done so much himself to frame the discourse of his own reception, to provide in advance the terms for critical engagement with the work; his fiction already practises a rather efficient sort of auto-exegesis that leaves the critic feeling a certain irrelevance (the posture of awestruck adoration that one finds in so much of the critical literature is, I think, one of the guises such irrelevance assumes).

In Santner's view, Sebald hasn't so much created the taste by which he wants to be judged as already established it – as though all we can really do when we write about Sebald is go on quoting him. But what bothers Santner, as it did Michael Hoffman, is the 'awestruck adoration' of Sebald, as though this in itself tells us something crucial about the writing, about how it works on us. Hoffman intimated that the extravagant celebration of Sebald was a way of overlooking the flaws in the work: 'Sebald's writing has been more often praised than accurately described,' he wrote, as though praise protects us from what might be revealed by further description. Or, to put it slightly differently, and rather more meanly, we might sometimes celebrate when we fear a fault-finding mission coming on. For Santner, the critic's 'awestruck adoration' of Sebald's writing is a kind of solution to 'the critic feeling a certain irrelevance', perhaps feeling he has nothing to add, can't really contribute, doesn't quite know what to say. By implication, then, 'awestruck adoration' gives the critic something to do, keeps a feeling of irrelevance at bay, cures redundancy. For both Hoffman and Santner the adoring praise of Sebald's writing is a solution to something, perhaps a problem posed by (or perceived in) the work. What Sebald is often telling us in his writing is that our solutions reveal the full extent of our problems; that our cures – or our imagined cures – expose the full nature of our suffering rather than making it disappear.

There is a small example at the beginning of *Vertigo* when the narrator, in talking about Stendhal's Italian adventures, enters into the very big subject of what he calls 'the various difficulties entailed in the act of recollection'. 'It was a severe disappointment for Stendhal,' the narrator learns from his notes,

> when some years ago, looking through old papers, he came across an engraving entitled *Prospetto D'Ivrea* and was obliged to concede that his recollected picture of the town in the evening sun was nothing but a copy of that very engraving. This being so, [Stendhal's] advice is not to purchase engravings of fine views and prospects seen on one's travels since before very long they will displace our memories completely, indeed one might say they destroy them.

This passage may allude to (or simply echo) Walter Benjamin's remark in 'Central Park' that 'the souvenir is the complement to isolated experience. In it is precipitated the increasing self-estrangement of human beings, whose past is inventoried as dead effects.' Sebald, through Stendhal, makes the dilemma more vividly immediate by making it simpler; we buy souvenirs to help us remember, and then what we remember are the souvenirs. Indeed, collecting souvenirs is an attack on memory, as though, unwittingly, we buy souvenirs in order to forget where we have been, to displace our memories; or perhaps we interfere with the workings of memory by trying to fix our memories in souvenirs. If the problem is, how can I remember where I have been? or, more interestingly, how can I remember what I want to remember? then the proposed solution is, buy a souvenir. But what the solution, the souvenir, reveals is the problem of remembering: we can't always remember what we want to remember, and in the ways we want to remember. Indeed, souvenirs reveal just how precarious memory is, how we want to pre-empt its workings, how distrustful we are of it, how we want to destroy it. Souvenirs disclose just how keen we are to forget things, how we can hate memory and want to ruin its works. What do you do with an object of desire? You try to remember it in its absence. But your very ways of remembering it reveal your wish to ablate it, reveal just how elusive, how unpredictable, it is in the way it works on you. The souvenir is not an aide-mémoire; rather, it reminds you how memory itself works, how it can work against you, and how it works beyond your calculation. Our solutions are redescriptions of our problems.

Again, Sebald is exercised by the paradox that only our solutions reveal our problems to us, or the full horror of our problems, Sebald's narrator might say. If a souvenir in some way celebrates an experience – 'extols' it, makes it 'publicly known', 'solemnizes' it, to use the *OED* definitions of 'celebration' – what it is celebrating is that one doesn't know what the experience was or even whether one has digested it; in a sense, a souvenir is celebrating the destruction of the memory, but in the guise of its preservation. Celebrations, as anybody who has had a birthday party they didn't want knows (birthdays being of some significance in Sebald's work), can feel like rather mixed experiences. Celebration, we can say – at least from a psychoanalytical point of view – is an ambivalent act pretending not to be one.

Our solutions show us our problems; our self-cures – as Sebald often makes patently clear in his mordantly witty way – bring on and bring out the real depth of our suffering. *The Rings of Saturn* begins with, and is born out of, this experience. It is, as often in Sebald's books, that the narrator is trying to help himself, walk himself out of what he is suffering from, and by doing so walks himself straight into it. The book begins:

> In August 1992, when the dog days were drawing to an end, I set off to walk the country of Suffolk, in the hope of dispelling the emptiness that takes hold of me whenever I have completed a long stint of work. And in fact my hope was realized, up to a point; for I have seldom felt so carefree as I did then, walking for hours in the day through the thinly populated countryside, which stretches inland from the coast. I wonder now, however, whether there might be something in the old superstition that certain ailments of the spirit and of the body are particularly likely to beset us under the sign of the Dog Star. At all events, in retrospect, I became preoccupied not only with the unaccustomed sense of freedom but also with the paralysing horror that had come over me at various times when confronted with the traces of destruction, reaching far back into the past, that were evident even in that remote place. Perhaps it was because of this that, a year to the day after I began my tour, I was taken into a hospital in Norwich in a state of almost total immobility. It was then that I began in my thoughts to write these pages.

His mobility ends up immobilizing him. His attempted cure for the emptiness of finishing a piece of writing works initially. He is carefree, at least at first, but there is some implied connection between his 'unaccustomed sense of freedom' and the 'paralysing horror' that comes over him 'when confronted with the traces of destruction, reaching far back into the past, that were evident even in that remote place'. On the one hand, he simply can't get away from the traces of destruction, even when he gets away from people; and on the other hand, it is almost as if his unusual sense of freedom can't protect him from these traces, or as if he is even freer to see them. It is not insignificant, though it is done as always in Sebald without portentousness, that freedom, perhaps our most highly valued political and personal ideal and aspiration – even when briefly achieved by the solitary walker – is impotent against the traces of destruction; it is not that his freedom can't hold at bay just how destructive even the traces of human destructiveness are, it is that his freedom is a freedom to see them as they are. He is in 'a state of almost total immobility'. Freedom is neither the cure nor a solution to his condition. And just as Sebald's books work like echo chambers – things are always resonating and returning and coinciding – so towards the end of the book, when the solitary walker goes to the strange and rather sinister island of Orfordness, he feels 'at the same time both utterly liberated and deeply despondent. I had not a single thought in my head.' Being free is not equated with feeling better – there are many traces of destructiveness on the island, which was full of 'military installations'.

Feeling utterly liberated, which is presumably cause for celebration, turns out to be radically depleting. Given the references to the war, there may be echoes in this passage of the liberation of concentration camps in which, once again, celebration becomes a peculiarly mixed thing. How can we celebrate, or what are we doing when we celebrate, in a world that is packed out with traces of destruction that are only reminders of the ongoing destruction that Sebald's narrators so relentlessly document? 'To what it was that I owed thanks for my utterly unexpected recovery late that winter, or whether thanks is the right word, I know as little as I know how one gets through this life,' the character Luisa writes in a memoir given to the narrator by Max Ferber in *The Emigrants*. Recovery (at least in English, and, of course, Sebald is a writer read in English translation) combines remembering and getting better. Sebald's narrators are sceptical about this connection, and indeed about whether 'thanks' is the right word. What is there to celebrate, and what is it to celebrate, when 'confronted with the traces of destruction, reaching far back into the past'? What is celebration a solution to, a self-cure for? These are the much celebrated Sebald's abiding questions.

Birthdays are important in Sebald's writing for their astrological significance, for the coincidences they provide, and for the celebrations that do and don't occur around them. So his own birthday, celebrated or at least recounted in *After Nature*, is of some interest. One's birthday is the most significant event in one's life in the sense that without it there aren't any other events; and yet the only memory of this significant event exists in the form of other people's accounts. A birthday is thus the celebration of an event that one cannot remember, an event in which one was the only person there who wasn't quite present. Birthdays, to begin with, are the history one depends upon other people for. As described in *After Nature*, on Sebald's birthday, unsurprisingly perhaps, celebration was tempered by catastrophe, presenting just the kind of absurdist coincidence that Sebald relishes:

> At the moment on Ascension Day
> of the year forty-four when I was born
> the procession for the blessing of the fields
> was just passing our house to the sounds
> of the fire-brigade band, on its way out
> to the flowering May meadows. Mother
> at first took this as a happy sign, unaware
> that the cold planet Saturn ruled this hour's
> constellation and that above the mountains
> already the storm was hanging, which soon thereafter
> dispersed the supplicants and killed
> one of the four canopy bearers.

Two celebrations, Christ's Ascension and Sebald's birth, were ironically juxtaposed and his mother naively took that as a happy sign;

both were spoiled by unexpected disaster; to celebrate his birthday is also to remember the death of one of the canopy bearers. What happened, in this case through no one's agency, meant that there would always be more to Sebald's birthday celebrations than the celebration of his birth. There is, Sebald will often intimate, an ominous excess in celebration, a storm in the offing. 'Benjamin at one point says,' Sebald remarks in an interview with Michael Silverblatt, 'that there is no point in exaggerating that which is already horrific. And from that, by extrapolation one can conclude that perhaps in order to get the full measure of the horrific, one needs to remind the reader of the beatific moments of life.' The beatific moments in life – and it is a not insignificant choice of words – remind one what one has lost or destroyed, or what has been destroyed. The beatific, the making blessed, may be the best way we have to get the full measure of the horrific.

In the account of his birth in *After Nature*, the blessing of the fields leads to the death of one of the canopy bearers. In *The Rings of Saturn*, the 'unaccustomed sense of freedom' brings with it the 'paralysing horror'. Both moments suggest that our celebrations are dark reminders. In Sebald's writing celebration can quite literally portend disaster, as though the celebration itself is the registration of the forthcoming catastrophe. 'Whenever one is imagining a bright future,' he writes in *The Rings of Saturn*, 'the next disaster is just around the corner.' Alternatively, signs of celebration are signs of loss, like the bridal gown made by the bizarre Irish spinster sisters in the same novel, a gown 'made of hundreds of scraps of silk embroidered with silken thread, or rather woven over cobweb-fashion, which hung on a headless tailor's dummy' and which, like all the things the sisters endlessly make and unmake, will never be used. As Penelopes without husbands, or betrayed Miss Havishams, the three sisters in all their literary and mythical allusiveness are reminders of horrific losses and destructions. It is indeed what the objects of celebration (like the wedding gown) allude to, what celebration refers us to, that preoccupies Sebald.

Celebrations can help us forget what will happen after the celebrations are over.

Celebration is what we do with the things and people we value; and the loss and traces of destruction that obsess Sebald in his writing matter only because there are objects of desire, people and things, we do love and value. So to cast suspicion on celebration, to wonder what we may be up to when we are celebrating, might seem like an unusually joyless task; not to celebrate celebration, not to 'praise whatever you can' (in the poet Stephen Dunn's words), is at best against the spirit of the age, and at worst the death of the spirit. And yet Sebald, I think, feels about celebration what he tells Arthur Lubow he feels about metaphysics: 'if one thing interests me it is metaphysics. I am not seeking an answer, I just want to say "this is very odd indeed." ' This sounds like the kind of ingenuous exclamation that Wittgenstein – another writer important to Sebald – tends to make in his philosophical enquiries. And as with Wittgenstein, it is not that Sebald has a theory about celebration (or metaphysics) in any sense, but that throughout his writing instances of it keep turning up: situations – like his many arrivals in empty hotels or meetings with people – in which celebration may or may not be the issue; or simply reminders that celebration is one of the things that we do in what he calls, in his lugubrious way, 'our history which is but a long account of calamities'. It is as if he wants to say about celebration, 'this is very odd indeed'.

So if it sometimes seems that a kind of plangent desolation is Sebald's expectable environment, that traces of destruction are everywhere in his landscape, there is also a great deal of avid energy and curiosity in his narrators. Indeed, one thing that confounds them is their undefeatedness. The relentless research and erudition of his narrators – at once a parody of the academic life, and a life-and-death struggle to keep going – is tempered by a reiterated gloom. On his way to Colmar in *The Emigrants* the narrator feels 'a kind of festive good spirits rising with me'; but by the end of the page, seventeen lines later, he is telling us, 'what is certain though is that mental suffering is effectively without end. One may think one has reached the very limit, but there are always more torments to come.' These, one might say, are the kinds of conclusions that Sebald's narrators tend to put their trust in, even if sometimes we can feel that they protest too much. But because the terror and the desolation and the general dismay are taken for granted – and this assumption has an obvious religious and historical provenance – the moments of relief and release can seem like moments of grace or revelation. In the fourth section of *Vertigo* the narrator is on a bus full of local women in the Tyrolean mountains. 'They talked mainly or indeed exclusively,' the narrator writes,

> about the never-ending rain, which in many places had already caused whole mountainsides to slide into the valleys. They spoke of the hay rotting in the fields and the potatoes rotting in the ground; of the redcurrants that had come to nothing for the third year in a row . . . As they went on discussing the effects of the ever-worsening weather, complaining that there was neither sunlight nor warmth, the scene outside brightened up, a little at first then more and more. One could now see the river Inn, its waters meandering through broad stony reaches, and soon beautiful meadows came into view. The sun came out, the entire landscape was radiant, and the Tyrolean women fell silent one after the other and simply looked out at the miracle passing by. I felt much the same myself . . . the steaming forests and the blue skies above, though I had come up from the south and had had to endure the Tyrolean darkness for only a couple of hours, were like a revelation even to me.

This sudden transfiguration of the landscape was a revelation even to him, and yet it is evident to the reader that the narrator of *Vertigo* – like the narrators of Sebald's other documentary fictions – has himself been talking 'mainly or indeed exclusively' about the never-ending rain and destruction of natural life; he is always haunted by the approaching state of 'after nature'. But perhaps it is more difficult – or difficult in a quite different way, as the parable says – to articulate one's thoughts about the desired object, the longed-for state, the time, when it comes, that you have been looking forward to. Like the women on the bus, the narrator can go on and on talking about 'the ever-worsening weather', but when the sun comes out they are struck dumb. It isn't necessarily that words fail them, but that they find themselves not speaking; it is, as it were, a silent celebration: 'the Tyrolean women fell silent one after the other and simply looked out at the miracle passing by'. At least in the translation this is a different kind of fall; the commentary stops, the storytelling fades out, and they start simply to look. And this too, it is intimated, is a kind of miracle. (The scene from Sebald parallels a striking pattern in psychoanalytic practice with older children. They tend to take good experiences with their parents for granted and talk about grievances. The frustrations return as articulated unhappiness; the good things, paradoxically, are not worth talking about, or there is just nothing to say about them.)

The Tyrolean women, like the narrator, celebrate the breaking through of the sun in silence; they just take it in. And that – even though, as always in Sebald, the scene is entirely convincing – is odd. In this instance, celebration is silent, grievance and fear are not. Here the beatific moment is not there 'in order to get the full measure of the horrific'; indeed, what is gained from that moment is not articulated. The solution, the sun, that calls up this silence in the women renders their suffering unfathomable; in this instance all we can know is that just looking is the form the celebration takes. One thing we might infer from this – though, rightly, no one in the book draws any conclusions – is that celebration resists language in a way that suffering does not; or that, sometimes at least, we celebrate more by looking than speaking, by attending rather than praising. As though we sometimes celebrate when we don't know what else to do.

Another instance in the book, however, suggests something

different again. The narrator has been recounting in gruesome detail the cruel history of silk manufacture and 'the great number of people', as he writes, who 'spent their lives with their wretched bodies strapped to looms made of wooden frames and rails, hung with weights, and reminiscent of instruments of torture or cages'. The work of these weavers makes it 'apparent' to him that 'we are able to maintain ourselves on this earth only by being harnessed to the machines we have invented'. And then he adds quite explicitly, in one of those Sebaldian moments when the reader isn't quite sure who the joke is on, that these weavers 'in particular' have 'much in common' with 'scholars and writers', all of whom, he writes,

> tended to suffer from melancholy and all the evils associated with it, [which] is understandable given the nature of their work, which forced them to sit bent over, day after day, straining to keep their eye on the complex patterns they created. It is difficult to imagine the depths of despair into which those can be driven who, even after the end of the working day, are engrossed in their intricate designs and who are pursued, into their dreams, by the feeling that they have got hold of the wrong thread.

It is an extravagant analogy, and typically provocative. If writers and scholars are like these weavers, then who are they being exploited by, and to what end? Is this torturous drudgery worth the suffering? This is a question the writers and scholars are in a better position to consider than are the weavers. If the lurking catastrophe is getting hold of the wrong thread, then there must be a fantasy about the right thread, and being able to get hold of it. What the reader is being induced to think about are tormenting forms of authority, of lives being sacrificed and spoiled for other people's profit.

And yet, the narrator tells us, there is something to celebrate; the manufacturing of silk, in and of itself, was more than merely a bad thing, even though the entire history of silk production is an unremitting story of tyranny. 'On the other hand,' the narrator writes, placing us on the verge of a familiar argument,

> when we consider the weavers' mental illnesses we should also bear in mind that many of the materials produced in the factories of Norwich in the decades before the Industrial Revolution began – silk brocades and watered tabinets, satins and satinettes, camblets and cheveretts, prunelles, callimancoes, and florentines, diamantines and grenadines, blondines, bombazines, belle-isles and martiniques – were of a truly fabulous variety, and of an iridescent, quite indescribable beauty as if they had been produced by Nature itself, like the plumage of birds. – That, at any rate, is what I think when I look at the marvellous strips of colour in the pattern books, the edges and gaps filled with mysterious figures and symbols.

There are in this passage stray thoughts and wrong threads; these commodities were produced by the human nature for whom Martinique was part of the slave trade. And the exotica of the list are recited with the relish of the aesthete and the knowingness of the scholar or connoisseur. When he concludes by saying, 'That, at any rate, is what I think,' he is determinedly reminding us, if we needed reminding, that not everyone thinks this way about these objects, and that, earlier in the passage, neither did he.

What is being celebrated in the list of beautiful words, and the paean to variety, is the mental illness and physical torment of the people who made the objects. What would we be thinking, or indeed doing, if we were not celebrating these objects that, unlike the plumage of birds, were made by exploited labour? Is celebration a way of dehistoricizing things, a mania, a determined thoughtlessness? What are words and phrases like 'variety', 'marvellous strips of colour' or 'mysterious figures and symbols' being used to rationalize or justify or legitimate? And of course the narrator knows what he is doing because he prefaces his celebration with the most elaborate historical account of this exploited labour, which he then compares with the work of writers and scholars. Is he, as a writer and scholar, complicit in legitimating this suffering? In this instance, celebration, the praise and enjoyment of beautiful, marvellous, wonderful objects, is also a cover story. In this instance, we use our pleasure to justify the suffering of others, as if to say, if I am enjoying these objects, or these marvellous words that describe them, then I am not thinking about how they are made. In this instance, celebration is a cure for history-taking. We celebrate as a way of diverting our attention from a history we would prefer not to know about.

So when we celebrate books – and the narrator is asking us to make the link – even books like Sebald's, with what, if anything, are we being complicit? Do we celebrate books by scholars and writers to keep the history of how they were made – the history of what went into their making – at bay? After the passage I have quoted, Sebald gives a characteristically scarifying account of silk manufacture under the Nazis, and mentions that he had come across, in his reading, 'an old master dyer by the name of Seybolt who, according to the file still in the Munich state library was employed for nine years in a silk factory'. Silk workers are like writers and scholars; and we are tempted sometimes to celebrate what they make in all its variety and marvellous beauty. The solution to the problem of exploitation is to celebrate what it produces, but the solution exposes the problem instead of curing it. What we are doing to objects and people when we celebrate them is one of the threads Sebald weaves into his books. Even Sebald's infamously odd photographs seem to be counter-celebratory. 'I am not seeking an answer,' he said, 'I just want to say "this is very odd indeed."'

There are, of course, two celebrations, two historically located celebrations, that haunt all of Sebald's writing, and each of them is a prelude to two different kinds of catastrophe. First, there is the celebrating of Hitler and his rise to power in Germany, and then there are the celebrations of the Allies at the end of the war. In Sebald's account, these celebrations are merely the beginning of an ongoing cultural trauma that post-war German society was unwilling or unable to acknowledge. The juxtaposition of celebration and catastrophe is integral to the kind of histories Sebald recounts, and it is done in his books more often by association than by contrivance, or, rather, by the contrivances of association that Sebald is so keen to recount. His narrators are always saying, 'this made me think of . . .' or 'this reminded me of . . .' or they are noting the free association of events called coincidences. In *Austerlitz*, for example – which reassured John Banville, writing in the *Irish Times*, that 'greatness in literature is still possible' – Austerlitz himself tells the narrator that 'only after the end of the war' could he, as a foster child from Germany, 'imagine any world outside Wales'. He knew nothing of what is referred to with appropriate understatement as 'the fighting on the continent of Europe'. 'A new epoch seemed to dawn,' he tells us, 'with the victory celebrations,' though it was also 'around the same time' that his adoptive mother Gwendolyn's 'state of health deteriorated, almost imperceptibly at first but then with increasing speed'. And it is also around this time that Austerlitz begins to know, he realizes in retrospect, about the preconditions of his own fate. He begins to realize where he has come from. The victory celebrations, and the newsreels he sees of them, are the first glimmerings he gets of his own defeatedness. And this is echoed later in the book when Vera – the neighbour who looked after him before his exile – recounts to Austerlitz how his own father, Maximilian, 'had described the Führer's prodigious reception at the Party rally' in Nuremberg:

crowds . . . stood shoulder to shoulder all agog with excitement . . . the sea of radiant uplifted faces and the arms outstretched in yearning. Maximilian had told her, said Vera, that in the middle of this crowd, which had merged into a single living organism racked by strange, convulsive contractions, he had felt like a foreign body about to be crushed and then excreted.

A few months later Austerlitz's father witnessed similar celebrations at Hitler's arrival in Vienna; 'In Maximilian's opinion . . . this collective paroxysm on the part of the Viennese crowds marked the watershed.' What is referred to later in the book as 'the roars of acclamation' greeting Hitler, 'the kind of euphoria such as one feels at high altitude', are simply the prelude to horror. Whenever birthdays or Christmas are referred to, or the words 'liberation' or 'freedom' are used – and this is usually the case in all Sebald's writing – something terrible is in the offing. In Sebald's fictional documentaries, celebrations are often a sign of something else. They are always ominous, though usually only in hindsight. When Vera and Austerlitz celebrate their reunion in Prague, one of the most overwhelmingly, silently poignant moments in Sebald's writing, a terrible recounting is about to begin – about the fate of the Jews in Prague, and the Kindertransport that separated Austerlitz from his parents for ever.

If the twentieth century was, to use Eric Hobsbawm's title, *The Age of Extremes*, then it was the age of extreme celebrations. The way Sebald stages celebrations in his writing, from meetings between people to Nazi rallies, from birthdays to victory festivities, tends to make them portents of catastrophic destruction, or forms of anticipatory mourning – as though we celebrate when we are about to do terrible things or when terrible things are about to happen, as though celebrations are transitions or thresholds. But Sebald, rightly, has no truck with this kind of explicit formulation. It is, indeed, what makes his books something other than essays or theoretical writings; the many ways in which he resists being polemical contribute to what makes his books so distinctive. And yet there is a moment in his piece 'Campo Santo', one of three sections of an abandoned book about Corsica that he wrote after *The Rings of Saturn* and before *Austerlitz*, when he makes a link between celebration and mourning, and in doing so becomes suspicious.

The narrator has been talking about Corsican funeral rites, observing that they are 'extremely elaborate and of a highly dramatic character', dramatic also in the sense of sometimes seeming like 'a hollow sham, a spectacle prescribed by tradition'. But, he assures us, 'there is no discrepancy between such calculation and a genuine grief'; the 'fluctuation between the expression of deeply felt sorrow . . . and the aesthetically, even cunningly modulated manipulation of the audience to whom the grief is displayed has been perhaps the most typical characteristic of our severely disturbed species at every stage of civilization'. The tentative 'perhaps' doesn't really offset the extremity of the statement, but what exactly is the nature of this disturbance? That we can make the contrived and the genuine inextricable? That authentic grief is a performance art? That we can't distinguish spontaneity from our cunning, from our wish to manipulate others? Given that mourning and, indeed, its absence, its failure in post-war Germany, are patently Sebald's themes, it is striking when these kinds of aspersions are cast – both on our own species and by implication on his own writing.

Through the idea of theatricality, Sebald then links mourning with celebration as though they were two sides of the same coin:

> Anthropological literature contains many descriptions . . . of the members of early tribal cultures who, while celebrating their rites of initiation or sacrifice, retained a very precise and ever-present subliminal awareness that the compulsive extremes to which they went, always connected with the infliction of injury and mutilation, were in essence mere play-acting, even though the performance could sometimes approach the point of death. Those in severe psychological conditions also have a clear idea somewhere, in their inmost hearts, that they are literally acting body and soul in a play.

Celebration is like mourning in that they are both 'in essence mere play-acting'. It may be psychobabble, but it could still be true to say that people in severe psychological conditions know they are acting as a way of distancing themselves from the immediacy of their predicament. This still leaves us, as do Sebald's actual words, with the questions, what is the play that is being acted? And whose play is it? These questions highlight something else that obsesses Sebald about the horrifying history he did and didn't live through, and that is the complicity that sponsored it, or what the political philosopher Norma Geras has called 'the bystander phenomenon' – those who go along with terrible things by not intervening, who witness atrocities without acting. In his essay 'Constructs of Mourning', Sebald describes 'the sense of complicity and fellow-travelling that lurks hidden everywhere' in Germany. Celebration, like mourning (like writing), can have the complicity of play-acting, or so Sebald suggests. And if celebration can be a form of complicity – a form, like mourning, that conceals the fact of its complicity – we need to know what we might be complicit with in our celebrations. Writing about Peter Handke's play *Kaspar*, Sebald once suggested, in one of very few such pronouncements, that literature should keep 'faith with unsocial, banned language'. Some of the language of celebration may be too welcome, too sociable, too easy to take.

WINNICOTT'S LEAR

I really don't know any author to whom I am half so grateful for
my idle self as Edward Lear.

John Ruskin, *Pall Mall Magazine*,
February 1886

Throughout more care than might be supposed has been given to
make the subject incapable of misinterpretation. 'Nonsense' pure
and absolute having been my aim throughout.

Edward Lear, Introduction to
More Nonsense, 1872

Unsurprisingly perhaps, or perhaps not, the Victorian nonsense poet
Edward Lear contributed the idea of nonsense to a tradition of British
psychoanalysis, a tradition initiated by the paediatrician and psychoanalyst D. W. Winnicott; a tradition in which 'nonsense' became a
key word, used to say something interesting and new about psychoanalysis, a profession obsessed by the making of sense and increasingly
hemmed in by a growing scepticism about the (therapeutic) value of
making sense; and a tradition that can itself be used to say something
about Lear and nonsense poetry, a literature obsessed by senselessness
and what sense to make of the making of sense. Winnicott's phrase
'organized nonsense' is pertinent here, as is the link between

intelligibility and significance in Johnson's two dictionary definitions of nonsense: 'Unmeaning or ungrammatical language . . . Trifles, things of no importance.' Lear can be described as wondering, as Winnicott was to do, what is the demand to make sense a demand for, what is it assumed that sense can do for us that nonsense can't? What psychoanalysis and Lear's nonsense poetry share – though it took Winnicott to see it in this particular way – is the acknowledgement that plausible intelligibility and self-estrangement can go hand in hand. Both psychoanalysis and Lear's nonsense poetry recognize that senseless things – frustrations and confusions and catastrophes – happened in childhood that making sense can't make up for or match, and that the commitment to the making of a certain kind of sense is (in the language of psychoanalysis) a phobic avoidance of something deemed to be essential, a fundamental disarray; something which could be called (again in psychoanalytic language) dependence, desire, aggressive vitality, the traumatic past – the cumulative trauma of childhood.

Lear himself, of course, was a writer all too aware of the depredations of his own childhood, of the trying not to think about it that psychoanalysis has made us think about. In a journal entry of 1874 Lear wrote, and inked out later, 'The . . . misery of some 55 or 56 years of past life before me – & ever I have to turn away from too much thought of it, by a decision that it was no fault of my making, but inevitable, and [growing] always from my 6th or 7th year – year by year.' What grows year by year is the misery as well as the child; the misery, as Lear put it in a psychoanalytic way before there was a psychoanalytic way, 'of some 55 or 56 years of past life before me' – the past being before us in the sense that it is at once behind us and in front of us. There was the misery – the lonely restlessness – that Lear recurs to in his letters and journals with such terrible unself-pitying poignancy; and then there was the nonsense, which was of his making, and was a kind of fault of his making. Definitions of the word 'fault' from the *OED* join Lear's nonsense to what became the preoccupations of psychoanalysis: 'deficiency, want (of something specified)', 'something wrongly done . . . a misdeed, transgression, . . . slip, error, mistake, . . . responsibility for an untoward occurrence, . . . a break in continuity, . . . a dislocation'. Lear's nonsense sometimes seems to be a deficiency of sorts, a want of sense, or about a want of sense; and about things going wrong, or going right in odd ways, and so on. So in his limerick about an old man with a beard – a poem about making and its cost – something has gone wrong, but not for everyone involved:

> There was an Old Man with a beard
> Who said, 'It is just as I feared! –
> Two Owls and a Hen, four Larks and a Wren,
> Have all built their nests in my beard!'

Lear suggests that the way things can go wrong exposes something wayward in our wish for things to go right. If a beard can be a nest, several nests, what is a desire to grow a beard a desire for? At its most minimal, Lear implies – as will the psychoanalysts who follow him – consequences exceed intentions. When something works, it works unpredictably.

If his nonsense was the fault of his making – itself an interesting phrase – then the fault that was not of his making was what Winnicott and others were to call, as shorthand, 'severe maternal deprivation'. Lear was the twentieth child in his family, and after he was four, his biographer Vivien Noakes writes, 'Mrs. Lear had nothing more to do with his upbringing . . . He lived in the same house as his mother, who had probably never wanted him, and his father, whom he practically never saw.' He was effectively brought up by his elder sister Ann: 'What I should have been unless she had been my mother I dare not think,' Lear wrote pointedly after her death. And it was between the ages of four and five – in the years he was adopted by Ann – that he became an epileptic (a fault of his making in the other sense). He was often ill as a child and as an adult suffered from asthma and other respiratory ailments. His nomadism, his endless restlessness and travel were driven by his health, by the professional need to make himself into a certain kind of artist, and possibly by a fear of the dependence he craved and was deprived of as a child, and needed to master.

And as a child and a traveller, of course, one hears a lot of language that doesn't make sense. Travel-writing is writing about not being at home, and writing about home by other means; Lear's travelling and travel-writing and painting life were increasingly dominated by a need for a home, a wife and a family, and by a dread and determined avoidance of all that. *Home Is Where We Start From*, to use one of Winnicott's titles, and one of the things that starts at home is the wish not to be there. The wish not to be there – whenever he was – seems to have been one of the abiding themes of Lear's life. Not so much the life of a wanderer – the subtitle of Noakes's biography – but a life on the run; his writing is not so much the cry of the heart against necessity but the (worse) cry of the heart against all the necessities created by all the unnecessary things that happened in his childhood. If Lear's limericks are not quite studies in hysteria, they are rhymes often about entrapment, about people stuck doing strange, unintelligible things, about people unable to give good reasons, or any reasons at all, for what they do. And we are left wondering about each of them, how has it come to this? – a question that inspires psychoanalytic enquiry.

I cite these well-known biographical facts and conjectures – the consequences of which can only be speculative – to suggest briefly just how much overlap there was, as it happens, between Lear and Winnicott: the preoccupation with maternal deprivation and absent fathers, the not always linked interest in childhood and in children, the relationship between solitude and geniality, the fear of and the need for compliant sociability, the terror of impingement and intrusion (in Lear hatred of noise and unwanted visitors), an appetite for fun (for play as the antidote to dutifulness and desire), a preference for the self-cure of humour over the self-importance and self-harm of tragedy, an inkling that sex may be the problem rather than the solution. And both Lear and Winnicott saw the point of nonsense.

If for Lear and Winnicott the intrusiveness of need and of the demands of other people is the problem, the privacy of the self becomes imperative. And nonsense is privacy; that is, nonsense verse is privacy publicly declared. It makes us interested in the fantasy of a private language as a pleasure and a provocation. (We have never heard these words before – scroobious, amblongus, the akond of swat – but unlike other words we haven't heard before we can't look them up in dictionaries; we are lost for authorities. There is no one we can turn to to make sense out of this nonsense.) Winnicott will say, in fact, that a capacity for nonsense is a primary sign of health; and that the psychoanalyst who cannot bear nonsense – who cannot let nonsense be nonsense – has a serious problem. Winnicott realized that the demand in psychoanalytic treatment that the patient speak and listen always had the potential to repeat or recreate the original trauma of intrusiveness, of the unchosen, invasive demands of the parents. And it is perhaps worth bearing in mind, in situating Lear's work historically, that anxieties about intrusiveness, whatever else they are, are also the signs and symptoms and sorrows of the urbanization and imperial colonialism that Lear lived in and through.

In Winnicott's version of psychoanalysis, nonsense is the heart of the matter, the making of it, the enjoying of it, and a capacity for it is essential for both the patient and the analyst. Winnicott, in other words, will redescribe nonsense (and by implication nonsense poetry, which he dubbed 'organized nonsense') as a way of revising something about psychoanalysis – something that could be called the will to understand and be understood, and that Winnicott saw as always potentially the saboteur of the wish and the need to experience. The word 'experience', like the word 'nonsense', is another key word in this version of psychoanalysis, which, like all versions of psychoanalysis, wants to show us how we use authority, among other things, to stop ourselves from having, and needing, certain experiences. It is probably not surprising that there are often remarkable and unsuspected, even unconscious, affinities between ourselves and the writers we are drawn to. Like the people we are drawn to, there is far more to them and about them for us than we realize. There is a real sense, I think, in which Lear and Winnicott shared a sensibility, or an aesthetic, or a tradition. As far as I know, Winnicott knew nothing about Lear's life – though Noakes's biography came out in 1968 and Winnicott died in 1971 – and little about his writing. But something about one of Lear's poems got to him, and got to British psychoanalysis through him.

The use of the word 'nonsense' – what it was used for, what it was used to do – became one of the understated but defining features of Winnicott's particular version of psychoanalysis: an interest in nonsense (and in experience) distinguished this psychoanalysis from its European and American rivals, and indeed from the Kleinian and Anna Freudian traditions within what became the dominant form of British psycho-analysis – traditions committed to interpretation and understanding. What psychoanalysis was for surrealism in France, nonsense was (or should have been) for psychoanalysis in Britain: both a prompt and an inspiration – and a kind of parallel text, surrealism being as much a commentary on psychoanalysis as psychoanalysis was on surrealism. Nonsense made all the difference to psychoanalysis in Britain, at least to those analysts who could use Winnicott's work; it made a new kind of sense of psychoanalysis. And I want to say something briefly about this as a way of saying something about the extraordinary poignant exuberance and genius of Lear as a writer who wanted to be a painter and an illustrator of pictures with words, as dreamers are when they tell us their dreams. This nonsense tradition in British psychoanaly-sis – committed above all to an idea of play – was not averse to delight nor to extending the repertoire of our pleasures. And it began and more or less ended with Donald Winnicott and Marion Milner.

The place to begin is 'The Owl and the Pussy-cat', a poem Win-nicott liked so much that he learned it by heart. Winnicott, his wife Clare wrote in a memoir after his death, 'enjoyed the fact that I knew more about the poets than he did, and that I could say a Shakespeare sonnet or some Dylan Thomas or T. S. Eliot to him on demand. He particularly enjoyed Edward Lear's "The Owl and the Pussy-cat" and couldn't hear it often enough. In the end he memorized it himself.' This is a small psychoanalytic parable about a man enjoying the fact that a woman has something he wants, though preferring to supply it himself – the familiar story in which men enjoy women knowing things that they don't, but want them on demand, and would rather, ultimately, not depend on the women for them.

> The Owl and the Pussy-cat went to sea
>   In a beautiful pea-green boat,
> They took some honey, and plenty of money,
>   Wrapped up in a five-pound note.
> The Owl looked up to the stars above,
>   And sang to a small guitar,
> 'O lovely Pussy! O Pussy, my love,
>   What a beautiful Pussy you are,
>   You are,
>   You are!
> What a beautiful Pussy you are!'
>
> Pussy said to the Owl, 'You elegant fowl!
>   How charmingly sweet you sing!
> O let us be married! Too long we have tarried:
>   But what shall we do for a ring?'
> They sailed away, for a year and a day,
>   To the land where the Bong-Tree grows,
> And there in a wood a Piggy-wig stood,
>   With a ring at the end of his nose,
>   His nose,
>   His nose,
> With a ring at the end of his nose.

'Dear Pig, are you willing to sell for one shilling
    Your ring?' Said the Piggy, 'I will.'
So they took it away, and were married next day
    By the Turkey who lives on the hill.
They dined on mince, and slices of quince,
    Which they ate with a runcible spoon;
And hand in hand, on the edge of the sand,
    They danced by the light of the moon,
        The moon,
        The moon,
They danced by the light of the moon.

Odd couples – men and women, mothers and babies, psychoanalysts and patients – were the stuff of Winnicott's clinical work and writing, and the 'The Owl and the Pussy-cat' is a poem about two creatures improbably making something work together, given who they are – different species, potential enemies and predators – and needing a certain amount of inventive nonsense to do it ('a runcible spoon', and so on). I want to suggest that Winnicott didn't merely learn this famous poem by heart but that he took something of what Lear was doing to heart and used it in a way that changed psychoanalysis, and by the same token gave us another way of talking and writing about Edward Lear.

And just as we are more likely to learn a poem by heart than we are to learn an interpretation of it by heart, Winnicott would describe the patient in psychoanalysis as suffering not only from a lack of understanding or insight, but also from experiences missed out on; so it was not only or simply explanations and interpretations that were required in psychoanalytic treatment – stories of causes and reasons about what did and didn't happen in a person's early life – but experiences, or a capacity for them, that had to be recovered as possibilities. Winnicott didn't want to replace self-knowledge with self-experience, but he was attentive to the ways in which so-called self-knowledge could sabotage self-experience, particularly the crucial self-experience of being able to forget oneself (a capacity for absorption was more of a sign of health and intelligence, for Winnicott, than an ability to understand and explain). And just as an explanation of a joke is no substitute for the experience of getting a joke, an explication of a poem cannot replace or displace the poem. This seems particularly true of Lear's nonsense poetry, in which the experience of reading or hearing the poems all too easily makes interpretation sound like misapprehension, tempting readers into a seriousness the poems distrust. Lear's nonsense poetry makes us think about the incongruousness of interpretation. As a psychoanalyst, Winnicott was alert to the disabling temptations of sense-making – all those forms of making sense that were destructive to a person's aliveness.

In *Playing and Reality*, Winnicott begins his unusual account of nonsense with a more Freudian account of free association. The Freudian demand on the psychoanalytic patient to say whatever comes into his head is a demand not for nonsense but a demand not to have to make sense. When the patient free-associates in the Freudian way, he is not being encouraged to talk nonsense. He is not, for example, in the business of coining nonsense words. He is just released from the burden of having to be coherent and intelligible in recognizable ways. 'Free association that reveals a coherent theme,' Winnicott writes, 'is already affected by anxiety, and the cohesion of ideas is a defence organization.' Coherence – compliance with narrative expectation – is a defence against whatever threatens to render one incoherent (in the psychoanalytic story, our coherence is a defence against or a compromise with what threatens to disturb us). So, in this context, a coherent theme is a sign of anxiety. Winnicott goes on:

> Perhaps it is to be accepted that there are patients who at times need the therapist to note the nonsense that belongs to the mental state of the individual at rest without the need even for the patient to communicate this nonsense, that is to say, without the need for the patient to organize the nonsense. Organized nonsense is already a

defence, just as organized chaos is a denial of chaos. The therapist who cannot take this communication becomes engaged in a futile attempt to find some organization in the nonsense, as a result of which the patient leaves the nonsense area because of hopelessness about communicating nonsense. An opportunity for rest has been missed because of the therapist's need to find sense where nonsense is.

Winnicott uses the term 'nonsense' non-technically. Nonsense here is simply whatever cannot be redescribed in a way that makes too much sense, whatever can't be added to the stock of intelligible available reality.

In this story, a capacity for nonsense is a resource and a resort; the picture is of relaxing into a state in which vigilance is not necessary because coherence is not required. This is the self idling; for this to happen privacy has to be guaranteed. Coherence is required, in this story, for the meeting of one's own needs, or for meeting the needs of others. What a person needs rest from, Winnicott implies, is demand. Nonsense is what one can say (or be) when there is no threat of intrusion, whether that intrusion is desire or frustration or other people's demands (intrusion, we should remember, was one of Lear's bugbears). It is as though we need to have access to a primal nonsensicalness. The analyst who demands sense from the patient – even if it is a sense and coherence that the patient is deemed to be unconscious of – is at best distracting him and at worse violating him. The demand that someone make sense – and the demand at the heart of psychoanalysis is that a person makes sense whether he wants to or not, that he cannot help saying what he means – can be a threat and a promise. So for Winnicott there is the nonsense that is release from compliance and from the meeting of demands (one's own and other people's), and then there is what he calls 'organized nonsense', which is what happens, what is done, when the original and originary nonsense is under threat. 'Organized nonsense is already a defence,' Winnicott writes, 'just as organized chaos is a denial of chaos.' Nonsense verse is organized nonsense. And Winnicott's psychoanalytic formulation allows us to ask what Lear's nonsense must be organized to both protect and ward off.

If we take Winnicott's words about psychoanalysis as instructions to the reader of Edward Lear, we might say that the reader of Lear's nonsense has to be a double agent: she has to accept the nonsense as nonsense, and not be a hyper-vigilant, over-attentive, super-subtly demanding reader; at the same time she has to be a version of that interesting and interested reader, perhaps wondering, in a more or less reductively psychoanalytic way, what the organized nonsense is defending against, and what the defence then makes possible. The reader of Lear's travel-writing, correspondence and journals, of course, has ample material for speculation, as Lear was acutely aware that he was defending himself and of what he wanted to defend himself for, and from: loneliness, depression (the 'morbids'), the misery of his childhood, epileptic fits, asthma, women, aristocrats, poverty, weather, lack of education, lack of recognition, and what he called, on his exhausting and relentless travels, 'the natives'. Winnicott believed that a person was at their most compliant when they were at their most coherent; that nonsense was a resource and a strategy; and that just as much as a person wanted to be understood there was a protest against being intelligible, against being drawn into intelligibility and acculturated into making sense. It is actually a very odd, counter-Freudian story in which the individual is organized and made coherent by her desire, and by the desire of others, but is freed or released or rested or refreshed by a primal nonsensicalness: an original privacy.

So for Winnicott 'nonsense' was a word he could make a lot of sense with. It meant for him a set of paradoxical and contradictory things. Nonsense was non-compliance, idiosyncrasy, a refuge for self-protection, a way of containing extreme demand, a way of hiding and a fundamental state of being. There was a world of need and demand and a world of nonsense. Each could be used as a cover story for the other, but need not be. Organized nonsense was a defence, but we can be at our most undefended when we are nonsensical. Nonsense is where we are between states of desire and meeting the demands of others; making sense is what we do to manage our desire and the needs of others. But nonsense is also something we can use or exploit as 'organized nonsense' when demand is excessive: on a trip to the island of Gozo, Lear wrote that 'the Coast scenery may truly be called pomskizillious & gromphibberous, being as no words can describe its magnificence'. 'Truly be called' because intelligible, sensible words wouldn't come close to describing it, the 'it' being what Lear felt about the coast. And given no words – no given words – can describe its magnificence, Lear is free to invent the words that can. Nonsense becomes improvisation, the best form that non-compliance can take, the mark of an attempt at singularity. 'So much are we creatures of habit,' Lear wrote to W. M. Rossetti in 1853, 'that we can hardly refrain from partly imitating what all about us save a few consider the "only right way".' Nonsense words are language partly imitated, the closest we can get to a private language. We have recourse to nonsense when we want to conceal or disguise or contain our desire, and when we are free of it. It can be used as a hiding place, but it can also be where we are least hidden. In our nonsense we are at our most defensive and utterly undefended.

Winnicott was interested in what being nonsensical could do for us, and in what nonsense could do for the language of psychoanalysis. After Lear, Winnicott could recognize that nonsense – the idea of nonsense and the organized nonsense of Lear's poetry – was an opportunity to describe ourselves differently. That a no-nonsense psychoanalysis could be more of the problem it was invented to address. Just as Lear's nonsense words invite us to work them out and sound them out – enjoying the sound – we could, for instance, begin to think of ourselves as interpreters *and* as free of the compliance of interpretation, as Winnicott wanted psychoanalysts to be. Or we could wonder whether there could be nonsense interpretation that was akin to nonsense verse, just as there might be work that was akin to (Freud's) dream-work. Or we could wonder what it might mean to take what Winnicott calls 'the communication of nonsense' without having to turn it into sense, or into a communication of a conventional kind; Winnicott warns us that making sense where sense can't be made leads to a sense of futility and hopelessness. Where the will to meaning does the work of the imagination, something essential, in Winnicott's view, is lost.

Very few of the interpretations of Lear's nonsense verse are going to give us anything like the pleasure, the pleasurable experience, however puzzling or enigmatic, of the verse. It is this that Winnicott wants us to wonder about. One can have the meaning but miss the experience, which is something that psychoanalysis, like all the interpretative arts, is prone to and that the reading of Lear's nonsense poetry could be a fitting emblem for. So, to Eliot's famous pronouncement about Lear in 'The Music of Poetry' — 'His non-sense is not vacuity of sense: it is a parody of sense and that is the sense of it' — we can add that Lear's nonsense is also a freedom not to make sense, or even to reinvent sense-making. It is the necessary relief, the fundamental pleasure, of pretending to a private language. So what Winnicott proposes that the analyst should do at certain times in some people's psychoanalytic treatment can also be read as a clue to the reading of Lear's so artfully organized nonsense. Psychoanalysis, in all its forms, radical and otherwise, has put its money on sense-making. Through Lear and Winnicott it is invited to consider what else it could do, what else a person might need. And we are invited, by the same token, to wonder what else Lear was doing by making so much nonsense so appealing, so distinctive, so eloquent, so telling.

Hamlet for Revenge

There is no point in disapproval of human nature.

Annette C. Baier, *The Pursuits of Philosophy*

When Hamlet first meets the ghost of his father it is as though he
wants the ghost to tell him what to do:

> HAMLET Whither wilt thou lead me? Speak! I'll go no
> further.
>
> GHOST Mark me.
>
> HAMLET I will.
>
> GHOST My hour is almost come / When I to sulphurous and
> tormenting flames / Must render up myself.
>
> HAMLET Alas, poor ghost.
>
> GHOST Pity me not, but lend thy serious hearing / To what I
> shall unfold.
>
> HAMLET Speak, I am bound to hear.
>
> GHOST So art thou to revenge when thou shalt hear.
>
> HAMLET What?
>
> (Act 1, scene 5)

In these opening lines of the fateful encounter Hamlet seeks instruction; he is 'bound' to hear, in the sense of destined and obliged. He
doesn't ask 'Why?' – why revenge? – but 'What?', what is he going

to hear that will make revenge imperative. And the ghost alerts him to the fact that if he doesn't concentrate on revenge he might feel pity, which would be a distraction. Though it is staged as a love-test, and there is always something vengeful about love-tests – 'if thou dids't ever thy dear father love . . . revenge his foul and most unnatural murder' – Hamlet needs little prompting. He just needs to know the facts, but the facts are, in a sense, after the fact, because his revenge is a fait accompli: 'Haste me to know't that I with wings as swift / As meditation or the thoughts of love / May sweep to my revenge.' And yet, as everybody knows – Hamlet without the prince is as unpromising as Hamlet without revenge – the play creates the space and time for us to see what else Hamlet might do if he doesn't take revenge, and what he does while he is, to all intents and purposes, waiting to take his revenge. There are always, as Hamlet shows us, two questions about revenge: why defer it? And, what else might one do, in the circumstances, other than take it?

Revenge, as so-called revenge tragedies make all too plain, must be plotted, but alternatives to revenge are less often plotted, or even considered (there are no anti-revenge tragedies, even though revenge tragedies can leave us feeling that the tragedy of injustice is when it leads to revenge). Revenge is second nature, virtually a reflex, when something we value is violated, as Hamlet's first encounter with the ghost makes explicit (it is as 'swift / As meditation or the thoughts of love'). And yet Hamlet makes us think about our resistance to revenge, about what can happen in the interim between the exhilarating certainty of the prospect and its execution. Indeed one of the things that Hamlet might make us wonder about is whether revenge is what we take when we don't want to know what has been done to us. We take revenge when there is something – many things – that we don't want to think about (which is one reason why we overhear Hamlet doing so much thinking). Why, after all, doesn't Hamlet decide to hear the ghost out, and make up his own mind, perhaps in consultation with others, about what has happened and what, if anything, he should do about it?

Revenge is a great narrower of the mind; it excites and oversimpli-
fies in one fell swoop. It answers the two essential questions – what
has happened? and what is to be done? – with militant certainty. It
answers the questions before a question has been asked. Revenge is
not, in other words, for the sceptical (it doesn't suit the more sceptical
side of Hamlet's character). Or, scepticism is something we have
invented to temper our vengefulness. Because it is, indeed, striking
how quickly and easily we (and Hamlet) find reasons for revenge as
though, a bit like Hamlet, we could be taken to be simply seeking
pretexts for the pleasures of revenge; that these are the opportunities
that we seek – to get even, to turn the tables, to make others feel what
they have made us feel, to turn trauma into triumph, and so on.

Revenge, we should remember – and revenge is nothing if not a
riveting way of keeping memories alive – is to vindicate again, from
the late Latin 'revindicare' (it is conservative in that it seeks to recover
a supposed status quo ante). For 'vindicate' the *SOED* has among its
earliest uses, 'to clear from censure, criticism, suspicion or doubt by
means of demonstration; to justify or uphold by evidence or argument'
(1653). It also has, of course, 'claim, set free, punish, avenge'. Revenge
is taken because, and when, we need to be right; madness, Winnicott
said, is the need to be believed, and so is revenge. There has been a
terrible misunderstanding. The unassailable has been attacked, something essential needs to be reinstated; certain truths need to be
re-established (my father's pre-eminence, my mother's love for my
father, my capacity to recognize and defend my parents' best selves,
or whatever else Hamlet, or anyone else, believes holds their world
together). It is a setting to rights. So if you were to write philosoph-
ically about revenge, in the blithe and bracing pragmatic way, you
could say – no truth, no revenge. If you live without foundations,
without any kind of essentialism, without any core beliefs, you don't
think of yourself as having much (or anything) to vindicate, and to
vindicate again (you won't be reiterating your truths, and even be
willing sometimes to kill and die for them). If you have nothing to

protect, you have nothing to repeat, nothing you have to keep saying (no revenge, no repetition). Where there was revenge there can be conversation; where there was an eye for an eye there could be new pictures of fairness. Thinking about alternatives to revenge is like trying to redo morality from scratch.

Whatever it is that matters most to us we want to avenge when it is violated. If you want to know what your real values are – what you believe to be true, or right, or good or necessary – you have to notice what inspires you to take revenge. This is more or less where we have got to morally. The paradox is that only values make us vengeful – once anything really matters to us, revenge is always on the cards – and that we are prone to betray our values in the ways we protect them. As though we want to attack and defend our values at the same time. As though what our instinct for revenge exposes is our ambivalence about morality, about having any values at all.

What, then, do we think our values are like if revenge is the way we ultimately protect them? Why does defaming them inspire this, of all things, at least in the first instance? What do we imagine revenge does if we believe it is, ultimately, the best sustainer of our values? What do we believe is recovered, or restored, by revenge? It is like asking why sexual jealousy doesn't make us kinder.

The Paris Review Interview

Adam Phillips was born in Cardiff, Wales, in 1954. He was educated at Oxford, where he read English. Later he trained as a child psycho-therapist and would become the principal at Charing Cross Hospital, in London. He also worked for seventeen years in the National Health Service; his one stated professional regret is leaving the public sector. His current private practice consists mainly of adults who see him at hourly intervals, mostly for fifty minutes each.

Phillips does not email. He uses the phone to stay in touch, making calls between patients. The time constraints and tight schedule are deliberate calculations: for two and a half decades, he has devoted every Wednesday to his writing. He is the author of nineteen books, among them: *Winnicott* (1988), *On Kissing, Tickling and Being Bored* (1993), *Monogamy* (1996), *Houdini's Box* (2001), *Missing Out* (2012), *One Way and Another* (2013) and, with his partner, Judith Clark, *The Concise Dictionary of Dress* (2010). A regular contributor to the *London Review of Books*, *Raritan* and *Threepenny Review*, Phillips is also the general editor of new translations of Freud's work published by the Penguin Press.

The following interview took place over several years and across two continents. Some sessions were conducted before large audiences at the New York Public Library; the Sun Valley Writers' Conference, in Idaho; Les Assises Internationales du Roman, in Lyon; and the Serpentine Gallery, in London. Private sessions were conducted at his offices in Notting Hill, a leisurely five-minute walk from his home. The space in which he sees patients is large and furnished with a couch and a straight-backed chair: Phillips sits at an angle across from his patients, looking mostly out of the window, at a point in the distance, while he listens. It helps him focus, he says. At the far end of the office sits a CD player with rock-and-roll classics. Down the adjoining corridor is a much smaller study where he does all his writing; here, his desk looks over rooftops. Both rooms are book lined: British and American poetry, essays and novels lie piled on shelves and floor, in some places three or four layers deep. On the days he sees patients, Phillips arrives at the office as early as six in the morning in order to read for an hour or two before his first appointment. (He claims to require very little sleep.) He also reads between consultations, whenever he can. As he puts it, 'I need to hear other voices.'

During our conversation, in public and private, Phillips spoke in whole paragraphs, but did not hesitate to take pause or to digress. 'Digression,' he has written, 'is secular revelation.'

– Paul Holdengräber

INTERVIEWER

How did you choose to become a psychoanalyst?

PHILLIPS

When I was seventeen, I read Carl Jung's *Memories, Dreams, Reflections*, and I thought it was an interesting, exciting life. And then I read D. W. Winnicott's *Playing and Reality* when it came out, and I had a tremendous feeling of affinity for the book. I don't exactly know what I thought of it – I can't remember exactly – but I felt that I completely understood it, and I knew then that I wanted to be a child psychotherapist. I don't know what that knowing was a knowing about. It wasn't a revelation, it was a conviction. I read the book and I knew what I wanted to do. It collected me.

Then I read Freud, who seemed to me a version of the Jewish family life that I knew. Here was a voice that felt very familiar to me – not that my parents spoke psychoanalysis at all. But there was something familiar about the voice. And so that bridged the gap, because Winnicott is chronically English, and obviously my family are not.

INTERVIEWER

I want to ask what you mean by that, but already I'm struck by the centrality of books in this story.

PHILLIPS

When I went to school as an adolescent, I had an English teacher who talked about literature with the same kind of passion that my family talked about each other. In other words, there was an intensity in this engagement that I'd never heard before. It was contagious and inspiring. My teacher had been taught by F. R. Leavis at Cambridge. Leavis was a literary critic who treated English literature as a secular religion, a kind of answer to what he thought was a post-Christian society. He had a fanatical assurance about literature that made you intrigued about the writers he didn't like. And my teacher at school felt something comparably zealous. It wasn't zealous in that we were told exactly what to read and what to think about the books, but it was conveyed to us that certain books really did matter and that you were involved in some rearguard action for the profound human values in these books. This was conveyed very powerfully – that the way to learn how to live and to live properly was to read English literature – and it worked for me. I was taught close, attentive reading, and to ironize the ambitions of grand theory. I was educated to believe that A. E. Housman was more interesting than Hegel, and I do. Marianne

Moore, the philosopher J. L. Austin and William Empson were key figures for me then.

Do you still feel that?

Yes, but not in the same way. Fortunately, I never recovered from my education, I've just carried on with it. If you happen to like reading, it can have a very powerful effect on you, an evocative effect, at least on me. It's not as though when I read I'm gathering information, or indeed can remember much of what I read. I know the books that grip me, as everybody does, but their effect is indiscernible. I don't quite know what it is. The Leavisite position, more or less, is that reading certain sentences makes you more alive and a morally better person, and that those two things go together. It seems to me that that isn't necessarily so, but what is clear is that there are powerful unconscious evocative effects in reading books that one loves. There's something about these books that we want to go on thinking about, that matters to us. They're not just fetishes that we use to fill gaps. They are like recurring dreams we can't help thinking about.

When you said 'the Jewish family life that I knew', what did you mean?

My parents were second-generation émigré Jews from Russian Poland. My father's parents were given the Welsh name Phillips because no one could understand the name Pinkus-Levy. My grandfather was a tailor and a travelling salesman. I grew up in an extended family in Cardiff, and the extended family consisted of my parents, my sister, my father's parents, my aunts and uncle, and my two girl cousins, from that side of the family. These were the people I saw three or four times a week.

INTERVIEWER

What did you talk about?

PHILLIPS

My parents were very left-wing, so there was a lot of talk about politics. There was a lot of talk among the men about sport. There was a lot of talk about sex and food and money and relationships. And there was a lot of . . . just sort of hilarity. I don't want to give too pastoral a view of this – everyone was anxious all the time – but there were a lot of laughs. And we were encouraged to do jobs that contributed something good to the culture, to be a doctor or lawyer, probably. This was a combination of acquiring social legitimacy and prestige – to be safe – and doing something that contributed to the common good.

INTERVIEWER

And you think that has something to do with being Jewish?

PHILLIPS

I think it has something to do with it, in the sense that my parents were keen to assimilate. They never remotely denied being Jewish, but they did want to be British. That was unequivocal. And they were not religious. I did have a bar mitzvah, but it was for my grandparents. That was the story, anyway. So I didn't grow up in a religious culture, but I did grow up in a *very* Jewish culture. And when I read

Freud, I thought, Freud's talking about the things they talked about in my family. Now, they didn't talk about it like that, but the issues were the same. I think that Freudian psychoanalysis recycles something for me about a Jewish past and a Jewish sensibility.

INTERVIEWER

Some things you knew and some things you were not really able to recognize.

PHILLIPS

Yes, because occasionally I would think it odd that my family had only properly been in England for one generation, and it was English literature I was learning about. I should be reading Dostoyevsky or Kafka, not *Gawain and the Green Knight*. So when I discovered Bellow and Roth and Mailer, it seemed closer to my heart in some way. When I read Bellow and Roth, and heard the tones and phrases in Bob Dylan's voice, I knew that was how I felt, even though I could not be more English. It was confusing but I wasn't at all confused.

INTERVIEWER

So by joining the psychoanalytic profession, you made a choice to go back to the family roots?

PHILLIPS

It was certainly being part of something for which I felt a strong affinity, an affinity which was unintelligible to me. I should say it wasn't only Jewish American writers who felt close to my heart. Reading Emerson was the most thrilling thing for me, for lots of reasons, but one was because it freed me from the wailing wall of Judaism.

The way Emerson says, Enjoy Shakespeare but don't worry about him, use him to do something new – we're here to write our own sentences. Or, when his son died, 'The only thing grief has taught me, is to know how shallow it is.' This was absolutely extraordinary to me, in a way not entirely dissimilar to Bellow or Roth or Mailer. In each case there was the tremendous energy and vigour, the feeling that sentences were cascading out of the writer as he wrote, and that things were turning up that the writer himself did not understand. That he went with it without knowing what it was saying. I found some of the same gusto and brio in contemporary American critics like Harold Bloom, Geoffrey Hartman, Richard Rorty. There was a sort of blitheness that I loved, a pleasure in the recklessness of one's own mind. And I liked Freud because he could make bad behaviour sound like good behaviour. I loved Whitman for the same reason.

It was in the music, too. Like everyone in my generation, I can remember the first time I heard Dylan's voice, Neil Young, J. J. Cale, Joni Mitchell – that music made me imagine myself. It was so evocative. It taught you nothing, but you felt you'd learned everything you needed to know. You would think, What kind of life might somebody have whose voice sounded like that? I don't mean rock-star life or money, nothing to do with that. Just unheard-of possibility. I got more from the Allman Brothers' *Eat a Peach* than from anything in Melanie Klein.

INTERVIEWER

Your first book was a study of Winnicott. How did that come about?

PHILLIPS

Christopher Bollas suggested that I write to Frank Kermode and propose it. Frank was editor of the Fontana Modern Masters series. It was a very prestigious series in England in those days. The idea that I would write a book on Winnicott seemed astounding to me. So did the idea that I would write to Frank Kermode. He had been a hero of mine at school. Anyway, I did it.

What did you write?

'Dear Frank Kermode, It's been suggested to me that I might send you a synopsis for a possible book on Winnicott for your series. Would you be interested?' And I sent him a paper I had written, 'On Tickling', the first thing I ever wrote. It was two and a half pages long. And he sent me a letter back saying, 'Dear Mr Phillips, No one wants to tickle old men. Your paper reminds me how much I miss it. Could we have dinner?' We had dinner. We got on very well. He said, I'd be delighted if you'd write this book. And that's how it started.

Of course, I had no idea how to write a book. I had never had any desire to be a writer. I wanted to be a reader. So, I thought, what you do is, you do all the research, which I did, and then you take a month off and you write the book. So I took a month off work, and for literally three and a half weeks, I did nothing. I sat around drinking coffee, reading the paper. I just couldn't do it. It was really terrible. And it was exactly like the way writers talk about writing – which is a feeling that I really wanted to do something and had a lot to say and I was a blank. It was as though there was nothing inside me, so I could no more write a sentence than I could stand on my head. It was absolutely impossible. No amount of willpower, no amount of resolution, determination, conversation with my friends made it happen. But it was as though, at a certain point, something literally got me to the typewriter, and I started typing. It just never stopped. It had a grip on me. And it gave me amazing pleasure to do it.

Since then, it's always been a version of that. When someone asks me to give a lecture, the minute I put the phone down, I know what I'm going to do the lecture on. There's nothing to you until someone sees something in you. It is as though I've got some latent preoccupations that are crystallized by somebody making a demand on me. And sometimes, of course, it isn't a demand. Things occur to me.

INTERVIEWER

It seems natural that an interest in literature and in Winnicott should go hand in hand. In Winnicott's essay 'On the Capacity to Be Alone', he writes that the goal for the child is to be alone in the presence of the mother. For a long time this has seemed to me the single best definition of reading.

PHILLIPS

That idea was one of Winnicott's most radical, because what he was saying was that solitude was prior to the wish to transgress. That there's something important about the early experience of being in the presence of somebody without being impinged upon by their demands, and without them needing you to make a demand on them. And that this creates a space internally into which one can be absorbed. In order to be absorbed one has to feel sufficiently safe, as though there is some shield, or somebody guarding you against dangers such that you can 'forget yourself' and absorb yourself, in a book, say. Or, for the child, in a game. It must be one of the precursors of reading, I suppose. I think for Winnicott it would be the definition of a good relationship if, in the relationship, you would be free to be absorbed in something else.

INTERVIEWER

In the Preface to *Promises, Promises*, you write, 'The version of psychoanalysis that I want to promote . . . is more committed to happiness and inspiration (and the miscellaneous) than to self-knowledge, rigorous thinking or the Depths of Being . . . Psychoanalysis does not need any more abstruse or sentimental abstractions – any new paradigms – or radical revisions – it just needs more good sentences.' What did you mean?

PHILLIPS

When I started in psychoanalysis – in British psychoanalysis – it was a very earnest and sentimental profession. There was a kind of vale-of-tears attitude to life, with the implication that life was almost certainly unbearable, that the really deep people were virtually suicidal, and it was a real struggle to believe that – in their language – love was stronger than hate. There were, of course, notable exceptions, including, fortunately, my analyst. But I hardly ever came across an analyst, when I was training, who made me feel that they really loved sex. So it was very difficult to be a relatively happy person training to become a psychoanalyst. I was then twenty-three, and it seemed to be held against me as a sort of shallowness that I was in some way 'happy'. I don't mean that I was happy all the time, but mostly in good spirits. I realize now, of course, that that psychoanalytic world was so grim because the owners of psychoanalysis were all middle-aged and older.

Also, I had assumed that anybody who would be interested in psychoanalysis would be interested in many other things as well, but a lot of psychoanalysts in Britain were very anti-intellectual. I assumed that Freud was one writer among many, whereas he was regarded by the establishment in British psychoanalysis as offering a kind of supreme fiction about contemporary life. So one of the dismaying things was reading contemporary psychoanalysis, which was so poor. There were some notable exceptions, for instance Wilfred Bion and Winnicott and Marion Milner. They were writers. Freud, to me, originally was a writer.

You have said, 'I read psychoanalysis as poetry, so I don't have to worry about whether it is true or even useful, but only whether it is haunting or moving or intriguing or amusing – whether it is something I can't help but be interested in.'

PHILLIPS

Yes, I was interested in psychoanalytic writing as being evocative rather than informative. At the time, the professional literature was written as if it was informing you either about how to practise psychoanalysis or about what people meant, broadly speaking. I couldn't read it like that. Partly temperamentally, and partly because I'd had a literary education. For me, Freud made sense then not in terms of the history of science or the history of neurology, but in terms of the history of literature. I had been lucky enough to read *Tristram Shandy* before I read psychoanalysis.

One advantage of thinking about psychoanalysis as an art, instead of a science, is that you don't have to believe in progress. The tradition I was educated in was very committed to psychoanalysis as a science, as something that was making progress in its understanding of people. As if psychoanalysis was a kind of technique that we were improving all the time. This seemed to me at odds with at least one of Freud's presuppositions, which was that conflict was eternal, and that there was to be no kind of Enlightenment convergence on a consensual truth. The discipline was practised, though, as if we were going to make more and more discoveries about human nature, as though psychoanalysis was going to become more and more efficient, rather than the idea – which seemed to me to be more interesting – that psychoanalysis starts from the position that there is no cure, but that we need different ways of living with ourselves and different descriptions of these so-called selves.

The great thing about the psychoanalytic treatment is that it doesn't work in the usual sense of *work*. I don't mean by this to avoid the fact that it addresses human suffering. I only mean that it takes for granted that an awful lot of human suffering is simply intractable, that there's a sense in which character is intractable. People change, but there really are limits. One thing you discover in psychoanalytic treatment is the limits of what you can change about yourself or your life. We are children for a very long time.

INTERVIEWER

So what's the point?

PHILLIPS

The point is that it's an experiment in what your life might be like if you speak freely to another person – speak and allow that person to show you the ways in which you stop yourself thinking and speaking freely. I don't mean by that that it doesn't change symptoms. I know by my own experience that it does. But I think the most interesting thing about it is its unpredictability. If you buy a fridge, there are certain things you will be guaranteed. If you buy a psychoanalysis, you won't be. It's a real risk, and that also is the point of it. Patients come because they are suffering from something. They want that suffering to be alleviated. Ideally, in the process of doing the analysis, they might find their suffering is alleviated or modified, but also they might discover there are more important things than to alleviate one's suffering.

INTERVIEWER

Do you feel, in some way, that you have failed when a patient leaves your office feeling better?

PHILLIPS

No. Relationships should make us feel better. Why else bother? But there are different ways of feeling better. And I don't think the project is to make people feel better. Nor is it to make people feel worse. It's not to make them *feel* anything. It's simply to allow them to see what it is they do feel. And then what redescription might change.

INTERVIEWER

And this is done through a conversation?

PHILLIPS

It's done through conversation, but it's also done through the medium of who the analyst happens to be. In other words, it's not a replicable technique. In that sense it clearly isn't scientific, because it's something to do with what goes on between two people, mostly unconsciously. An analyst should be someone you have an appetite to talk to and who has a desire to listen to you. Not a professional desire, which is a contradiction in terms. Analysts are people who don't speak on the patient's behalf, don't speak for someone, unlike parents and teachers and doctors and politicians.

INTERVIEWER

'Appetite' is a word that often comes up when you talk about psychoanalysis.

PHILLIPS

Analysis should do two things that are linked together. It should be about the recovery of appetite, and the need not to know yourself. And these two things –

The need *not* to know yourself?

The need not to know yourself. Symptoms are forms of self-knowledge. When you think, I'm agoraphobic, I'm a shy person, whatever it may be, these are forms of self-knowledge. What psychoanalysis, at its best, does is cure you of your self-knowledge. And of your wish to know yourself in that coherent, narrative way. You can only recover your appetite, and appetites, if you can allow yourself to be unknown to yourself. Because the point of knowing oneself is to contain one's anxieties about appetite. It's only worth knowing about the things that make one's life worth living, and whether there are in fact things that make it worth living.

I was a child psychotherapist for most of my professional life. One of the things that is interesting about children is how much appetite they have. How much appetite they have – but also how conflicted they can be about their appetites. Anybody who's got young children, or has had them, or was once a young child, will remember that children are incredibly picky about their food. They can go through periods where they will only have an orange peeled in a certain way. Or milk in a certain cup.

And what does that mean?

Well, it means different things for different children. One of the things it means is there's something very frightening about one's appetite. So that one is trying to contain a voraciousness in a very specific, limiting, narrowed way. It's as though, were the child not to have the milk in that cup, it would be a catastrophe. And the child is right. It would be a catastrophe, because that specific way, that habit, contains what is felt to be a very fearful appetite. An appetite is fearful because it connects you with the world in very unpredictable ways. Winnicott says somewhere that health is much more difficult to deal with than disease. And he's right, I think, in the sense that everybody is dealing with how much of their own aliveness they can bear and how much they need to anaesthetize themselves.

We all have self-cures for strong feeling. Then the self-cure becomes a problem, in the obvious sense that the problem of the alcoholic is not alcohol but sobriety. Drinking becomes a problem, but actually the problem is what's being cured by the alcohol. By the time we're adults, we've all become alcoholics. That's to say, we've all evolved ways of deadening certain feelings and thoughts. One of the reasons we admire or like art, if we do, is that it reopens us in some sense – as Kafka wrote in a letter, art is the axe that breaks the sea that's frozen inside us. It reminds us of sensitivities that we might have lost at some cost. Freud gets at this in *Beyond the Pleasure Principle*. It's as though one is struggling to be as inert as possible – and struggling against one's inertia.

Another of the early analysts, a Welshman called Ernest Jones, had an idea that, interestingly, sort of disappeared. He believed that everybody's deepest fear was loss of desire, what he called aphanisis. For him that's the thing we're most acutely anxious about, having no desire. People now might call it depression, but it wouldn't be the right word for it, because he's talking about a very powerful anxiety of living in a world in which there's nothing and nobody one wants. But it can be extremely difficult to know what you want, especially if you live in a consumer, capitalist culture which is phobic of frustration – where the moment you feel a glimmer of frustration, there's something available to meet it. Now, shopping and eating and sex may not be what you're wanting, but in order to find that out you have to have a conversation with somebody. You can't sit in a room by yourself like Rodin's *Thinker*.

Why not?

Because in your mind, you're mad. But in conversation you have the chance of not being. Your mind by itself is full of unmediated anxieties and conflicts. In conversation things can be metabolized and digested through somebody else – I say something to you and you can give it back to me in different forms – whereas you'll notice that your own mind is very often extremely repetitive. It is very difficult to surprise oneself in one's own mind. The vocabulary of one's self-criticism is so impoverished and clichéd. We are at our most stupid in our self-hatred.

As a writer you work mainly as an essayist. Do you see any special kinship between psychoanalysis and the essay form?

Very much so. Psychoanalytic sessions are not like novels, they're not like epic poems, they're not like lyric poems, they're not like plays – though they're rather like bits of dialogue from plays. But they do seem to me to be like essays, nineteenth-century essays. There is the same opportunity to digress, to change the subject, to be incoherent, to come to conclusions that are then overcome and surpassed, and so on.

An essay is a mixture of the conversational and the coherent and has, to me, the advantages of both. There doesn't have to be a beginning, a middle and an end, as there tends to be in a short story. Essays can wander, they can meander. Also, the nineteenth-century essayists who I like, like Emerson and Lamb and Hazlitt, are all people who are undogmatic but very moralistic, though it's not always quite clear what that moralism is. That's to say, they are clearly people of very strong views who are trying not to be fanatical. The essay is very rarely a fanatical form, it seems to me, partly because you'd just run out of steam. It would just be propaganda of the most boring sort. In order to write a compelling essay, you have to be able to change tone. I think you also have to be reflexively self-revising. It's not that these things are impossible in other genres, but they're very possible in essays. As the word 'essay' suggests, it's about trying something out, it's about an experiment. From the time I began writing – although this wasn't conscious – I think that was the tradition I was writing in.

INTERVIEWER

Digression is crucial?

PHILLIPS

If one looked into digression, what would begin to fall apart very quickly would be the idea of *non*-digressive prose and conversation. It seems to me that digression may be the norm, the invisible norm, in conversation. Because if you believe in digression as something separate, you must believe it's possible to be coherently focused and purposive. What psychoanalysis shows is that one is digressive whether or not one wants to be. Indeed, the digressions one is unaware of are the most telling. Even in normal conversation it's very interesting how we pick up on each other's digressions, not only in terms of content, but also in terms of tone of voice, so that it's actually extremely difficult to stay on a subject. To stay on a subject you've got to know what the subject is.

INTERVIEWER

Would it be right to say that what interests you most is actually when people are off subject?

PHILLIPS

What interests me most is when people are trying to be on the subject and can't help but go off it. When somebody is really trying to articulate something, genuinely struggling to articulate something, as if they will know when they've done it. And in the process of trying to do that, they say all sorts of other things.

INTERVIEWER

Give me an example.

PHILLIPS

I can't, because you'd have to be the one hearing me do it – I can't give myself as an example. But if you try to articulate anything, the hesitations in it and the difficulty will produce spin-offs. In ordinary conversation, the spin-offs are often ignored. One thing psychoanalysis does is listen out for them, because they're roads not taken.

INTERVIEWER

In your essay 'On Not Getting It', you write, 'We are, in actuality, something we don't have the wherewithal to recognize.'

PHILLIPS

The trouble is not that we can't or don't know things. The trouble is that we use *knowing* in bits of our lives where it doesn't work, or where it's actually not the point. I don't mean to argue against knowing things or knowing people. But when you say you know someone, it's very hard to know what it is you want by doing that.

INTERVIEWER

In love, for instance?

PHILLIPS

Yes. We really do know the other person in some profound sense – and also we really don't. And you could think that the fantasy of knowing is spurred by or prompted by something like 'this person has a powerful effect on me and it's so overwhelming that I'm going to manage this through a fantasy of knowledge'. For Proust, for example, knowing people is often very much about dealing with the anxiety that one can't control them. As though, if I know or understand you, then I will have some sense of what you're doing and where you're going when you're not with me. The question is what we use *understanding* to do.

As young children, we listen to adults talking before we understand what they're saying. And that's, after all, where we start – we start in a position of not getting it. It's true of listening to music, too. The emotional impact of music is so incommensurate with what people can say about it, and that seems to be very illustrative of something fundamental – that very powerful emotional effects often can't be articulated. You know something's happened to you but you don't know what it is. You'll find yourself going back to certain poems again and again. After all, they are only words on a page, but you go back because something that really matters to you is evoked in you by the words. And if somebody said to you, Well, what is it? or What do your favourite poems mean?, you may well be able to answer it, if you've been educated in a certain way, but I think you'll feel the gap between what you are able to say and why you go on reading.

In the same way, a psychoanalysis bent on understanding people is going to be very limited. It's not about redescribing somebody such that they become like a character in a novel. It's really showing you how much your wish to know yourself is a consequence of an anxiety state – and how it might be to live as yourself not knowing much about what's going on.

INTERVIEWER

And how much perhaps you need to live that way, not knowing.

PHILLIPS

Or that there's no other way *to* live. That's what's happening anyway, actually, but it's concealed or covered up or assuaged partly by fantasies of knowing who we are. When people say, 'I'm the kind of person who', my heart always sinks. These are formulas; we've all got about ten formulas about who we are, what we like, the kind of people we like, all that stuff. The disparity between these phrases and how one experiences oneself minute by minute is ludicrous. It's like the caption under a painting. You think, Well, yeah, I can see it's called that. But you need to look at the picture.

INTERVIEWER

There is a quotation in *Missing Out* that haunts me, from Randall Jarrell – 'The ways we miss our lives are life.' What does this mean to you?

PHILLIPS

Well, this is an example of the thing we're talking about. Because when you say, What does this mean to you?, I think, What is it about?

INTERVIEWER

But isn't analysis precisely asking somebody, What is it about?

PHILLIPS

It can be that. But it's also having a sense of when that's the wrong question to ask. There are some areas where it's useful to make meaning, and there are other areas of one's life where the making of meaning is a way of pre-empting an experience. If you go to a concert or listen to a piece of music thinking, What does this mean?, you won't have experienced the music.

But about Jarrell's line, tell me, what do *you* think it's about?

INTERVIEWER

I don't know what it's about, but it strikes me as true, and painful because it's true.

PHILLIPS

What's painful about it? It could be extremely comforting, couldn't it? It could be a way of saying, Actually, that's what a life is, it's the lives you don't have. As if to say, Don't worry, because that's what a life is. Or just that missing all our supposed other lives is something modern people are keen to do. We are just addicted to alternatives, fascinated by what we can never do. As if we all had the wrong parents, or the wrong bodies, or the wrong luck.

INTERVIEWER

Are you telling me not to worry?

PHILLIPS

I'm saying there could be a comfort in that line. And the comfort would be something like, You don't have to worry too much about trying to have the lives you think you're missing. Don't be tyrannized by the part of yourself that's only interested in elsewhere.

INTERVIEWER

Really?

PHILLIPS

Well, you could just think it's terrible, and start believing that mourning is the reallest thing we ever do. But one is going to feel different things at different times. As Emerson said, 'Our moods do not believe in each other.'

There's a mood in which you'll feel, This is a terrible fact about life. We're always going to be preoccupied by what we're missing, by what we've lost, and there's no way around it. And in other moods we can think, Well, that's what it is to live a life, so get used to it, that's the point. That's not a problem, it's the point.

INTERVIEWER

My favourite line in 'On Not Getting It' is from John Ashbery – 'The worse your art is, the easier it is to talk about it.'

PHILLIPS

The real reason one does what one does is precisely because one can't give an account of it, if you see what I mean. It is often the case that people who are really absorbed in something can only do the thing that they do, which is why people who write or paint or whatever often find critics very difficult. Either because, obviously, they're not being praised enough, or, alternatively, because it feels irrelevant. It feels necessary because clearly art is buoyed up by responses to it, but it is also somehow irrelevant.

And again, the same is true, in a different way, in psychoanalysis. There's a whole range of analysts who can give extremely fluent, elaborate accounts of how they do psychoanalysis, and I – one, you – always think, If it's like that, then surely they're not doing it, because psychoanalysis is about the unconscious, how could you know what you were doing on that scale? So it seems to me that the better your psychoanalysis is, the less able you'll be to talk about it.

INTERVIEWER

Is this the way in which you approach your own work? It seems to me you haunt your subjects, you approach them from different angles, you surprise them, you try to encircle them – and you can't quite get to them, you release them, and, with other quotations or the same quotations, you come back to them in the subsequent book.

PHILLIPS

I'm sure what you're saying is true – it sounds true. My experience of doing it is I just write it. One's style is like one's smell – because you can't smell it, you need other people to tell you about it.

INTERVIEWER

Do you write about your patients?

PHILLIPS

I never write about people I see, and there are very few clinical vignettes. I think what happens in analysis is entirely private, and I also wouldn't want people to be thinking they are material for my books. Because they're not. Very occasionally, in *Houdini's Box*, for example, something is quoted verbatim. When it is, obviously, I ask the person if I can use it.

INTERVIEWER

Do you feel that you write your essays to satisfy something that was absent in your work as a psychoanalyst?

PHILLIPS

Partly, yes, although that makes it sound too calculated. In the doing of it, it wasn't like that. Retrospectively, I think I began by writing the kind of essay on psychoanalysis that I wished I could read. Or perhaps I was, as it were, unconsciously appealing to the kind of psychoanalytic readers I would want. Or trying to make an audience of people who might be interested in this way of talking and writing. Or to find out if they were.

INTERVIEWER

What do you want people to take away from your books?

PHILLIPS

Obviously, it's not up to me. But what I want is for people to enjoy the experience of reading the books and then forget about them. I'm not trying – consciously, anyway – to promote a set of theories or ideas. There's a spirit, I think, in the writing. There must be. But really, I hope you read one of my books because it gives you pleasure or because you hate it – you read it for those sorts of reasons – and then you discover what you find yourself thinking, feeling, in the reading of it. That's it. I don't add anything to psychoanalytic theory at all. Or any other kind of theory.

INTERVIEWER

You're talking less of your critics and more of your readers. Do you make a distinction?

PHILLIPS

I get two kinds of reviews. One kind of review says, This is narcissistic, self-indulgent, pretentious, empty. Don't be impressed and don't be fooled. And then I get another kind of review which says, These books are interesting. It's always one of the two things, and clearly from their own points of view, they're both right – though I prefer the second view. You have to be really good at masochism to welcome criticism. But you know, you can't write differently, even if you want to. You just have to be able to notice when you are boring yourself. And I am fortunate, because I don't have to earn my living by writing, so I really don't have to think about it. I don't mean it doesn't impinge upon me, but I don't have to be preoccupied by it.

INTERVIEWER

Now you're writing a biography of Freud. I wonder what it is you think you might discover – which is a wrong question, because you don't know.

PHILLIPS

I don't particularly want to discover *anything*, in that sense, about Freud. Nobody needs another biography of Freud. There are very good ones already. What I want to do is write a short biography, in the light of the previous biographies, that can say something about Freud's doubts about what is in some ways a very absurd but very absorbing genre – that is, biography.

I'll give you a simple example. Freud makes a huge palaver about not going to Rome. He desperately wants to go to Rome. Can't go there, for all sorts of reasons. In 1901, he finally goes with his brother. Peter Gay says something like, In 1901, Freud eventually conquered Rome. But he went as a tourist! Ernest Jones, who wrote an early biography of Freud, says something like, Freud entered Rome in triumph. It's astounding. And you can see obviously what's going on here.

INTERVIEWER

What is?

PHILLIPS

Well, what seems to me to be going on is there's a rhetorical enforcement of a fantasy of Freud as a hero. When people write biographies they often idealize their subjects or demonize them, depending on what they are using their subjects to do or say. Understandably, Jones and Gay want Freud to be an extraordinarily masterful person who, by undertaking his self-analysis, is doing some great heroic thing. And it *was* an impressive thing to do, but plenty of people had done things like that in the past, as Freud knew. People had gone through crises in their lives and tried to work them out through writing and through conversations. Now, what came out of this particular crisis was the invention of psychoanalysis. And of course that is very remarkable to the people who love psychoanalysis. But Freud was writing in a long spiritual, religious tradition of crisis writing. It's not the Adoration of the Magi. It's a limited thing.

Not that I want to write a sort of anti-heroic, disparaging book at all. I just want to see whether it's possible to entertain Freud's fantasy of a realistic biography.

What would that mean?

I'm doing it to try to find out. It may not be a possible thing to do.

In *Monogamy*, you write, 'There are fundamentally two kinds of writer, just as there are two kinds of monogamist: the immaculate and the fallible. For the immaculate every sentence must be perfect, every word the inevitable one. For them, getting it right is the point. For the fallible, "wrong" is only the word for people who need to be right. The fallible, that is to say, have the courage of their gaucheness; they are never quite sure what might be a good line; and they have a superstitious confidence that the bad lines somehow sponsor the good ones.' Do you find yourself in one or another of those?

By aspiration, obviously, I would want to be the fallible kind. Because I would want to feel that in the writing I could try things out and could risk being pretentious, gauche, naive, brash – things I would rather not be seen to be, in order to find out what it's like. Anybody who writes knows you don't simply write what you believe. You write to find *out* what you believe, or what you can afford to believe. So when I write something and it sounds good, I leave it in, usually, to see what it sounds like to someone else. To somebody else it might sound awful or brash, but I want to be able to have the courage of my brashness. I don't leave things in that I know to be terrible, or that I don't, as it were, find interesting – I don't do that – but if there's a doubt about it and it sounds interesting, I'll leave it in. And I want to be free to do that, because that's why I write. When I write, things occur to me. It's a way of thinking. But you can perform your thinking instead of just thinking it.

INTERVIEWER

You are very productive for someone who spends four days a week seeing patients and two days at home with his family. When and how do you write?

PHILLIPS

That's easy to talk about, but difficult without either sounding precious or glib – because there is no creative process. I mean, I sit down and write. That is really what happens. I sit down in the morning on Wednesday and I write. And sometimes it doesn't work and almost always it does work, and that's it. Like everybody else, I sometimes have a problem starting, but it passes quickly. I sometimes get stuck and then I just abandon it. I don't try. I'm not somebody who works hard at writing. I wouldn't know how to do that. I wouldn't know what to do, if you see what I mean. I just write until it runs out, and then I start again when I can do it again, but I do like to be able to do it regularly, simply because I love the experience of doing it.

INTERVIEWER

Do you go into the office to write?

PHILLIPS

Yes, I can only write in my office. I love the romance of people who can write anywhere, who can write in hotels, but I can't write anywhere but in that room. At least, so far I can write only in that room.

INTERVIEWER

The office where you see patients is fully covered with books – not just the shelves but the floor. They are everywhere. Do you think the extraordinary amount of books has an effect on your patients?

PHILLIPS

It must do. Some people speak about it. And of course one's room is a powerful communication and demand. Not a known demand, but a demand. I mean, the books are here because I like books and I like having these ones to hand. They are, in a sense, current. I don't mean I'm reading all of them all the time, but they're linked to things that I'm thinking about writing. Or they're just books that I love from the past, that I read and reread. I think there must be some real reassurance for me – the bourgeois, cultured-middle-class fantasy of the reassurances of culture. In any case, they are integral to my life, to my sense of myself, and they have been for a very long time.

INTERVIEWER

Do you think that the great decline in the popularity of psychoanalysis has been a good thing for psychoanalysis or a bad thing?

PHILLIPS

I think it's the best thing that could have happened to psychoanalysis, because it means there is now no prestige in it, no glamour, no money, no public for it, so you'll do it now only if you really love it, if it really engages you. I hope that the disaffection with it — even though it's bad economically for people who do it, obviously — will free people to work out what it is. It's too new for anyone to quite know what it is yet. I don't at all feel that there was a heyday and then it all fell apart. I think it's beginning to dawn on some people what it might be good for, that it might actually help us to live differently, and in unforeseen ways. To me it's one of the best things around. I don't need anybody else to agree with me, but I do feel that's true. And I think it's a very good thing that people have become extremely sceptical. Psychoanalysts used to hide behind mystifications of language, they hid in their societies, they never spoke to anybody else. The moment they started speaking to people outside, the whole thing looked vulnerable, which was the best thing for it to be.

You can't just hold forth about human nature now. You have to talk to anthropologists and sociologists and historians and philosophers, to patients and critics, to anyone who is interested. Really, to anybody who has a view and can open it up. Psychoanalysis is everything that anyone says about it. I think eventually it will get better, or it will disappear.

INTERVIEWER

If psychoanalysis were to disappear, what would you like to do for a living?

PHILLIPS

Well, if it disappeared I'd go on doing it. But I would be . . . I could imagine being a teacher, I could imagine being a primary-school teacher. I'd like to do that. I wouldn't want to be a writer. I couldn't do that.

You once said that you would like to live in a world where there were fewer artists and better relationships. What did you mean by that?

PHILLIPS

I think partly it was a daft thing to say, but one bit of it seems right to me, which is that if you live in a culture which is fascinated by the myth of the artist, and the idea that the vocational artistic life is one of the best lives available, then there's always going to be a temptation for people who are suffering to believe that to become an artist would be the solution when, in fact, it may be more of the problem. There are a number of people whom you might think of as casualties of the myth of the artist. They really should have done something else. Of course some people get lucky and find that art works for them, but for so many people it doesn't. I think that needs to be included in the picture. Often one hears or reads accounts in which people will say, Well, he may have treated his children, wives, friends terribly, but look at the novels, the poems, the paintings. I think it's a terrible equation. Obviously one can't choose to be, as it were, a good parent or a good artist, but if the art legitimates cruelty, I think the art is not worth having. People should be doing everything they can to be as kind as possible and to enjoy each other's company. Any art, any anything, that helps us do that is worth having. But if it doesn't, it isn't.

Appendix: On Translating Freud

> It's never, in any way whatever, by another person's excesses that
> one turns out, in appearance at least, to be overwhelmed. It's always
> because their excesses happen to coincide with your own.
>
> *The Seminar of Jacques Lacan Book XVII:*
> *The Other Side of Psychoanalysis*

Now that the Freud wars are over it seems a good time for a new translation. This is certainly a good time for psychoanalysis: because it is so widely discredited, because there is no prestige, or glamour, or money in it, only those who are really interested will go into it. And now that Freud's words are so casually dismissed, a better, more eloquent case needs to be made for the value of his writing, by those who value it. Though likely to be largely ignored – and ferociously contested by the few remaining devotees and owners of psychoanalysis – a new translation should be something of a new start for anyone still curious. An opportunity, at its most minimal, to see what's left of Freud after the gossip and after his writing has been put through the mill of the psychoanalytic institutions and the universities. Now, at long last, there could be a Freud only for the people who liked him, whether critically or uncritically.

When Penguin first approached me about the possibility of a new translation, there was no suggestion that I would be involved. Freud had come out of copyright in the EU, and they were consulting with various people, they told me, about the viability of a new version. They already had, as the Penguin Freud, most of the Standard Edition in paperback, with the exception of the papers on technique, and it was not obvious what a so-called new Freud could be like, what could be sufficiently new about it to make it marketable, at a time when Freud-bashing and Freud wars were more notorious than Freud-reading, and psychoanalysis was no longer every middle-class person's therapy of choice. What Penguin wanted to know from the people they consulted was how one might go about re-editing, redoing Freud; how one might make a 'Freud for the new century'. I can't pretend that at the time this was of great interest to me. I am not a linguist, I am not a scholar by nature or inclination; I have never done anything that looks like what people call research, and I am far more interested in doing psychoanalysis than in close readings of its texts. I have also always admired the Strachey translation, and like many people really did think of it as the Standard Edition. Like the King James Bible, if I can use that unfortunate analogy, it is so good – or we have been so educated to see its goodness – that it seems like the real thing. It's true that I wondered, when Penguin first phoned me, whether Freud *sounded* different in other translations; but, then again, reading Brill and Joan Riviere and Katherine Jones and Robson-Scott had not been illuminating. I didn't, in other words, really think that Strachey was the problem with Freud. I was quite happy to be locked up in Strachey's Freud and the myth of the Standard Edition and assume that it was more or less for all time.

Just as the risk of psychoanalytic training is that it might make people more interested in psychoanalysis than in other people, the risk of the Freudian texts is that they might make readers more interested in Freud than in other writers. That all writing might become, one way or another, Freudian. I wanted to find out if there was a Freud usable for something other than – for something as well as – more psychoanalysis. The young Auden, for example, was fascinated by

Freud but did not end up writing Freudian poems, or indeed, at least as a young man, poems that sounded much like anybody else's. Psychoanalysis can inform projects that do not themselves have to sponsor psychoanalysis.

My conscious assumption that I would be exempt from the work of the project freed me to say what I thought a new Freud could be like; I wouldn't have to face the consequences of my suggestions, and I could try things out under the guise of being more dogmatic than I felt. In fact, of course, no one involved in psychoanalysis, no one embroiled, is ever nonchalant or insouciant when they are talking about Freud. I did, though, find talking to publishers about Freud often more pleasurable than talking to psychoanalysts. After all, they only wanted to persuade people to buy Freud, not to believe him. Whether psychoanalysis is a language that requires the kind of assent given to religious language – whether there are ways of using it that are not ways of being utterly convinced by it – is still a question for the future readers of Freud.

I suggested, over lunch, the following things to the people at Penguin: that it should not be a complete edition because, as with all so-called great writers, some of Freud was boring, and some of it repetitive; that it need not be a forbidding corpus, need not be in volumes, not intimate that if you hadn't read all of it you hadn't read any of it; that the demand need not be, as Joyce's was of *Ulysses*, that one might devote one's life to it. There is no reason why Freud can't be dipped into; and if people are moved, or intrigued, or gripped they will read on. The selection should be generous but not diligent; but the papers on technique should be included because they are among the most revealing of Freud's writings, not only about psychoanalysis but about what it might be to help someone. Freud is a great writer about our misgivings about helping and being helped. I said that I thought each of the books should be translated by a different person, and that there should be no consensus about technical terms, each of the translators writing a preface in which they might say something about choices made, about the pleasures and the puzzles and the difficulties of translating Freud. Ideally, I thought, the translators would be people who had previously translated literary texts, and need not have previously read Freud: Freud could then be given a go as the writer he wanted to be, and is, as well as the scientist he wanted to be, and might be. And the translators would, presumably, know what the word 'Saussure' meant. I suggested that each book should be introduced by a writer in the so-called humanities, and that there should be two stipulations: the introducers should not be practising analysts nor affiliated with psychoanalytic societies, and they should be asked simply to write their own essays around and about the texts selected by the editor. The introductions would introduce the reader to reading Freud, not to Freud.

The avoidance of analysts, I hoped, might mean that the people involved would not be hung up on what is still called psychoanalytic politics, and would not be overly mindful of what people within the profession would think of as the issues, especially of terminology. People within psychoanalytic groups, unsurprisingly, have a very strong transference, both negative and positive, so to speak, to Freud's texts; I wanted people who were not quite so embroiled, or who were embroiled in other things. I wanted them to be people who were used to reading and interpreting texts, not just to learning and using them as instruction manuals. And I thought the project would have life in it only if the editor got pleasure out of it.

Presumably the character, for want of a better word, of people doing such projects matters; I have always been haunted by a story about Winnicott's analysis with Strachey. Winnicott saw Strachey five times a week and for the first six months of his analysis Strachey supposedly never spoke. Eventually Winnicott got up from the couch, having talked for six months, and said something to the effect that he had been coming for six months and Strachey still hadn't said anything, to which Strachey apparently replied: 'But neither have you.' I have never known whether this is an impressive story or not, but it is a story about a man with a rigorous sense of what he is listening for, of what he wants from analysis. People might want all sorts of things from Freud's texts, and the editor's choices, I thought, might reflect this, might assume that this was possible, that Freud's work is of indeterminate use. I said I thought that the general editor should not read German, so he or she would simply read the translations for readability – for false notes, verbal infelicities, syntactical awkwardness – not for accuracy; the good faith and skill of the translators (with track records) would be assumed, rather than there being, as it were, a senior translator they were answerable to or collaborating with (the sticklers for accuracy would have their chance to pounce on publication). The general editor should be available for consultation, but the translators and introducers should have the last word about their own texts. This would not be a project in which the authority, or even the vision of the general editor, should be stamped too soundly. The books, even Freud's texts themselves, would be in different voices (which, of course, they can never be for people who can only read Freud in the so-called original). Translation could multiply the Freud we think we know.

I thought that, as a rule of thumb, only people who keenly accepted the invitation to work on this project – as everyone did – should be employed; that it should be framed as an experiment and should not be done dutifully, as mere careerism. And I thought it should be made clear that the project was not to usurp, or aim to replace Strachey, but to see what alternative versions sounded like. It would not be organized to compete with Strachey in format, selection or comprehensiveness. Territorial imperatives should be set aside – which was one reason I wanted analysts excluded from the project – partly because Strachey is mostly wonderful, and partly because the field needs airing. The very real advantages, and the very obvious limitations, of having a so-called Standard Edition of Freud in English didn't seem to me, so late in the day, to be worth reciting. And in so far as these issues are still of interest, they are of interest only in the rather narrow world of the profession of psychoanalysis (having been disappointed over the years by what, with some notable exceptions, the profession of psychoanalysis made of Freud, I was more and more interested in what those outside the profession, hostile and otherwise, make of his writing). There was not, after all, something called a standard interpretation in psychoanalysis; and new translations might undo the mystique, the aura of a single, standard translation. I thought it unlikely there could be a new Freud, but that there could be surprises: that there might even be things Strachey got wrong. I thought it was important, given the signs of the times, that the books should be shortish, not tomes (presenting Freud as neither forbidding nor too easy, not a soft touch), and should look attractive. The kinds of book you would like to see yourself with, the kinds of book you liked the idea of yourself being able to read. They should be recognizably part of the Penguin Modern Classics series, aligning Freud with other Modernist writers, in the same format as Joyce, Conrad, Stein, Ford Madox Ford, Woolf and so on. And there should, as with Penguin Modern Classics, be as little scholarly apparatus as possible: only Freud's notes, if possible; and no indexes, given what indexes imply about a book and its genre.

I thought the books needed to be properly marketed; that a splash should be made; that it would be an experiment to see just who, if anyone, wanted to read Freud now, and write and talk about him; and who, if anyone, thought new translations were worth having when a more than good one was available. It was, I suppose, in the language of my education, an appeal to the common reader, even if there is no such thing, and perhaps never has been. My thoughts about this, when I spoke them, seemed liberal, upbeat and rather worthy; probably the kind of thing someone of my generation who had a Leavisite literary education at public school in the 1960s, and an anti-Leavisite literary education at Oxford in the 1970s, would come up with. In the back of my mind, for some reason, was a series that Orwell might have admired: unpretentious accessible editions of a writer worth the trouble he caused the reader, but without highfalutin' claims having to be made. If, as Harold Bloom once suggested, Freud's writing will outlive the profession of psychoanalysis, and if the idea that Freud is in fact a translated writer for the English-speaking world is taken seriously, then new versions seemed to me potentially of value. No more and no less. We didn't and don't *need* new translations of Freud, but we might want them.

If there was a problem – and even to call it a problem seems a little dramatic – it was not with Strachey but just with the idea of there being something that called itself, that wanted to call itself, the Standard Edition. All one's misgivings about Strachey cut both ways, and are evident in Strachey's General Preface. 'When the Standard Edition was first planned,' he writes,

> it was considered that it would be an advantage if a single hand were responsible for shaping the whole text; and in fact a single hand has carried out the greater part of the work of translation, and even where a former version has been used as a basis it will be found that a large amount of remodelling has been imposed. This unfortunately has involved the discarding, in the interests of this preferred uniformity, of many earlier translations that were excellent in themselves. The imaginary model which I have always kept before me is of the writings of some English man of science of wide education born in the middle of the nineteenth century. And I should like, in an explanatory and no patriotic spirit, to emphasize the word 'English'.

Strachey, in translating Freud, imagined himself as an English equivalent of Freud, presumably something a novelist might do; but there is nothing in this statement of intent that isn't debatable. The scientism of Strachey's Freud, which Bettelheim so regretted, saying that the soul had been taken out of his writing, confirms Freud's often stated commitment to psychoanalysis as a science. And the coining of unfamiliar terms (most notoriously, 'cathexis' and 'super-ego') serves to defamiliarize the Freudian texts in instructive ways (Deleuze and Guattari's point that philosophy should be coining new, unfamiliar terms – that the rebarbative opacity of the language could be the point not the problem – could apply to psychoanalysis as well). And the advantage of a (more or less) single-handed translation is, obviously, that it at least seems to replicate Freud's single-handed writing.

Strachey's decision to name his version the Standard Edition was offering a hostage to fortune. Who says that this is the standard, and why do they need to say this? Who has set the standard and what are the criteria? Is calling it the Standard Edition a provocation; could there be another one? And what would it then be called? The Non-standard Edition, the Sub-standard Edition? And who authorizes the authorizers? Why would anyone want to fix the text, once and for all? Is uniformity being asserted because disarray is so acutely sensed? Why, in other words, didn't the English settle for a debate, for a series of possibly disparate and competing translations? What had they suffered, what had the psychoanalytic profession suffered, such that they sought a solution in this kind of dogmatic canon formation? And, by the same token, why haven't the copyright holders allowed the translation of Freud to be a free-for-all? The New Penguin Freud translations couldn't not be part of the broaching of these questions. And even though the questions seem to me, probably now more than then, of some interest, my heart was not in all this; talking about Freud translation is talking about too many other things. And not talking about what seems to me to be most interesting about psychoanalysis.

I was offered the job of general editor and took it. Everything I suggested was agreed to; but we couldn't find enough translators, so we had, in the end, ten translators for sixteen volumes. And there was a practising analyst involved: me. When I was offered the general editorship, and when I accepted it, I was surprised; it sounds ingenuous, and perhaps it is. And it is something I am glad to have done, but it was always something, I thought, I would be glad to have done. It was more work than I wanted to do, and the kind of work that mostly doesn't appeal to me. I have always read for the pleasure of reading and for the experience of reading, and to some extent now with a view to writing. And I read only whatever happens to interest me, which not being an academic or a teacher frees me to do; all this was interfered with by the Freud project. I never knew when a translation might arrive, and very often I read several drafts (I read three drafts of *Interpreting Dreams* in a year). The reading of the translations, though often thrilling in its way, and usually interesting, involved the kind of diligence, the kind of thoroughness, that I don't want for myself. There is for me the kind of freedom in reading – in reading, and not attending – that editing inevitably precludes; the attention required is the opposite of free-floating attention, and ordinary distractedness.

I am offering all this special pleading as a way into the larger question of why bother to do a new Freud, given the vested interests in his work, and its increasing marginalization. We would not, when talking about translations of Mann or Kafka, talk about the translator's entitlement to translate the texts; nor would we think of new translations as a provocation, or, to use Perry Meisel's terms in *The Literary Freud*, as 'fraught with the dangers of disorder and decay'. The problem, we would assume, that was being solved by new translations of Kafka or Mann would be that the previous translations were felt to be inaccurate or misleading, or both. Adequacy would be the issue, not official sanction. There may be heated debates among Kafka scholars, or among his translators, but they would not have the kind of charge that Freud translation seems to have. What could it be about Freud as a writer that can get people so worked up about translation; and worked up in a way that both threatens to kill people's pleasure in the new and experimental, and makes them over-defend the Standard Edition? What is the problem with translating Freud such that, when the new Penguin Freud translations were announced, the Institute of Psychoanalysis in London, which owns the copyright of the Standard Edition, should send a solicitor's letter to the managing director of Penguin making it clear that the new translations should not draw on the existing translations?[*]

Apart from the obvious question – why would a new translation draw on a previous one when it was going to be, by definition, a new translation? – it is worth considering, if we use this as an exemplary instance, what we might fear, and what we might lose, in retranslating Freud. And how is Freud a special case – if he is? I don't think these questions are adequately or interestingly answered by saying that new translations free the texts from institutional control. In producing and promoting and defending the Standard Edition, the institutes of psychoanalysis were not in any way controlling the interpretation of Freud's texts. I think it is possible, to put it in psychoanalytic language, that there is a wish to control – odd as it might sound – the diversity of personal histories that are brought to bear on Freud's texts by having a variety of translators, none of whom may have been analysed (Strachey, we should remember, was a patient of Freud's), and many of whom may have different views about Freud's language. The Standard Edition, whatever else it is, is one man's transference to Freud's words, a transference that Freud himself was acquainted with and had, to some extent, analysed; and it was supervised by a committee of senior analysts. Given what analysts know about the power of transference – the power of transference to translate its objects – there could be real fears about what might be done to Freud's texts in the apparently innocent name of new translation.

What is dismaying about this, if it is right, is that it is such a narrow view of transference: narrow-minded and perhaps unduly fearful, as though transference was only, ultimately, a form of spoiling or

---

[*] When I read a version of this essay as a lecture at Harvard, Mark Solms from the Institute of Psychoanalysis helpfully told the audience that the Institute's letter was prompted by their fear of loss of income from the Standard Edition, which sounded entirely plausible; though, at least from a psychoanalytic point of view, it is assumed that people tend to do what they do for more than one reason and that the reasons they give are not the only reasons they have.

distorting. Transference, the psychoanalyst Joseph Smith writes in *Arguing with Lacan*,

> was first understood as the capacity to misread or distort a new object
> in terms of prior objects. Analytic experience has taught us to see
> this first sketch of its meaning as transference in only the narrowest
> sense. Similarly analysis conceived as a mode of correcting transfer-
> ence distortions would be an impossibly limited concept of the process
> of analysis . . . the current emphasis is not on transference as a failure
> in reading but on transference as the power to read and relate to a
> new object or situation. It is the power to invest and enter into a
> relationship or situation in one's own way, in the light of one's prior
> experience. It is the power to be open to new experience in a way that
> not only allows the old to affect the new but also allows the new to
> affect the old.

In this account transference is not only the problem: it is also the point. Anyone can read Freud, but – at least until recently – not anyone could translate Freud. But if translation, whatever else it is, is a func- tion of transference (psychoanalysis inevitably organizes itself around its transference to Freud), and if transference brings new things into being, makes new things possible rather than simply foreclosing them, then a range of transferences brought to bear on the Freudian texts is also going to be a way of making it new. Freud's writing will be like the patient in psychoanalysis who wants to change by remaining the same, and wants to remain the same by changing. Each of the new translators entered into a relation with the Freudian text, in their own way, in the light of their prior experience; and what resulted, the given translation, was available in the public realm for consideration.

Until recently readers of Strachey's Standard Edition had little to compare him with. After the new translations there can be more of a conversation – both about Strachey and about the new versions – where once there was either fight or flight, so to speak. I have never met an analyst who had such serious misgivings about Strachey that they were canvassing for new translations. But then, of course, unless they knew German, they had very little to argue with. Translation, like transference in Smith's account, is unpredictable and idiosyncratic, and given the requisite conditions, can be made available for reflection, as something to be thought about. The New Penguin Freud translations are a new set of transferential relations to the Freudian texts. So what? Why are several better than one? One answer is that many translations make comparison possible. It may, for example, be instructive for clinicians and Freud readers alike to discover, as John Reddick writes in his Translator's Preface to the Penguin *Beyond the Pleasure Principle and Other Writings*, that if the opening paragraph of Strachey's translation of *On Narcissism*

> were handed in by a student as a translation exercise, it would end up covered in red pencil, with everything from light squiggles to heavy underlinings and multiple exclamation marks, for it is so full of slips and shifts and omissions as to be a travesty of Freud's original . . . Whilst none of these infelicities [which Reddick lists] makes much difference on its own, their cumulative effect is to alter the whole tone and thrust of the passage . . . They are as nothing, however, by the side of the two quite startling mistranslations that reveal themselves in these [opening] few lines . . . Much more serious, however, is the garbled title . . . The agenda here (and elsewhere) is clear, and not a little pernicious: Freud's writing is to be presented not as a hot and sweaty struggle with intractable and often crazily daring ideas, but as a cut-and-dried corpus of unchallengeable dogma.

If Freud's wildly speculative work in progress is translated as a set of scientific inferences or true beliefs, Strachey is misleading us; and, of course, shaking our confidence in the rest of his translation. There is no way I would have known this – known, as a non-German speaker, that there was a problem – without a new translation, and indeed a

Translator's Preface. Nor would I have known that Freud's important paper on technique, entitled by Strachey 'Observations on Transference Love', was apparently more accurately translated by Alan Bance in the New Penguin Freud as 'Observations on Love in Transference' – a title that suggests (as indeed does Freud in the paper) that there may be no essential difference between transference love and the other kind of love. In other words, all love may be transference. Reddick's critique and Bance's revision have considerable consequences. Clearly one of the things the New Penguin Freud does is to raise these, and many other issues, for consideration. Strachey alone – though there is no reason to assume that this was his intention – conceals what may be at issue, or that there are issues at all.

I want to consider what kind of excess might be entailed by having one standard translation of Freud's work, and what kind of excess might be involved in having many translations. Or, to put it slightly differently, why, when it comes to translating Freud, consensus might be preferred to coexistence, why one Freud may or may not be better than many. Freud, I think, provides a useful redescription of this in his famous account of how and why monotheism successfully superseded polytheism. Of course, chronologically, this is the opposite of the situation vis à vis the Freud translation, and indeed of Freud and his so-called followers: initially, despite the fledgeling attempts of Brill and Riviere et al, there was one English Freud – Strachey's – and now, there are many. So, to begin with, we need to look at Freud's account of the triumph of monotheism; and to read this account in terms of the excess that turns out to be overwhelming. As usual with Freud, a story about the sacred sheds light on the secular.

Most of the references in Freud's writing to monotheism and polytheism, and their relative merits, are in his late, strange text of 1939, *Moses and Monotheism*; even in *Totem and Taboo* the terms are not used (that is, the English terms; I don't know about the German). And, interestingly enough, Freud concludes his second prefatory note to the text, written in London in June 1938, with a misgiving, an anxiety about translation. Freud himself has just been translated to London, and is finally ready for *Moses and Monotheism*, in its now complete version, to be translated into English. 'In the few weeks of my stay here,' he writes,

> I have received countless greetings from friends who were pleased at my arrival, and from unknown and indeed uninvolved strangers who only wanted to give expression to their satisfaction at my having found freedom and safety here. And in addition there arrived, with a frequency surprising to a foreigner, communications of another sort, which were concerned with the state of my soul, which pointed out to me the way of Christ and sought to enlighten me on the future of Israel. The good people who wrote in this way cannot have known much about me; but I expect that when this work about Moses becomes known, in a translation, among my new compatriots, I shall forfeit enough of the sympathy which a number of other people as well now feel for me.

The translation of this work, by making Freud known, might make him too well known: he is being welcomed now, in what he calls 'lovely, free, magnanimous England', by even unknown and uninvolved strangers, but translation – both his own, by implication, and that of his book – gives more new people a different kind of access to him; and Freud fears that this may lose him their sympathy (the more one is known, the less sympathy one inspires). It is as if Freud is wondering, at least to himself and his German readers, whether, given his circumstances, he might be better off not having *Moses and Monotheism* translated, let alone, presumably, all the rest of his writing. Translation can be dangerous, and there is a resistance to it; and he mentions later in *Moses and Monotheism* how the patient in analysis does not understand the symbols in his dream, 'unless an analyst interprets them to him, and even then he is reluctant to believe the translation'. What is gained by access is tempered by the suffering involved.

I am not concerned here with the intricacies of Freud's argument – his attempt to prove that Moses was an Egyptian, the evolution of Jewish monotheism from Egyptian monotheism and so on – but simply with the way Freud in this text characterizes the supposed differences between polytheism and monotheism. (One thing one learns from Freud's writing, and indeed from the practice of psycho-analysis, is the value of weak theory: theories that are obviously not quite right invite conversation; strong theory creates a fight-or-flight situation.) Freud tends to describe these religious forms in terms of their excesses; and this might be a neat and instructive analogy for – or simply another way of talking about – the difference between there being the one Freud translation, the Standard Edition, and there being many. Bearing in mind, of course, the theologically complicated fact that even though Strachey has seemed to be Freud, there is the original behind Strachey's authoritative translation. So, there is the desire for the one, and the desire for the many.

In *Moses and Monotheism* there is what Freud often describes in the text as 'rigid monotheism', the two words almost always yoked together, and what he refers to once in the text as 'unbounded poly-theism'. In the Jewish religion, as traced back to Moses, Freud writes, 'there is but one god, he is unique, all-powerful, inaccessible; humans cannot withstand the sight of him, may make no image of him, may not even speak his name'; whereas in the Egyptian religion there is 'an almost countless host of deities of varying degrees of merit and diverse origins . . . The hymns in honour of such gods . . . unreflect-ingly identify them with one another in a way that we should find hopelessly confusing . . . magic, ritual acts, spells and amulets dom-inated the service of these gods.' The one god of the monotheists has an excess of power, an excess of mystery, an excess of privacy and unknowability, and an excessive intolerance of rivalry. The many gods of the polytheists are of excessively variable value and origin, are excessively and confusingly similar to each other (i.e. not always sufficiently distinct), and excessively allied with magical practices.

Freud's misgivings, as we know, are reserved for the monotheists: 'It was a rigid monotheism,' he writes, 'the first experiment of its kind in the history of the world, as far as we know, and with belief in the single god, as it were inevitably, religious intolerance was born, something that had been unknown to the ancient world before.' By making, as he writes, 'this universal god the one god, everything told about other gods is deception and lies'; alongside the one god 'any other was inconceivable'. Like the ego, the one god constitutes himself through repudiation: he defines himself by what he rejects. And in explaining anti-Semitism, towards the end of the text, Freud makes an impassioned plea about the resentment created, the violence incurred, by imposed unification, coerced consensus: 'It should not be forgotten,' Freud writes,

> that all the nations currently distinguished by their hatred of Jews became Christian only in recent historical times, often having been forced into it by violent coercion. They were all, one might say, imperfectly baptized; beneath a thin veneer of Christianity they remained what their ancestors had been, subscribing to a barbaric polytheism. They had still not overcome their resentment that the new religion had been foisted on them, but they had shifted that resentment onto the source from which Christianity came to them.

Coercing the many versions into one, foisting or imposing a consensus where one did not exist, Freud asserts, unleashes a deferred violence (as does a too worked out, too coherent narrative of the patient's life in psychoanalytic treatment). Polytheism is barbarous in this translation, in the sense that 'barbarians' were 'not Greeks'. Monotheism, in Freud's account, creates outsiders to hate and destroy, or makes outsiders – that is, competing, alternative versions – literally unthinkable, inconceivable (believing in one god being a calculated attack on the individual's capacity to think or imagine). There is a world of excessive confusion and multiple loyalties, and a world of excessive clarity and mutually exclusive belief.

It is not, and could never be, as stark as this; and even Freud doesn't suggest that polytheism is without violence, just that it required excessive violence to create monotheism, and that this engendered excessive violence. I don't, of course, feel that violence has been done to me by the one and only Standard Edition; but I do think, in the psychoanalytic way, that retroactively, in the light of the new Freud translations, we can begin to see what has been done to us and to Freud by the Standard Edition and its sponsors. It should be the psychoanalytic way to prefer coexistence to consensus, and to privilege variety over uniformity.

When it comes to evaluating the relative efficacy of available forms of therapy – psychoanalytic and otherwise – we need only acknowledge that if anything worked we would all be doing it. We should by the same token be promoting a variety of therapies, a variety of translations, and indeed a variety of religions.

Acknowledgements

'Psychoanalysis for Poets' was given as a talk at the universities of Oxford and of York, and published in a slightly different version in *Salmagundi*. 'Tribute to H. D.' was an Introduction to a New Directions edition of *Tribute to Freud*; 'Barthes by Himself' was an Introduction to a new Farrar, Strauss and Giroux edition of *Roland Barthes* by Roland Barthes. 'Against Biography' was given as the Empson Lecture at the University of Sheffield, and as a talk in a series at Wolfson College, Oxford, and at the University of York. 'Byron on the Run' was published in a slightly different version in the *London Review of Books*. 'Emerson and the Impossibilities of Style' was published in *Thinking Through Style* edited by Michael Hurley and Marcus Waithe, published by Oxford University Press. 'The Soul of Man under Psychoanalysis' was given as the T. S. Eliot Lecture at the University of Kent and at the University of York. 'Isaac Rosenberg's English' was given as a lecture at YAKAR in London. 'Celebrating Sebald' was given as a lecture at the University of East Anglia and published in *Raritan*. 'Zeno Getting It Wrong' was given as a lecture at the University of Oxford and published in *Raritan*. 'Winnicott's Lear' was given as a lecture at the University of Oxford and published in *Raritan* and in *Edward Lear and the Play of Poetry* edited by James Williams and Matthew Bevis, published by Oxford University Press. 'Johnson's Freud' was given as a talk at the University of Oxford and published in *Samuel Johnson: The Art of the Pendulum*, edited by Freya

Johnston and Lynda Mugglestone and published by Oxford University Press. 'Clough's *Amours*' was published in *The Oxford Handbook of Victorian Poetry*, edited by Matthew Bevis and published by Oxford University Press. 'Hamlet for Revenge' was published in *Threepenny Review*. 'After Strachey: On Translating Freud' was given as a lecture at Harvard and published in the *London Review of Books*. Minor changes have been made in some of these essays.

I am very grateful, as ever, to the editors of these books and journals, and to all those people who invited me to talk; without them this writing wouldn't have been done. The *London Review of Books*, *Raritan*, *Salmagundi* and *Threepenny Review* – and originally also the *Nouvelle Revue de Psychanalyse* – have made much of my writing possible.

Matthew Bevis and David Russell have been essential readers (and friends) for some of the most recent writing in this book. I have relied on their more than reliable judgement and suggestions. Judith Clark and Hugh Haughton are always my real and imagined first readers. Simon Prosser is my essential editor.

I have dedicated this book to two great editors who really took me under their wing when I began writing, and from whom I got an abiding sense of what writing could be; and also, of what psychoanalysis need not be.